The Maya Sites

Hidden Treasures of the Rain Forest

A Traveler's Guide to the Maya Sites on the Yucatán Peninsula, in México and Guatemala

Second Edition - 2018

With 155 illustrations, 91 in color

Imprint

The Maya Sites - Hidden Treasures of the Rain Forest
A Traveler's Guide to the Maya Sites on the Yucatán Peninsula, in México and Guatemala
2nd Edition
2018

Christian Schoen
Luisenstrasse 59
76137 Karlsruhe
Germany

Email: crischo@goldpilz.de
Web: http://AmazingTemples.com

ISBN 978-3-00-060142-2

Map 1 is an edited version of https://commons.wikimedia.org/wiki/File:Maya_civilization_location_map-blank.svg

Dedication

I dedicate this book to all explorers and all those who go through life's journey with open eyes.

Content

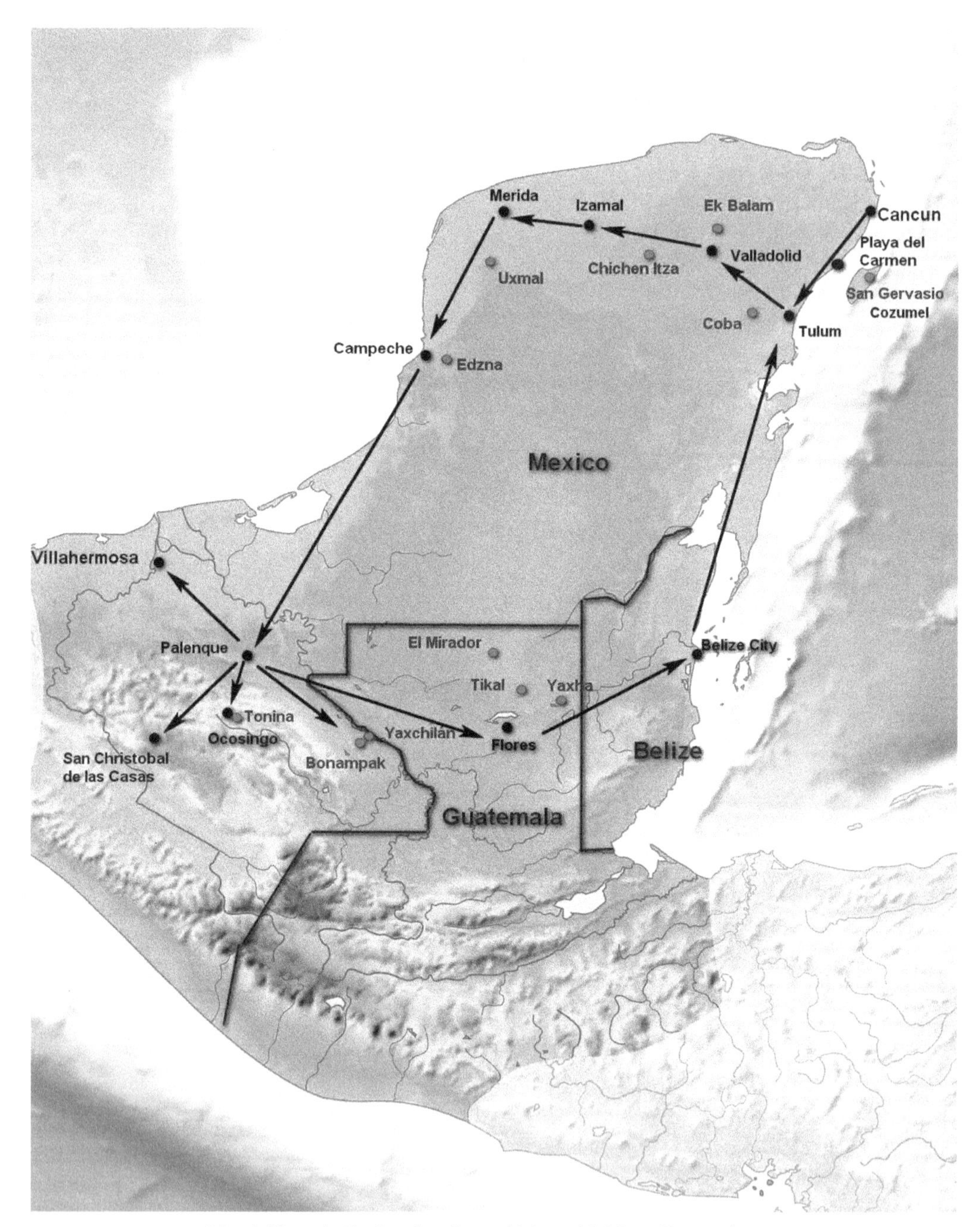

Map 1 - Yucatán Peninsula - General Map with Maya Sites and Route

Introduction

I was missing one important thing during my travels through the Maya world: A travel guide providing a list of all the exciting Maya sites, suggesting appropriate travel recommendations so I could quickly get to these places,and offering some additional maps and plans of each individual Maya site to inform me, in advance, about the essential things to see there. Unfortunately, what seemed most appropriate to me didn't exist yet. So I decided to write such a guide on my own, hoping that other travelers might benefit from this work.

Basically, I have written a book as I would have liked it during my travels: short, concise, crisp, having at hand the most important facts about the most important Maya sites without a long search for it. Such a book is priceless for someone who travels in an unknown area. Where the Maya sites are, how to get there and in which order to visit these places best, is the content of this book.

Conventional travel guides excel in long lists of hotels and restaurants, half of which no longer exist when the book is finally published. Other "recommended" spots increase their prices immediately after they are listed in one of the famous travel books or the quality of the food acclaimed by the travel book author is lowered dramatically. Yes, nothing is as ephemeral as a lonely planet.

Therefore, I have omitted all this gadgetry. It is usually sufficient if you ask for reasonable accommodation on site. For restaurants, just pay attention to where the locals go and follow them. At such places, price and performance often match. Again, this book provides answers to the following questions:

- Which are the most important Maya sites?
- Where are they located?
- How to get there?
- What can you see there?
- What should you know about it?

This book is ideal for all kinds of tourists; from the globetrotter focused on his budget to the explorer interested in art history or ancient architecture. The content has gaps because there are only those Maya sites listed that I visited myself. I hope that I can still add one or more locations in future releases.

After section 1 gives a short overview of the possible routes and the second section describes the sites in detail, I added two new parts. Section 3 provides a brief description of the history and the culture of the ancient Maya. In section 4, I will explain how the Maya calendar system works and how to read a simple date inscription.

Karlsruhe, Germany, in March 2018

Christian Schoen

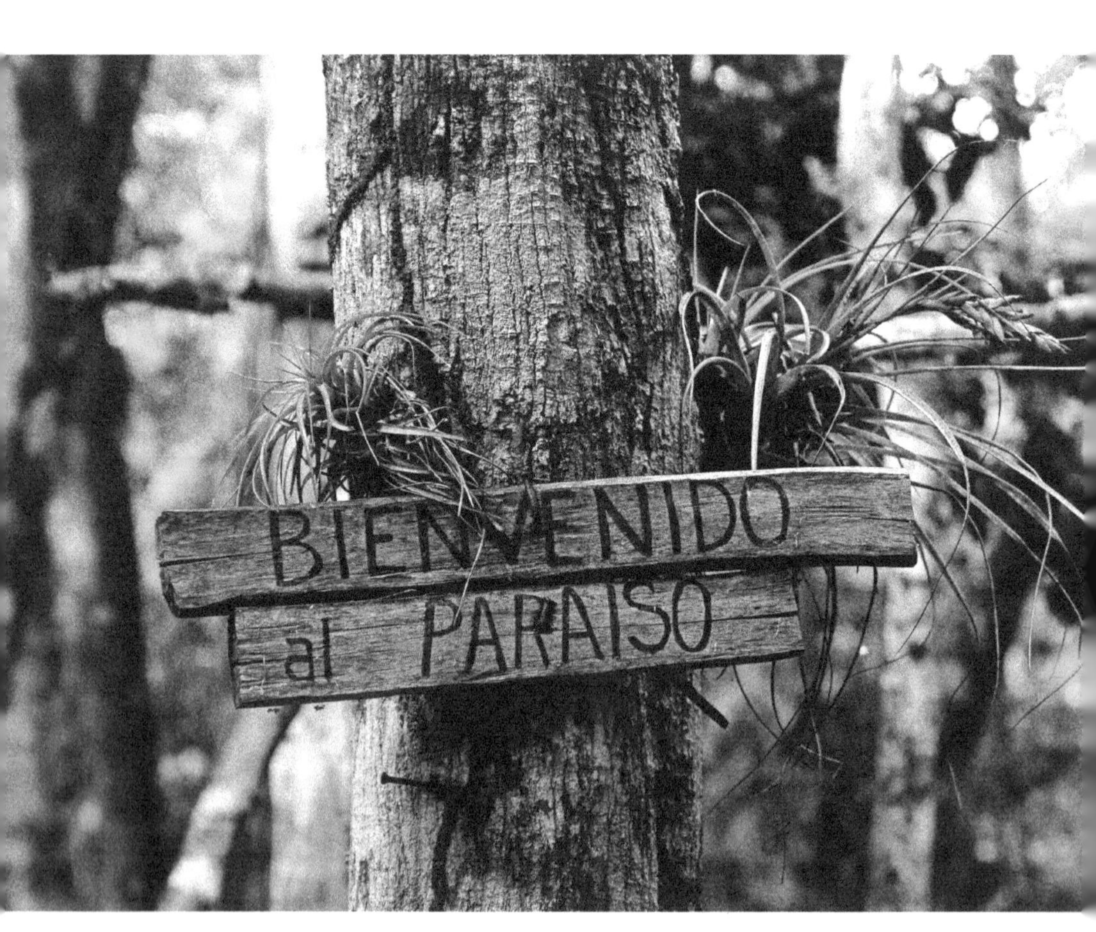

Figure 1 - Welcome to Paradise - Wooden Sign in the Jungle of Petén near El Mirador

Section 1

–

Routes and Short Descriptions

The Maya inhabited the entire area of the Yucatán peninsula in Mexico and Guatemala, in addition to the highlands of Chiapas and Guatemala down south to the Pacific coast in historical times. The southernmost settlement traces of this early civilization have been detected in Honduras and San Salvador.

It is convenient for the traveler to divide the region into three major areas to get a first rough overview of the Mayab, the land of the Maya, and its significant Maya sites.

The first area includes the present states of Yucatán and Quintana Roo in the north of the peninsula. This area is superbly developed for tourists. Many of the lovely ruin cities can easily be visited during a day trip. Moreover, tourist agencies offer day excursions to these places. Chichén Itzá, Ek Balam, Tulum, and Cobá are the best known name here. But Uxmal, Izamal or San Gervasio on Cozumel Island are worthy to take the trouble of a short journey as well.

The climate in the north of the peninsula is relatively dry; the ground is composed of limestone. In many places there are cenotes, water-filled collapses of the karst ceiling also called sinkholes.

Due to the geographical pattern - a semicircle extending across the peninsula and along which the cenotes are located scientists assume that the impact of a large meteorite in the Gulf of Mexico north of the Yucatecan coast is responsible for the formation of the cenotes. That impact took place about 65 million years ago and led to the extinction of the dinosaurs at the end of the Cretaceous period.

The second middle range is from Campeche in the Gulf of Mexico to the highlands of Chiapas. Here are longer distances to overcome than in the north and especially the Maya sites Edzná, Palenque, Bonampak, Yaxchilán, and Toniná have to be highlighted. Because of the proximity, I included Villahermosa, with the outdoor museum at La Venta Park dedicated to the Olmec, in my descriptions.

The landscape around Campeche resembles the arid north of the peninsula but transforms gradually to the rainforest the farther south you go. The country becomes increasingly humid and the vegetation denser especially in the often flooded estuary area of the Río Usumacinta. Further south, the mountain ranges of the Sierra Madre del Sur, the central highland of Chiapas, arise. Evergreen pine forests determine the view to a great extent.

The third area is located in the lowlands of the province of Petén in Guatemala. There, in the neighborhood of the island city of Flores in the Lago Petén, the Maya sites Tikal, Yaxhá and El Mirador can be found. A more comprehensive description of the environment can be found in section 3 of this book.

Usually, the history of the Maya is divided into three distinct main phases, the Pre-Classic, Classic and Post-Classic periods. These, in turn, are subdivided into early, middle and later portions. I've entered a separate chapter at the end of the book for a brief and rough outline of the different cultural epochs, ranging over the considerable period of 5000 years, from about 3000 v. Chr. to the modern times.

Perpetual sunshine, beautiful beaches and the perfect turquoise waters of the Caribbean cause the Yucatán peninsula to be a desirable tourist destination. The traveler can rely on a lot of different travel lodgings along the Caribbean coastline suitable for all travel budgets. Different types of all-inclusive resorts located between the cities invite the tourists to spend a relaxing time with the sun, beach, Mexican mariachi music, and exotic cocktails.

Countless restaurants, bars, and clubs with live music offer the best entertainment or unique culinary delights to tourists in the major cities. Unfortunately, many tourists almost never leave their holiday domicile, and so miss the most beautiful attractions they could have reached with only one or two hours of driving. Beautiful temples and huge pyramids are waiting to be explored by the curious in the hinterland of the tourist areas. The ancient lost cities of the classic Maya culture with its 2000-year-old ruins, walls, streets, and palaces could be visited. Most of them are accessible by public transport. Just a few of the essential sites can be reached only after days of marching through the jungle.

Holá! I talk about the oldest stone buildings of the Americas!

Why do so many people miss to visit these exciting places? The answer is simple: Travelling in Yucatán seems to be an adventurous undertaking. It is cozier to spend the day next to the hotel pool sipping a glass of Frozen Marguerita. But is it really less comfortable on the road? The answer is clear: No – with an "if" - behind. The "if": If you are aware of what and where...

Ok, I admit, outside the tourist centers you won't have a swimming pool available most of the time and the beaches are far away. But when you finally return to your hotel or beach resort, then you will bring not just a few super photos of an adventurous trip with you. The most significant benefit is the travel experience that you were able to gain! And you can tell great adventure stories to your travel buddies who preferred to stay at the beach. Believe me; they will go green with envy while listening to your accounts.

In the following three chapters, I will describe three possible routes, according to the geographical division that I have made before, enabling you to visit about 15 different Maya sites throughout the Yucatán peninsula in Mexico and Guatemala. Some of them are world famous, others you've probably never heard of. Subsequently, in the following section, I will describe the various sites in more detail then. Except for one, all can be easily reached by car. As you will see, these three routes expect very different fitness levels from you.

I start with the simple route.

THE STANDARD ROUTE – NORTHERN YUCATÁN AND THE RIVIERA MAYA

I call this route the standard route because it affects all the sites in northern Yucatán, which are usually visited by tourists in the Riviera Maya. Most of these Maya cities are actually ranked in the classic period of the Maya culture, even though most of them had their heyday during the post-Classic.

Most people reach Yucatán by a flight to Cancún. This is the place where our trip through the world of Maya begins. After your arrival in Cancún, you will probably want to acclimate for a few days. Usually, I go directly south to the rather cozy Playa del Carmen, where I spend two or three nights.

You could just choose to spend the first days in Cancún, Tulum or in one of the beach resorts as well. It makes no difference to the onward journey. In this way, you can quickly get used to the higher temperatures, the humidity, and the Mexican food and you can overcome the jet lag if you flew in from overseas.

TULUM AND COBÁ

Tulum and Cobá are the first two Maya sites on our list whose visit is worthwhile. For both places, it is advantageous if you search for lodging in the modern city center of Tulum. Tulum City is manageable in size and offers several accommodations and catering facilities.

The archaeological site of Tulum is just a few minutes' drive north of the modern city. The extent of the ruins is not very big. They are located on a cliff facing the Caribbean Sea. You can use a rented bicycle or a taxi to get there from the city center.

The Maya site Cobá, on the other hand, is about 40km west of Tulum and offers the possibility to climb the big pyramid, what is unusual at the Riviera Maya. The reward for these efforts is a fantastic view over the jungle to another pyramid that rises up from the rainforest.

Cobá has a considerably large area, and within the complex, you will have the possibility to rent a bike or a bicycle taxi. This might be useful if your condition doesn't allow walking the distances between the buildings, that quickly sum up to 10km and more. Cobá can be reached by public bus or a colectivo bus. Some hotels offer guided tours. Sturdy shoes are very advisable for Cobá in any case.

COZUMEL AND SAN GERVASIO

San Gervasio is a relatively extensive Maya site on the island of Cozumel. The number of tourists there is low, although Cozumel is approached by cruise ships. Most "crusaders" prefer to spend their time with a trip to the mainland, to buy a China-imported plastic replica of Maya handicrafts...

The ferry to Cozumel departs from Playa del Carmen. The best thing is to use the first possible ship of the day. In Cozumel, you rent a cab or, as I have done it, a scooter. San Gervasio is located in the center of the island. Using a motorcycle, you are about 30 - 45 minutes on the road until you reach the entrance.

San Gervasio had great importance as a sanctuary of the Maya goddess Ixchel in historical times, but the building complexes are rather unspectacular regarding size. Situated on a Carribean island, the cultural meaning and the uniqueness of the buildings turn this place into a location that is worth seeing. Sturdy shoes are recommended.

EK BALAM AND VALLADOLID

You can reach Valladolid efficiently using the public bus from Tulum. The trip takes about 1.5 hours. In Valladolid, you could plan your next stay.

Valladolid is a lovely Mexican colonial city, with plaza and cathedral. Tourism doesn't take place in Valladolid, so this location is also suitable for shopping. I bought my best hammock ever - with the size "Familiale" at an excellent price there.

The archaeological site of Ek Balam is located about 30km north of Valladolid. It is famous for the beautifully preserved Maya stucco friezes on the Great Acropolis. In Valladolid, there are colectivo taxis that can take you there.

The expansion of the facility is not significant, but when climbing the Great Acropolis, you might become dizzy. Sturdy shoes are recommended. Ok, sturdy shoes are almost always advisable for these sightseeing tours!

CHICHÉN ITZÁ

From Valladolid, the path leads to Chichén Itzá. I strongly recommend that you look for a hotel the day before your visit, and then access this archaeological site early in the morning.

Chichén Itzá is by far the most famous Maya city and is therefore visited by numerous tourists accordingly. Many come as day-trippers from Cancún just about 100km away. Early entry is therefore recommended. If you want to make some attractive photos, then the best approach is to wait for the opening in front of the entrance gate. Around noon, Chichén Itzá is so densely populated that you can hardly think of photography unless you like pictures of crowds of tourists. Subsequently, Chichén Itzá is one of the few sites that can be visited in sandals or flip-flops...if you want that.

IZAMAL

Izamal is special. You pass this small town in the north of Yucatán on your way towards Mérida. The least tourists take the advantage to stop here, although the city has some significant attractions.

In historical times, the two bulkiest Maya pyramids of northern Yucatán were here and still are partial. One of them was destroyed by the Spaniards. Instead, a monastery was built on top of it. The other is relatively well preserved and still worth seeing. The sheer size of this pyramid is impressive.

Izamal was the first bishopric in Mexico. Accordingly, the fourth bishop in Mexican history lived here. Diego de Landa was his name. He gained dubious fame in that he had not only burned nearly all ancient books and documents of the Maya, but also for the documentation of the Maya history that he recorded later. He did this presumably as a sort of compensation. The monastery is worth seeing next to the big pyramid. Izamal itself is a small town in colonial style and is well-suited for an overnight stay. The two mentioned buildings are located in the center because Izamal was built precisely at the same place as the ancient Maya city. In Izamal, you could stay overnight if you do not prefer to visit the town during a day trip from Merida.

UXMAL

For a visit to Uxmal, I recommend scheduling a stay of a few days in Mérida, the capital of the state of Yucatán. This allows you to initially visit this old colonial town with its cathedral, which is one of the oldest on the American continent. Also, the city's museums and the massive, modern National Monument are worth seeing. While you linger in Merida, you can plan your trips to Uxmal, Izamal or to other Maya sites in the region.

The most impressive building in Uxmal is the Pyramid of the Magician. A legend says that this building was built by a magical dwarf

Figure 2 - Cozumel - San Gervasio - Spider near the Entrance >>>>

overnight. All structures, pyramids, palaces and temples in Uxmal are in excellent, restored condition.

With Mérida and Uxmal, our first trip to the north of the Yucatán peninsula comes to an end. Now, you can return to the Riviera Maya or proceed to the second section of the tour. I call the second part "The Exotic Route."

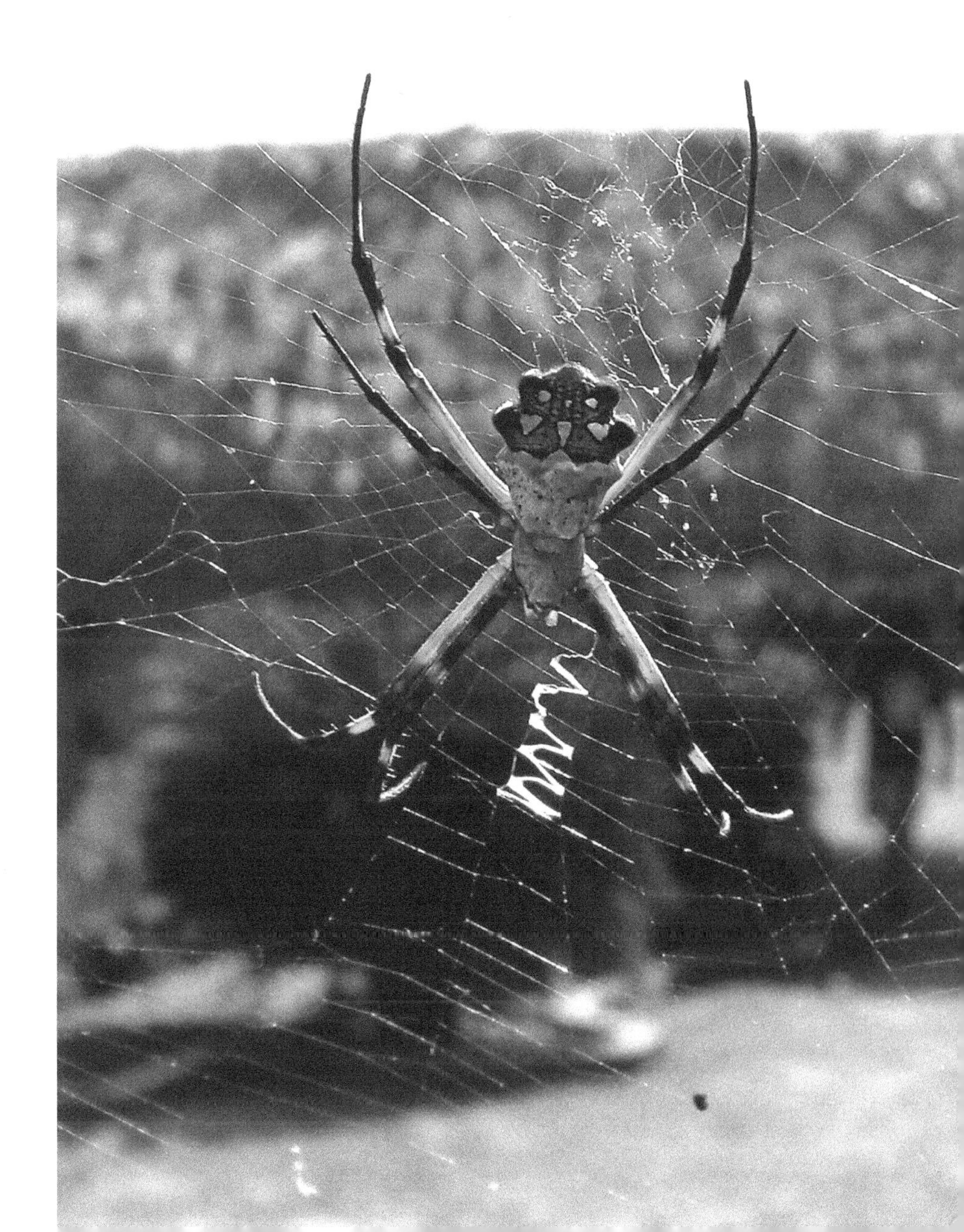

THE EXOTIC ROUTE

–

CAMPECHE AND CHIAPAS

The second part of the trip is what I call "The Exotic Route" because we leave the well-beaten tourist path at this point and head into the "wilder" and more exotic parts of Mexico. Many of the Maya buildings that you will see on this route have an age of more than 2,000 years. The origins of some of these Maya sites are in the pre-classic era of the Maya culture.

EDZNÁ AND CAMPECHE

From Mérida, it is only a short hop to Campeche. Public buses of the large overland lines complete the course in about three hours. Campeche is the most significant city on the west coast of the Yucatán Peninsula and also the capital of the Mexican state with the same name. It is a UNESCO World Heritage Site famous for the colorful facades of the beautifully preserved colonial city houses and for seafood dishes. The people of Campeche remember, especially, pirates who have attacked and conquered the city repeatedly during the 16th century.

Edzná is a sprawling Maya site with significant buildings and well-preserved temple pyramids. Unfortunately, transportation from Campeche to Edzná in the hinterland is poorly developed.

It is best to ask in Campeche for a guided tour or hire a taxi for a day, which definitely pays off, especially if you are traveling with several people.

PALENQUE

We continue from Campeche southwards. The bus will take you to Palenque in about three hours. About the other locations, Palenque is so conveniently located, that it is outstandingly suitable as a "base camp" for several short trips, and therefore the right place for a more extended stay. From here, you can visit the nearby attractions in short one- or two-day trips. A rest of five days up to a week should be taken into account.

With the arrival in Palenque, you reach a predominantly subtropical area and find yourself in the Mexican state of Chiapas. By now, you should equip yourself with bug spray, because mosquitoes are increasingly expected in this area.

Although Palenque is just a small town, it is very well prepared for tourists. There are numerous hotels and hostels and of course, restaurants and bars. Just outside the city, you can find luxury resorts, in case you prefer to stay more comfortably.

The archaeological site of Palenque is stunning. Surrounded by the jungle, the massive temples, pyramids, and palaces will impress you. The calls of the howler monkeys in the dense forests around the ruins will give your visit an extraordinary, mystical character.

The ruins of Palenque can be reached easily by public transport. Small colectivo buses run from Palenque City to the ruins several times an hour. They are marked with a sign "Ruinas" and stop on a show of hands.

BONAMPAK AND YAXCHILÁN

Bonampak and Yaxchilán are fantastic examples of art and architecture of the Classic Maya period. They are located close together.

Yaxchilán can be accessed from the small town of Frontera Corozal. However, the ruins can be reached by boat only. The boat trip on the untamed Usumacinta River along the subtropical gallery forests is an experience that you will remember for a long time – especially during the rainy season when the water level is high.

Bonampak, on the other hand, is famous for its murals. These murals, with scenes from the daily life of the Maya,were discovered just a few years ago. They are in excellent condition. Bonampak is located in the territory of the Lacandon Indians in the Selva Lacandon, the "Forest of the Lacandons."

I recommend booking a guided tour to Yaxchilán and Bonampak from Palenque to visit both sites "in one go." There are one- or two-days tour offers. It should be noted that the price of the boat trip is always referred to the boat, no matter whether you are alone or a group of people. For this reason, I recommend an organized tour.

TONINÁ

Toniná consists of a single pyramid, essentially. But this is an awe-inspiring one, not only because of its overwhelming size. In fact, the builders have used a mountain and covered it with stones.

With 74 meters in height, rising in seven stages over the surrounding pastures, Toniná can boast of being one of the tallest buildings in the Maya world – maybe the tallest at all. The individual layers are so large that there were several more temples built on the existing free space.

Toniná is located in the highlands of Chiapas, few kilometers off the

road from Palenque to San Cristobal de las Casas near Ocosingo.
You can plan the visit of Ocosingo and Toniná as a day trip via bus from Palenque, which is what I would recommend. The ruins are situated around 4km from the city center and can be reached within 30 minutes by a colectivo bus. The colectivos start beside the marketplace in Ocosingo. Incidentally, the colorful market of Ocosingo is worth seeing too.

SPECIAL: THE OLMEC AT THE LA VENTA MUSEUM PARC

Another day trip that you can do from Palenque is a bus ride to Villahermosa, a city in the state of Tabasco. Using one of the big bus lines, you can be there within just two hours and visit an almost tourist-free town, do some regular shopping or enjoy a delicious meal in one of the numerous restaurants.

But that is not the main reason why you should go to Villahermosa. The most impressive place you can see in this mid-sized city is the "La Venta Museum Parc," an open-air museum where the finds of the excavations of the nearby wetland of La Venta are exhibited.

Impressive giant stone heads, which were once created by the Olmec culture more than 2,000 years ago, are among the artifacts. Tropical plants, jungle trees draped with lianas and a small zoological garden determine the jungle-like atmosphere of the park. Even a rare black jaguar can be viewed here.

SAN CRISTOBAL DE LAS CASAS

A trip to Chiapas would not be complete without a visit to San Cristobal de las Casas in the highlands of Chiapas. It's best to plan for a three to four days stay.

The fabulous city has several old churches from the colonial period, a museum about Maya medicine, a museum about the indigenous group of the Lacandon and an excellent tourist market. A bus manages the route Palenque to San Cristobal in the heart of the highlands of Chiapas in about three hours.

A visit to the village San Juan de Chamula situated about 20km from San Cristobal completes this tour. Chamula is the most significant indigenous community in Chiapas. The colorful market is worth seeing, but the Maya church in which you find the center of religious events in the region, especially during the San Juan festival in mid-June deserves particular interest. In this church, Christian ceremonies are celebrated in addition to those of the Mayas in an unusual mixture.

Important note! It is entirely forbidden to take pictures inside the church! Even outside of the building, restraint is advisable. People there can be outraged, and the loss of the camera is one of the harmless

Figure 3 - Palenque – Horse in the Jungle

consequences. The best is to ask a local before you bring out your camera and take photos.

The “exotic route” ends after returning to Palenque. Now you can take the bus, preferably overnight, to return to the Riviera Maya or you turn to the third part, the somewhat adventurous journey through the Petén.

THE ADVENTUROUS ROUTE

–

PETÉN - GUATEMALA

The third and last section of our tour will allow you to immerse yourself deep in the pre-classic period of the ancient Maya culture. Therefore, we leave Mexico and cross the border into the Petén area of Guatemala.

In the second section, we had visited Maya sites in Chiapas. Our last stop was Palenque. And there, in Palenque, our trip starts. Our next stop is the small island town of Flores in the lake Lago Petén.

FLORES AND THE LAGO PETÉN IN GUATEMALA

The travel from Palenque to Flores in Guatemala takes a whole day. I strongly recommend that you do not perform this part of the journey on your own but to ask one of the travel agencies in Palenque for appropriate opportunities. The trips to Flores offered by the local travel agencies in Palenque are organized excellently. Without planning, this part of the trip will take two days or longer. A Mexican bus takes you to the border in Frontera Corozal, where a Guatemalan bus picks you up and transports you directly to Flores in Guatemala.

The distance is actually not that big as it might appear from this description, but the time cost is enormous for two reasons:

First, before you arrive in Guatemala, you have to cross the Rio Usumacinta. Surprisingly, there is no bridge, and you have to perform the distance between the two border towns by boat. Not enough! The Guatemalan village is located about 45 boat minutes upstream!

In fact, the river crossing is a real adventure, and it will not be the last one on this tour. In the same moment in which you reach the Guatemalan side, you step into the Petén.

El Petén is also the name of the Guatemalan government district and the name of this landscape in the lowlands of Guatemala. First, you will drive for hours on bumpy, dusty or muddy roads depending on the weather conditions before you finally arrive in the island-town of Flores in the Lago Petén. Have you noticed it? By crossing the Rio Usumacinta, we returned to the Yucatán Peninsula. Flores is a colonial town in the Petén area. The small town is located on a small island in the lake and is well prepared for the arrival of tourists. Connected to the mainland by a bridge, the city offers numerous hotels, restaurants, and shops that invite tourists to stay a little bit longer. Flores should be used as a central base camp because from here it is straightforward to reach the surrounding Maya sites. I recommend stopping by the restaurant "Café Yax-Ha," because they offer guided tours to nearby ruin cities, but there are several other tour operators in Flores as well, providing the same kind of day trips.

TIKAL

Tikal is the best known Maya site in the region of Petén, about one hour drive from Flores. In any case, the pre-classic Tikal should be visited first while you stay in Flores.

For my own visit, I merely took a public bus. You can catch it at the central bus station in Flores/St. Elena. If you want to have the extraordinary experience of a sunrise on the pyramid, then you will need to use an organized tour.

YAXHÁ

Yaxhá is less famous than Tikal but worth a visit in any case. Several pyramids, temples and other buildings can be seen in excellent restored condition.

Yaxhá, situated between two lakes, offers a breathtaking insight into the sub-tropical nature and Maya architecture at the same time. For a trip to Yaxhá, you can ask in the already mentioned Café Yax-Ha or one of the tour operators in Flores.

EL MIRADOR

El Mirador is an ancient Maya city that unites several superlatives. It was by far the largest city of the Maya which has been discovered yet, and it contains some of the highest pyramids ever built by the Maya.

The city is located in the jungle and cannot be reached with a vehicle. You have to hike to get there. The best way to do this is to visit one of the tourist offices in Flores to keep yourself informed about how to get to El Mirador. They organize such tours.

It's a two-day walk through the jungle until you arrive in El Mirador. After a stay of a single day that serves to explore the ruins, you will walk back during the additional two days. The entire trip takes five days. While you're hiking in the jungle, you'll feel like Indiana Jones himself! Do not worry, your luggage is dragged by mules over muddy mule tracks, and of course, there are possibilities to ride the trail on a mule too.

Here in Petén, our tour on the Yucatán Peninsula and in the world of the Maya finds its end.

BACK TO THE RIVIERA MAYA

From Flores, you can go back to the Riviera Maya now. The easiest and fastest travel option is to take a bus to the border between Guatemala/Belize and then further to Belize City. From there, you continue the travel by bus north to Playa del Carmen, Cancún or Tulum in Mexico. I needed 18 hours for this drive. Apparently, it is recommended that you catch the first possible bus in the morning.

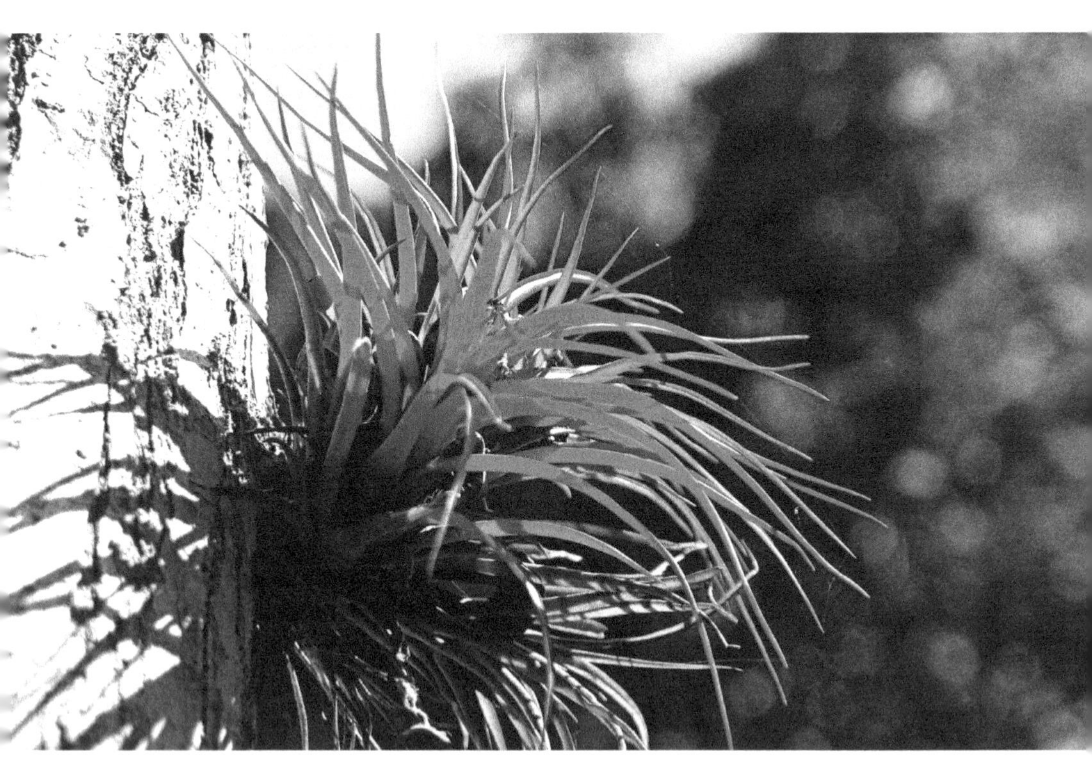

Figure 4 - Tikal - Blooming Tillandsia

Section 2 - The Maya Sites

Region: Yucatán and Quintana Roo

TULUM - TURQUOISE SEA AND TEMPLE RUINS

Tulum is the first of the Maya sites I'm going to discuss here, in this book. It is located directly on the coast of the Riviera Maya, about 60 kilometers south of Playa del Carmen. Tulum is the most easily accessible ruin city on this stretch of coastline and, next to Chichén Itzá, the most popular tourist attraction.

In the books of Chilam Balam, Tulum was called "Zamá." The word means "dawn," which is due to the unique location and orientation. Situated directly on a cliff on the coast, Tulum offers a clear view of the Caribbean to the east, to watch the sunrise.

According to Maya standards, Tulum was founded relatively late. The buildings were all built in the post-classical period between 1200 and 1450. An architectural style typical of the east coast was used for their construction. A low platform is the basis on which the building is erected. Between the building's base and the platform below, a step has been placed enclosing the entire structure. The doors are low and are framed by columns. Tulum was a small settlement of the Maya. The population barely exceeded the number of 1,600 people. Only the ruling class lived within the city walls. The ordinary people settled scattered all over the surrounding countryside.

Jade, obsidian and other finds from the entire Maya area show that Tulum occupied a prominent position on the Caribbean coast as a

Figure 5 - Tulum - The Temple of the Wind

Figure 6 - Tulum - The Palace

trading post. In addition to the sea trade along the coastal line, Tulum had access to trade routes leading into the interior of the peninsula. However, Tulum was not the only seaport in the region.

At the time of the arrival of the Spaniards, Tulum was inhabited. The Catholic priest Juan Diaz, who accompanied the Spanish Grijalva expedition to Mexico in 1518 and approached the city from the sea, compared Tulum with his hometown of Sevilla:

> *"... a city or village so large that Sevilla could not be better or greater, and in it was a very high tower visible ... "*

Around 1560, just 20 years after the arrival of the Spaniards, Tulum was abandoned by its inhabitants. It is believed that at this time, diseases that might have been dragged in by the Spaniards decimated the population to the extent that the city was abandoned.

First reports by researchers are from Stevens and Catherwood, who visited the city in 1842 and roughly explored it. Catherwood is the creator of several drawings of the temple buildings. A stele, on which the calendar date for the year 564 was registered, was sent to London in the British Museum. Since the city was founded much later, it is assumed today that this stele is an artifact from elsewhere, which was brought to Tulum then. For what reason this has happened is not known. From 1913, Sylvanus Morley and George How began to examine Tulum scientifically.

Tulúm, which is located above a rocky coastal section, is protected by a high wall from three sides. Due to this fortification, Tulum got its name. Tulu'um in the Mayan language means "wall." The height of the wall in the countryside varied between three and five meters. It had a total length of almost one kilometer and was eight meters thick. Undoubtedly, the construction served to increase the defensiveness of the city.

THE MAIN BUILDINGS:

El Templo del Dios Descendente - The Temple of the Descending God

The Temple of the Descending God received its name from the depiction of the god of bees, Ah Mucen Cab on his façade above the lintel in the roof frieze. The name of this god means "honey gatherer." The god is represented with the head down, the angled legs point upwards. The asymmetrical design of the west facade of the building is striking.

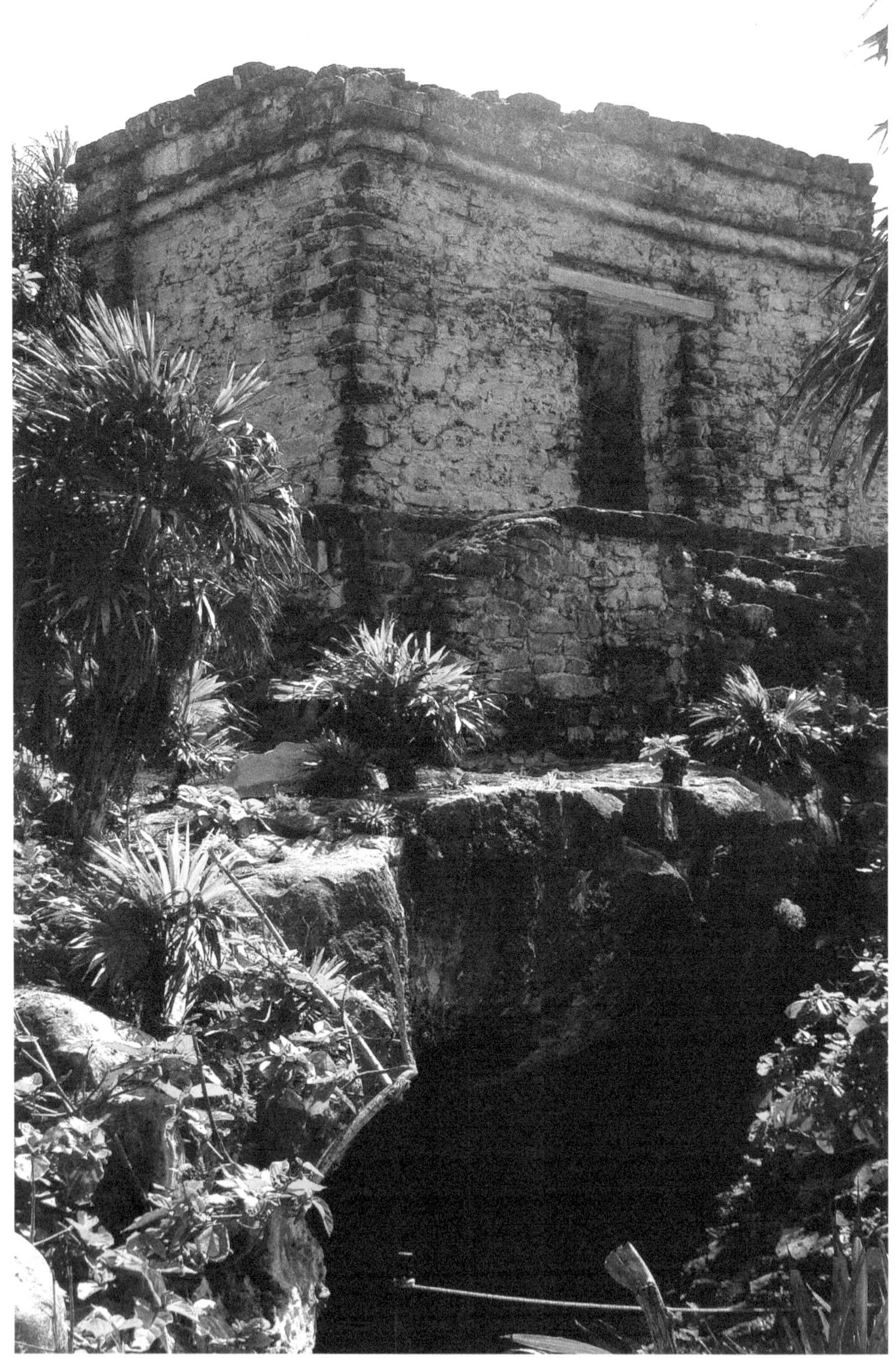

Figure 7 – Tulum –The House of the Cenote

El Palacio - The Palace

It is thought that the initially rather large but poorly preserved building served as the residence of a ruler. There are numerous stone columns on the side of the building. In contrast to the title "Ahau" of the classical period, the rulers in the post-classical period were named with the title of "Halach Huinik." This is why the building is also called "House of HalachUinik."

El Castillo - The Castle

At 7.5 meters, El Castillo is the tallest building in Tulum. There are two pillars in the three-fold doorway of the temple building. At the base of these two pillars, initially two snakeheads were mounted, but they do not longer exist. In its interior are two rooms, the walls of which were initially adorned with paintings, but only a few remain. The building is located on the east side of the site, directly on the cliff and is assumed to be the one that was designated by Juan Diaz as a "tower." The upper temple building, including the staircase, stands on a platform erected earlier. On this base, there are two smaller temples on the right and left.

El Templo de las Peinturas - The Temple of Paintings

The almost square building is two-storied. Around a smaller temple, another temple was built. The lintel is supported by four pillars, creating five openings. On this lower part, a second, upper building, which is considerably smaller, was erected in later times.

The structure was named after the wall paintings found inside. The oldest of these paintings date back to the 11th or 12th century. They can be seen on the facade of the inner temple. In some cases, however, it is assumed that they were created at a time when the Spaniards had already conquered the country. The paintings show people performing various activities, such as a woman milling corn. One figure shows the goddess Chak Chel, another one shows a god originating from Central Mexico named Tezcatlipoca. The predominantly used color is blue against a black and white background. The figures are framed by representations of intertwined snakes.

On the outer façade, there are numerous reliefs depicting fish, snakes, and reptiles. These were originally painted. Only red, blue and yellow were used as color. Contours were painted black. The top part of the building had just red handprints as ornaments. There is also a representation of the descending god at this temple.

El Templo del Dios del Viento - The Temple of the Wind God

The Temple of the Wind God is a small building that has only one room. Because of the rounded platform on which it was built, it is assumed that it served to worship the Wind God. Due to its picturesque location

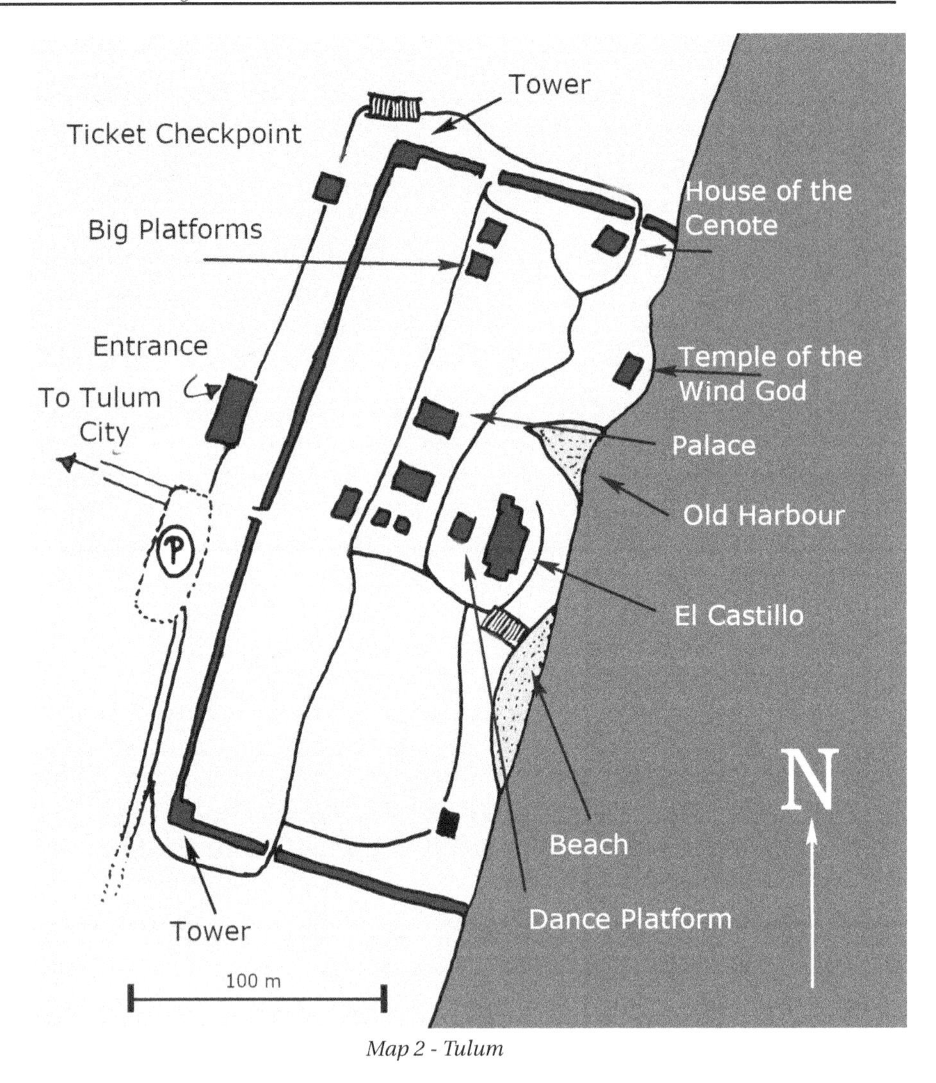

Map 2 - Tulum

directly on the coastline with the turquoise Caribbean sea in the background, this building is mainly Tulum's landmark.

TRAVEL TIP:

Tulum is a still small but fast-growing town, just two hours driving time south of Cancún, right on the Riviera Maya of the Yucatán peninsula in Mexico. The modern city with about 15000 inhabitants is about two kilometers from the beach in the interior of the country. On the beach itself, a "beach resort" joins each other over a distance of almost seven

Figure 8 – Tulum - El Castillo – Back Side >>>>

kilometers. If you don't like the hustle and bustle of beach resorts or the big cities on the Riviera Maya, you can also get to know the more tranquil life of the country's inhabitants during your stay in Tulum. In addition to various hostels, hotels, and restaurants, there are also a few small shops in the town of Tulum.

The beach can also be reached from here because in various places you can rent bicycles. Another advantage is that the prices for accommodation in Tulum itself are much more moderate.

I recommend performing the visit of the ruins of Tulum on a weekday. During the day more and more buses from the tourist centers reach the rather small area. On weekends, the local visitors will also get there. If you are interested in capturing the ruins in beautiful, tourist-free photos, you should start as early as possible. South of the ruins you can easily access the beach and complete the day with a beach walk.

NATURE

Just a few hundred meters from the coast is the Mesoamerican Barrier Reef. This Caribbean coral reef is the second largest reef in the world. It breaks the waves from the open sea and thus protects the beaches from destruction. Many people come to the Riviera Maya to explore the perfect underwater world of the reef. South of the modern Tulum begins the nature reserve of Sian Káan. Sian Káan is a UNESCO World Cultural Heritage. Travel agencies in the tourist centers offer the opportunity to visit this spectacular natural habitat. If you are lucky, you can see some of the largest mammals in Mexico; a jaguar, a puma, a tapir or a Caribbean manatee. In the vicinity of Tulum, several large cenotes can be visited, perfect places to swim in freshwater or to experience the underwater world of Yucatán.

OTHER MAYA SITES IN THE VICINITY

An excursion to Valladolid in the province of Yucatán to visit the Maya site Ek Balam can be carried out from Tulum easily. The road from Tulum to Valladolid is new and in excellent condition. The regular bus takes about two hours for the distance. So you can start in the morning, then in Valladolid take a Colectivo taxi to Ek Balam, return to Valladolid around four o'clock and go back to Tulum using the last bus after a shopping trip and dinner.

Also, Cobá, a substantial Maya city with an imposing pyramid, is easy to reach from Tulum. Cobá is located about 40 kilometers west of Tulúm. I described the details for both sites in the following chapters.

In any case, remember that Yucatán's east coast is an entry point for hurricanes. The likelihood of Tulum being hit by a cyclone rises significantly during the autumn hurricane season. The best times for a trip are in winter and spring.

Figure 9 - Cobá - The Ball Court >>>

COBÁ – RULED BY WOMEN?

Cobá is a Maya site located on the Yucatán Peninsula in Mexico and about 40km west of Tulum. Cobá is different from the other two known pyramid cities of the Maya, Chichén Itzá, and Tulum, in its vast expansion and the fact that you can find here the highest pyramid in the northern part of the peninsula.

The fact that the ruins of Cobá are surrounded by dense jungle and that it is allowed to climb on the giant main pyramid makes the site a worthwhile tourist destination at the Riviera Maya.

Cobá fills a unique position among the Maya cities of northern Yucatán due to its architectural style. The design used here is more reminiscent of the pre-classic structures of Petén in Guatemala. The buildings show little resemblance to those in the other classical sites of the North with their usual Puuc style.

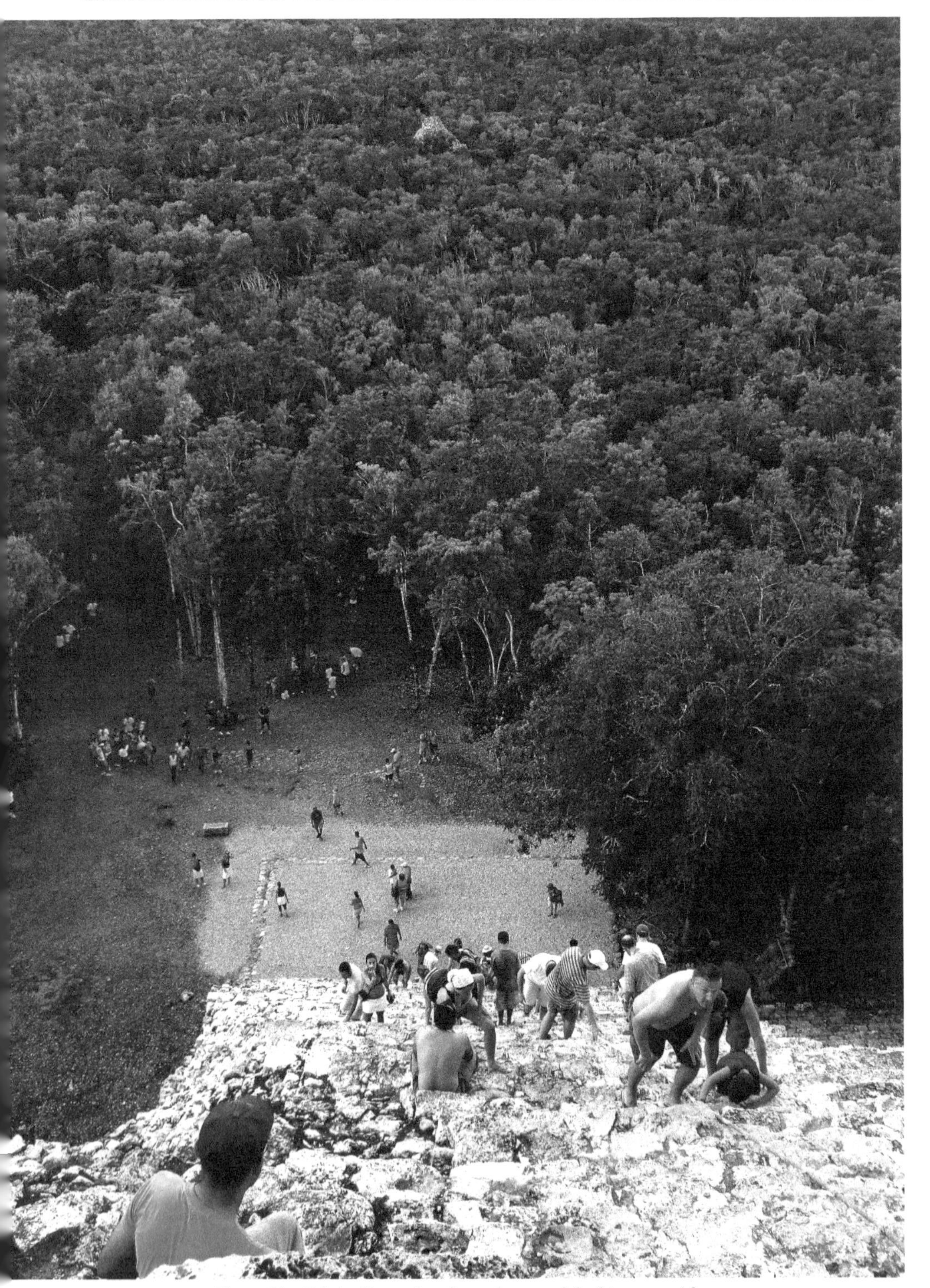

Figure 10 - Cobá - Great view from the top of the big pyramid

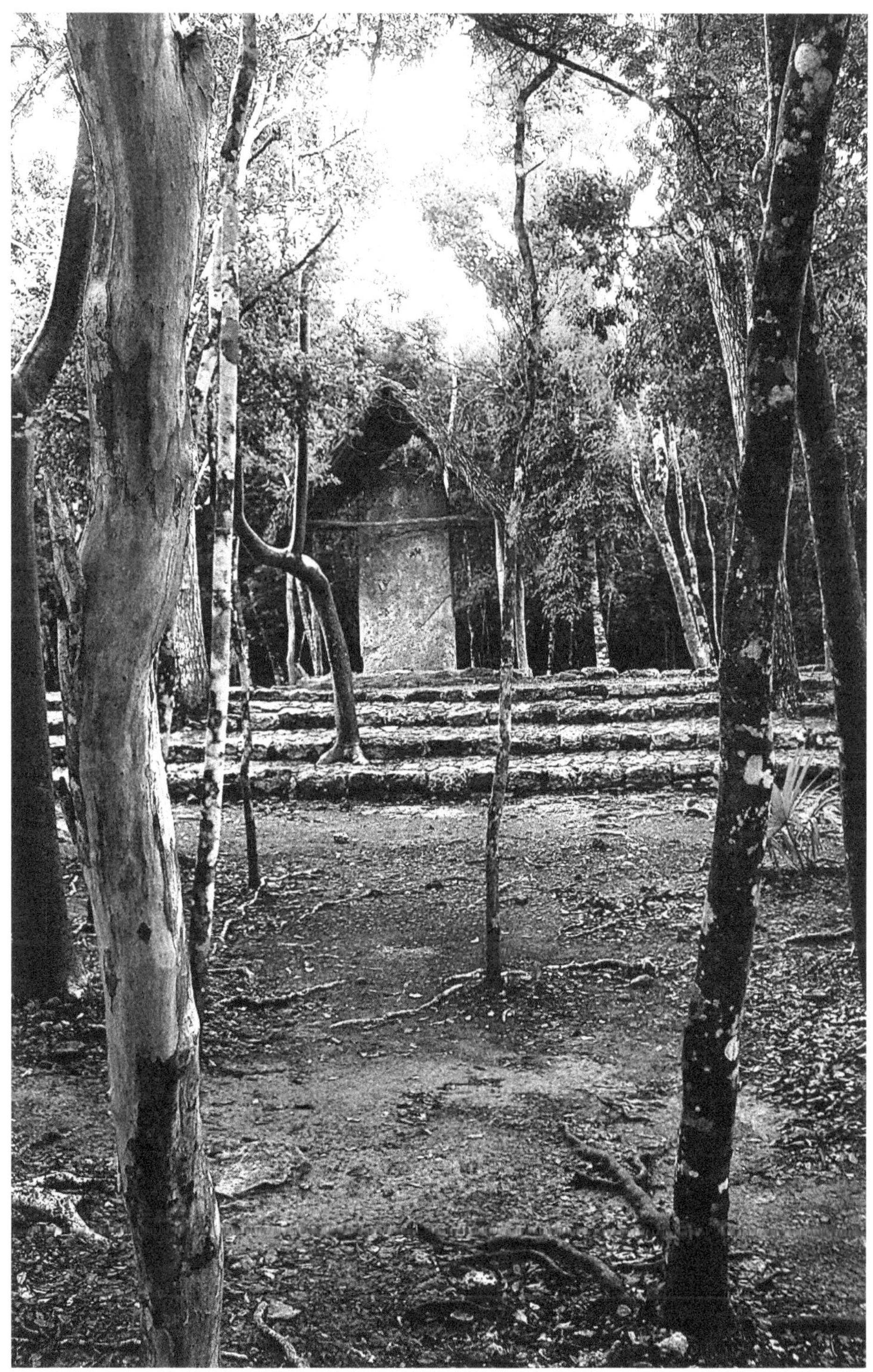

Figure 11 - Cobá - A Stele in the Forest

Figure 12 - Cobá - The Power of the Nature at the Ball Court

The colonization of Cobá might have already begun at 200 BC. This hypothesis is supported by ceramic fragments that were found during the excavations.
Approximately in AD 1500, the city was abandoned. Cobá was already unsettled when the Spanish conquistadores arrived in Yucatán.

During its heyday, Cobá might have had a population of about 50,000 people. Today, about 1500 people live in the same place within the margins of the old city. It is believed that Cobá had control of Tulum and took advantage of this small city on the Caribbean coast as a port.

Numerous steles and inscriptions have been found in Cobá. Unfortunately, the limestone prevailing in the surrounding area which was used to produce these memorial stones is of such poor quality, that many inscriptions are dimly discernible. Many of them cannot be deciphered because of natural erosion. Due to the few decipherable inscriptions, archaeologists believed for a long time that Cobá was governed primarily or at least for an extended period by women.

The climbing of the big pyramid is a unique experience. With its height of 42 meters, it towers high above the treetops of the surrounding jungle and allows for a broad panoramic view. The view of other pyramids towering above the fresh green of the canopy of leaves is impressive. The small temple, situated on the top of the pyramid, is well preserved.

Figure 13 - Cobá - Bicycle Taxis Waiting for Customers

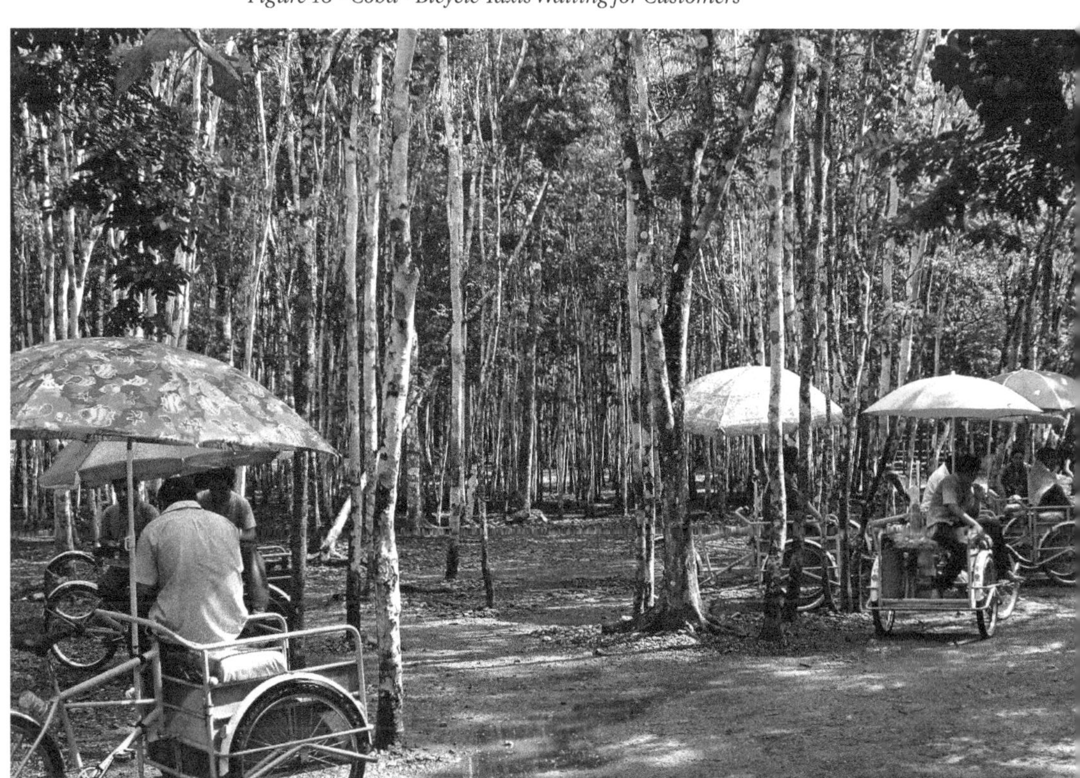

TRAVEL ADVICE - COBÁ:

For the visit of Cobá, it makes sense to stay in Tulum in one of the many hotels or hostels due to the short distance. Also, you can visit the ruins of Tulum then.

You can reach Cobá efficiently using public transportation from Tulum. Colectivos are the preferable option rather than the rare main buses. A rental car is an excellent choice too, or you opt for a guided tour. The center of the ancient city is located between two lakes. Due to the extent of the city, the associated distances and the more or less well-developed long forest trails, it is advisable to wear sturdy shoes, especially if you intend to climb up the main pyramid. Also, you have the opportunity to rent a bike taxi at the entrance of the site. This lets you quickly get around, chauffeured even over longer distances. For the sporty type, there are also bicycles for rent.

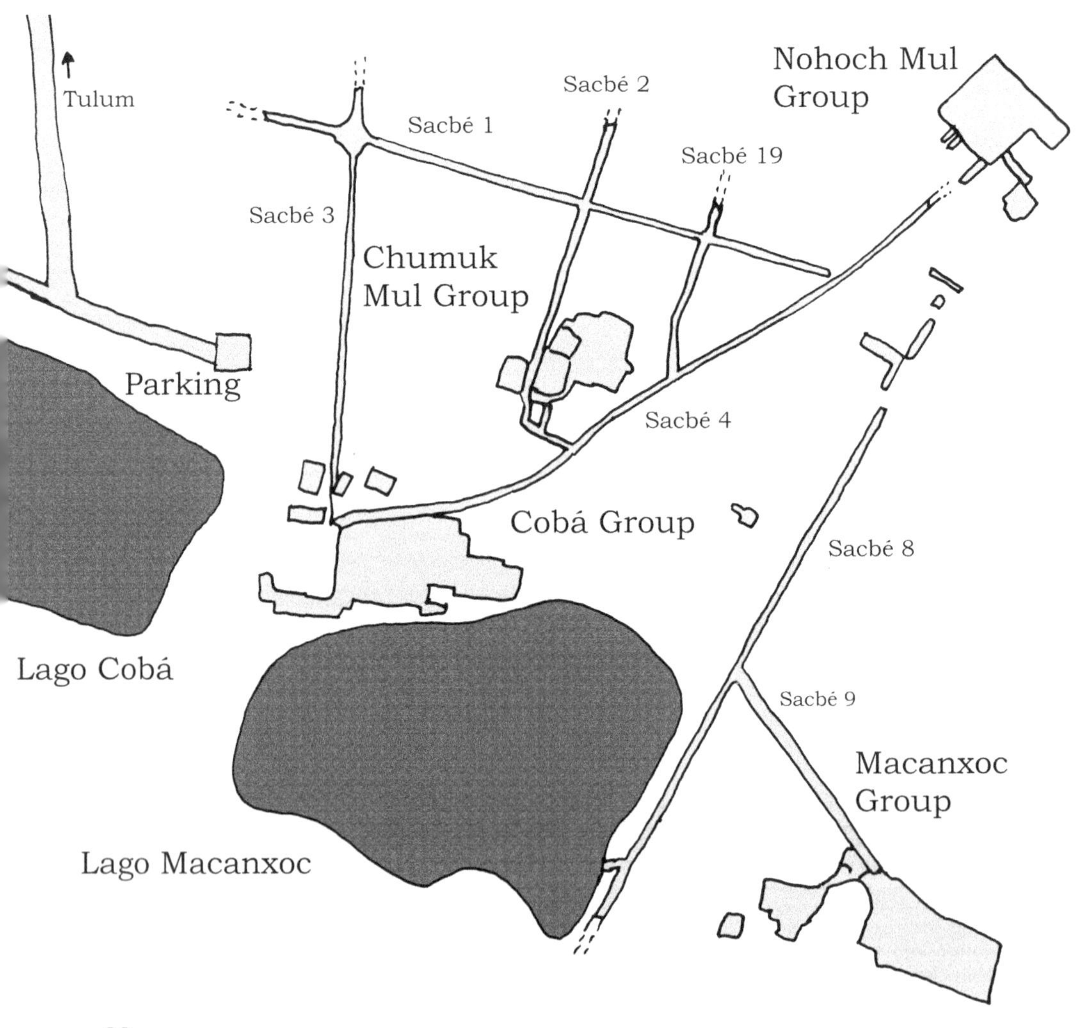

COZUMEL - PILGRIMAGE TO IXCHEL - SAN GERVASIO

Ixchel was the goddess of fertility of the ancient Maya. Various attributes and symbols, like the moon, water, childbirth or the rainbow were associated with her. Ixchel appears in different shapes and ages. An illustration in the Codex of Dresden shows the goddess as an old woman, with claws instead of toes, on the head a slithering snake instead of hair, pouring liquid from a vessel onto the floor. Other traditions speak of a young woman who invented the art of weaving. She was also one of several jaguar deities, to which the Maya worshiped. The island of Cozumel was probably the principal place for the worship of Ixchel. San Gervasio was a religious point of similar importance to the ancient Maya in post-Classic time like Chichén Itzá. Female pilgrims from the entire Maya area, most especially, even from locations as far away as Honduras, traveled to Cozumel to worship the goddess.

In AD 1560, the Spanish historian Diego Lopez de Cogolludo wrote about Tulum:

> *"The pilgrims come to Cozumel, to offer sacrifices, to fulfill their vows, to ask for help in their interests and for the outrageous worship of their false gods."*

Most of the population of Cozumel died shortly after the arrival of the Spanish conquistadores during an outbreak of smallpox, as Spanish chronicles report.

The pre-Columbian name for San Gervasio was "Tantun Cuzamil," which means as much as "Flat Rock at the place of the swallows." Few significant buildings have been preserved in San Gervasio, and only a

<<< *Map 3 - Cobá*

Figure 14 - Cozumel - San Gervasio - Ka'na Nah - The High House

Figure 15 - Cozumel - San Gervasio - Nohoch Nah - The Big House

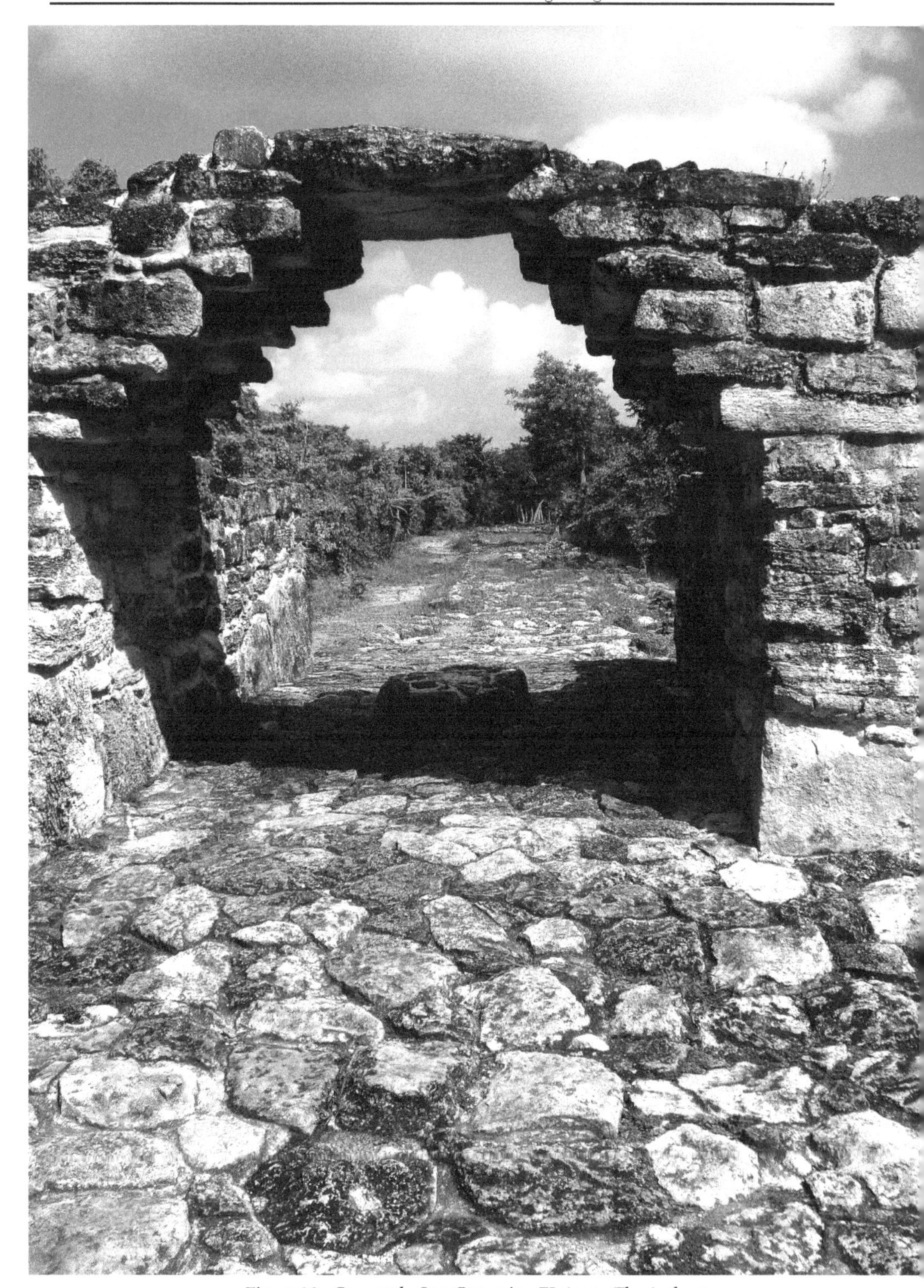

Figure 16 - Cozumel - San Gervasio - EL Arco - The Archway

part of the archaeological area can be visited.

The most massive building is the Pyramid Ka'na Nah, which means "Tall House" in the Mayan language. Priests there used a hollow figure that had an opening according to the records of the Spanish. Unnoticed by the pilgrims, the priests slipped into this figure to announce the will of the gods to their astonished audience.

An impressive monument is El Archo, a portal that has been reconstructed according to other preserved archways of this kind. Directly behind the gate begins a long causeway, a 'Sac-Be ', that was used for ceremonial purposes leading to another temple building, the Nohoch Nah. Nohoch Nah means "big building" in the Mayan language.

TRAVEL ADVICE – SAN GERVASIO:

The distance from Cozumel to the mainland is about 25km. Ferries that leave from Playa del Carmen accomplish this in just about 30 minutes.San Gervasio is located in the northern part of the island. To reach it, you can take a taxi or, if you're the more adventurous type, rent a scooter near the port. The drive to the entrance of San Gervasio takes about 40 minutes.Most tourists reach Cozumel with a cruise ship, but few find their way to this ancient Maya site. Cozumel is also better known as diving paradise.

I recommend that you schedule a visit to San Gervasio as early as possible during the day and to take the first ferry to Cozumel. To do this, you might want to stay in Playa del Carmen the night before and after.

There are just a few tall trees, and therefore little shadow can be found at the whole site. The storms that sweep over the island during the hurricane season are responsible for the low vegetation. Consequently, you should definitely use headgear to protect you against sunstroke!

Figure 17 - Ek Balam - The Gate of the Snake Mouth >>>>

EK BALAM - THE BLACK JAGUAR

Ek Balam in the Mayan language means "Black Jaguar". It was a city of the ancient Maya in the Mexican state Yucatán around 30 km north of Valladolid and 150 km west of Cancun.

In 1997 the excavation was started. According to legends that were recorded by the Spanish government during the 16th century after the conquest of Yucatán, the city was founded by a ruler with the name Ek'Balam.

Figure 18 - Ek Balam - The Acropolis

Figure 20 - Ek Balam - Fresco on the Acropolis

<<< Figure 19 - Ek Balam - The Gate

In its heydays, the city was the capital of the kingdom of Talal. The first king, of who we have the knowledge, named Ek'Balam, was murdered after forty years of rule. The earliest traces of settlement in the area date back to a time of about AD 200 to 300. The descent of Ek Balam began 1000 years later around AD 1200.

The ceremonial center of Ek Balam covers an area of about one square kilometer. It is surrounded by several concentric walls, which are currently interpreted as a defense system. The surrounding area with numerous structures occupied an area of twelve square kilometers. It is not much examined yet.

The most substantial building in Ek Balam is the so-called "Acropolis." With a length of 160m, a width of 70m and a height of 31m, this pyramid is definitely one of the most massive monuments in the northern Yucatán Peninsula due to its volume.

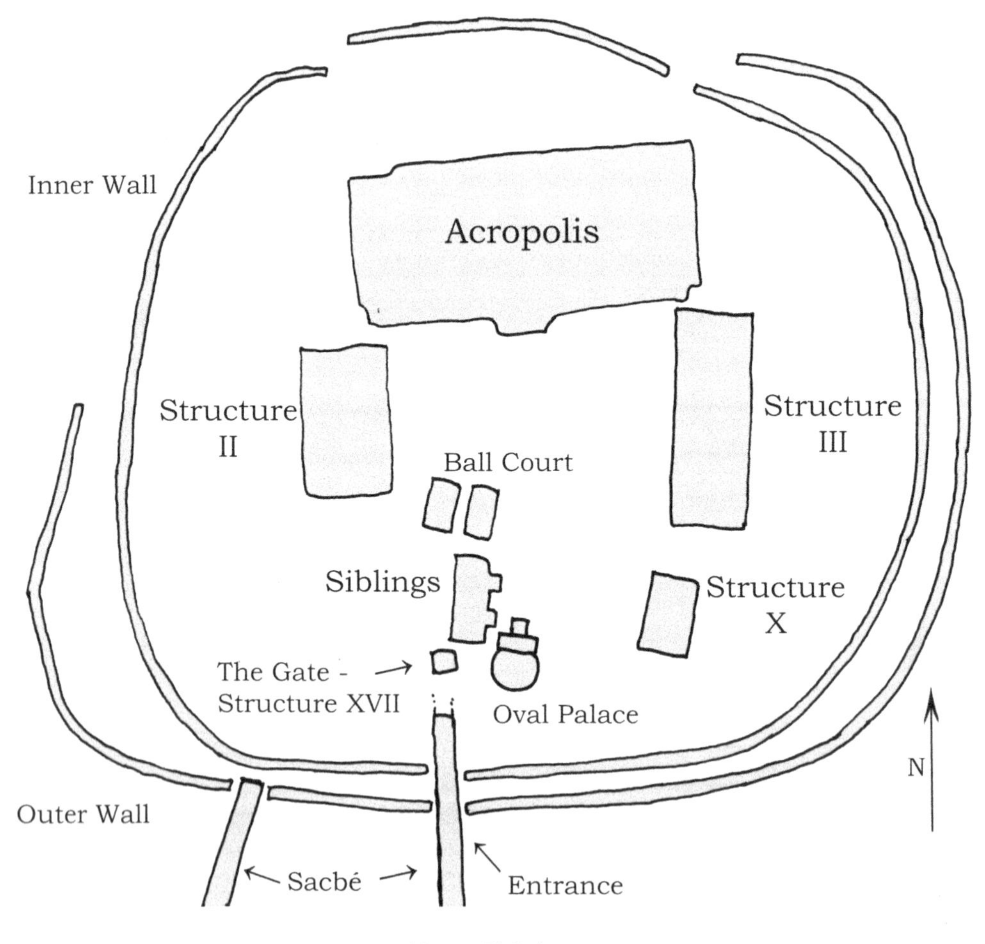

Map 4 - Ek Balam

The building consists of six levels. A total of 72 rooms, which were built into the structure, were found during the excavation work. In one of these rooms, the archaeologists discovered the grave of the ruler Ukit Can Le'kTok. Inscriptions indicate that it was Ukit Can Le'kTok who began the construction of this pyramid during his reign in the years AD 770-801.

In addition to the Acropolis, there are other impressive structures. The "Oval Palace" allows a good view over the Acropolis from its top level.

The building named "Entrance Arch" is a very special gate that opens on four sides. Its roof was reconstructed.

The absolute highlights of Ek Balam are the considerable stucco reliefs, excellently preserved, showing figures of the religious and everyday life of the ancient Maya.

TRAVEL ADVICE

I combined the tour to Ek Balam and Valladolid with a visit to Tulum and Cobá. For this, I decided to stay in Tulum for a couple of days. From there, I took the bus to Valladolid early in the morning. The trip took about two hours. But it is easy to reach Ek Balam from Cancun or Playa del Carmen as well. The distance from Cancun to Valladolid is about 150 km. The public bus from Cancun to Valladolid needs 1.5 hours for the distance.

From Valladolid then, you can take a colectivo or a taxi to reach Ek Balam.

Another option would be to choose Valladolid as an overnight spot and to travel from here to Chichén Itzá after visiting Ek Balam.

Valladolid is a charming town with friendly people and architecture in Spanish Colonial style. Also, visitors can shop here very well since Valladolid does not attract many tourists. Most prices are (still) moderate.

CHICHÉN ITZÁ - THE STAR AMONG THE MAYA SITES

Chichén Itzá is by far the most famous archaeological site with ancient Maya temples and pyramids in Mexico. It is a popular destination for tourists who spend their holidays on the Riviera Maya. From Cancún, Playa del Carmen or Tulúm, Chichén Itzá can be easily reached within two to four hours by rental car or bus. Shortly after the opening of the gates, it will fill up with tourists It is therefore advisable to plan your trip carefully to ensure that you arrive early in the morning before the stream of visitors floods the area. The weekend is not recommended for the visit. It is best to reach Chichén Itzá the day before

the actual tour and stay overnight in the immediate vicinity. The name of the village next to Chichén Itzá is Pisté.

Chichén Itzá is a Maya settlement from the late classical period. However, the urban area shows traces of settlements between 600 BC and 1500 AD. The ruling group of Maya known as the "Itzá" is the origin of the city's name. In the Mayan language, Chichén Itzá means "At the edge of the fountain of Itzá." A large cenote, which was also used by the ancient Maya for sacrificial ceremonies, can be seen on the site. The inscriptions found in Chichén Itzá, various Maya traditions and records of the Spanish conquerors, provide only incomplete and partly contradictory insights into the history of the city. Few things seem to be sure.

Construction work began only in the late classical period around 750 AD. Around 1500, at the end of the Postclassical period, Chichén Itzá was gradually abandoned. The architecture of Chichén Itzá is exceptional in that it combines the style prevailing in the Puuc region with a style variant known as "Toltec," the origin of which is to be found in central Mexico. Researchers discuss the theory that this could be due to the control of Toltec conquerors from Tula, north of Mexico City. Some assume a diffusion model of artistic influence.

Initially, Ek Balam controlled the whole northern area. However, Chichén Itzá, which took control of the area replaced this influence. Following a confrontation with the city of Mayapán, Chichén Itzá was conquered and lost its power. The Itzá finally emigrated to the south and founded the city of Nojpetén, which means "big island," on the site of today's Flores in Lago Petén in Guatemala.

The first modern-day illustrations of Chichén Itzá have been painted by the British architect and painter Catherwood, who visited Yucatán in 1841 together with the American diplomat Stephens.

EL CASTILLO - THE PYRAMID OF KUKULCÁN

The most famous building in Chichén Itzá is undoubtedly the monument "El Castillo," also known as the pyramid of Kukulcán. Twice a year at the time of the equinox, light, and shadow create, combined with the giant snakeheads at the foot of the stairs of the building, the illusion of a snake moving down the building. This spectacle is very popular with tourists, even if it is not clear whether the builders had planned the effect or whether coincidence played a role here.

The pyramid consists of nine levels and has 91 steps on each of the four sides, which together make up the number 364. If you add the base of the temple on the highest level, 365 steps result, which correspond to the number of days in a year. However, this calculation should be done with caution, because the steps were rebuilt during the reconstruction of the pyramid. It is not sure whether the monument in its original state

<<< *Figure 21 - Chichén Itzá – El Castillo – The Temple of Kukulkan*

Figure 22 - Chichén Itzá - Temple of the Warriors

Figure 23 - Chichén Itzá - Serpent head at the big ball court

had 91 steps on each side. There are also signs that there were no 91 levels.

The outer Kukulcán pyramid, visible today, was constructed around 1100 AD. Excavations have shown that it was built over an older nine-level temple. This first pyramid is thought to have been made around 700 AD. There are indications that there is a further overbuilt pyramid structure hidden inside this second pyramid. At the top of the pyramid is the temple of Kukulcán. Unfortunately, the pyramid has been closed to visitors for many years, so you can't climb it anymore.

TEMPLO DE LOS GUERREROS - THE TEMPLE OF THE WARRIOR

The Warrior Temple is named after a series of columns on which the relief-engraved depictions of Maya warriors can be seen. The temple was built over an older structure, the temple of Chak Mol. The columns have a square cross-section and are sculptured. The pictures show Maya warriors, snakes, and birdmen - a mixture of warriors and birds.

This kind of figure is also found in Tula, north of Mexico City. Because of the similarity in architecture and art between Chichén Itzá and Tula, it is believed that a connection between the Maya people living here and the Toltecs from Tula can be established.

GROUP OF THOUSAND COLUMNS

The group of a thousand columns is a large collection of stone columns that join the warrior temple to the south and east. In ancient time, these columns were the pillars of a massive vaulted roof, but it has not been preserved.

TEMPLO DE LAS MESAS - TEMPLE OF THE GREAT SACRIFICIAL TABLE

The temple of the sacrificial table is a small pyramid stump, the base of which consists of four levels. A temple building is found on the upper platform.

JUEGO DE PELOTA - THE BIG BALL COURT

The big ball court is one of the twelve ball courts discovered in Chichén Itzá. And it is the largest ball court ever found in the Maya world. This one has a length of 168 meters and a width of 38 meters (6384 square meters). The side walls are eight meters high. By way of comparison, an international soccer pitch is only slightly larger. It measures 105 x 68 meters (7140 square meters). The way the ballplayers of the Maya managed to move the massive rubber ball, which they were only allowed to touch with hips, shoulders, and knees but not with their hands or feet, through the two rings just below the top of the side walls, will remain a mystery forever.

Figure 24 - Chichén Itzá - The Snail Tower - El Caracol

Figure 25 - Chichen Itzá - La Eglesia

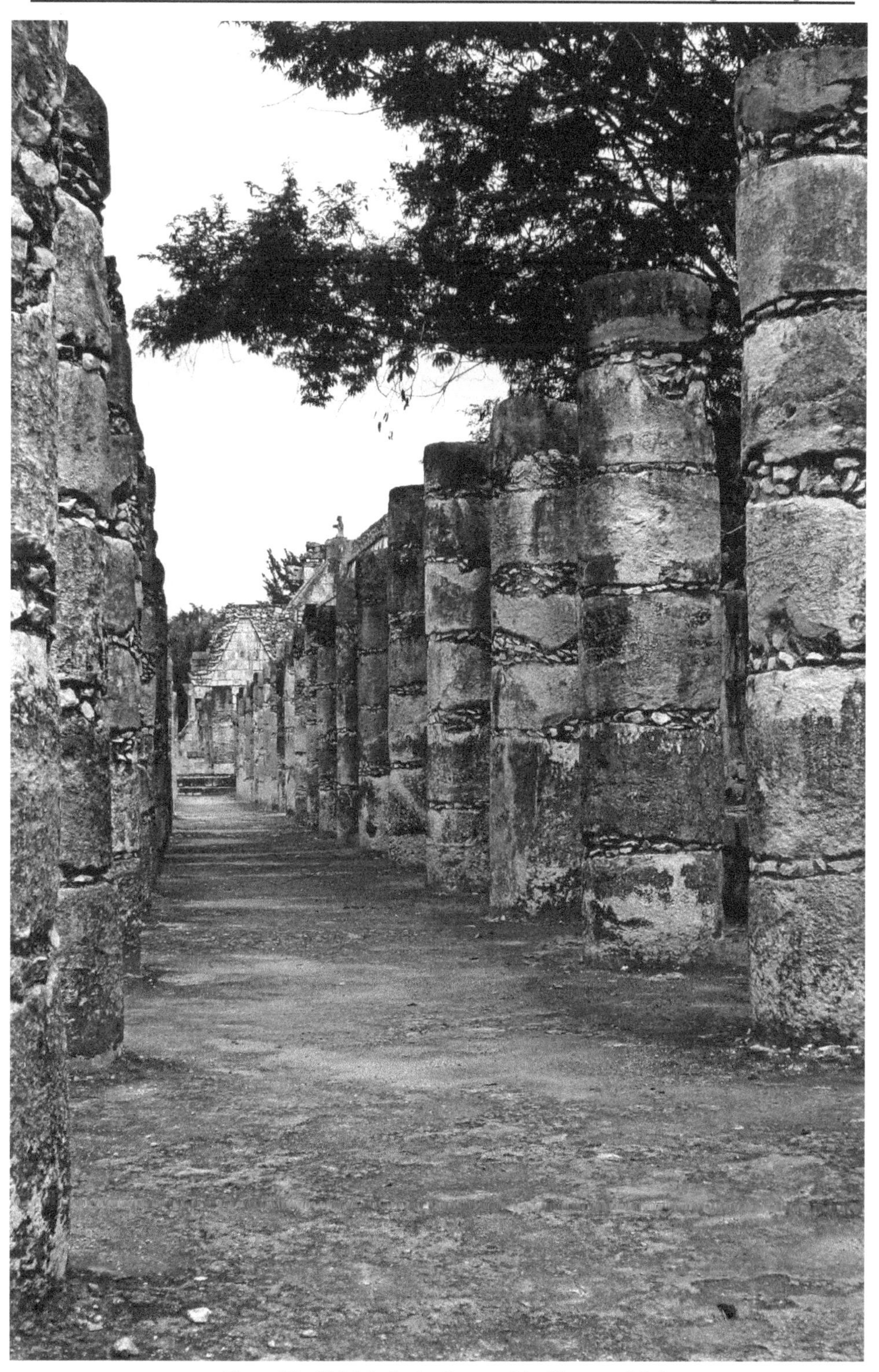

Figure 26 - Chichén Itzá – Group of the Thousand Columns

Figure 27 - Chichén Itzá - Cenote Sagrado

Due to the weight of the ball, violent injuries might have been common for ballplayers. The losers or the winners, as some historians assume, had the honor of being sacrificed on the pyramid of Kukulcán after the game.

TEMPLE OF THE JAGUARS

Several temples were built around the large ball playground on the enclosure walls. The most striking of these is the Jaguar temple on the south side of the eastern wall.

TZOMPANTLI

The word Tzompantli, borrowed from the language of the Aztecs, the Nahuatl, originally refers to a platform on which the skulls of the ritual victims were exhibited, fastened to wooden frames. The base of the Tzompantli is decorated with relief skulls.

VENUS PLATFORM

This structure is a small square-shaped platform. Snakeheads form the upper end of the stairs leading upwards on all four sides.

CENOTE SAGRADO - THE SACRED FOUNTAIN

The Cenote Sagrado is located about 400 meters north of the Castello. The path leads through sparse forest and is lined by all kinds of stalls of artisans and traders. The cenote also served as a place for sacrifice. In addition to various objects of art, several human skeletons have been found on their bottom during dives.

The diameter of the cenote is about 60 meters. The distance from the upper edge to the water surface is about 15 meters. Like probably all cenotes, the Cenote Sagrada of Chichén Itzá is connected to the subterranean water system of northern Yucatán.

CARACOL - THE SNAIL TOWER

The Caracol or snail tower is one of the most prominent buildings in Chichén Itzá. According to an inscription found on its surface, the construction time of this monument built for astronomical observation dates back to 906 AD. The tower got its name because of the spiral staircase that leads upwards inside. The builders erected the round tower on several superimposed platforms.

Archaeologists and historians assume that a total of 29 astronomical events were of interest to the Maya priesthood. These include the day-and-night equals, solstices and solar eclipses. For 20 of these events, the Caracol has established lines of sight for observation. Probably, the number of these lines of sight was initially even higher. However, due to the temporary deterioration of the building structure, they are no longer detectable today.

Figure 28 - Chichén Itzá - Column at the Temple of Warriors

IGLESIA - THE "CHURCH"

The building called Iglesia is relatively small and has only one doorway. It stands out for its façade decorations with several masks of the rain god Chaac.

TRAVEL TIP:

Chichén Itzá is a very frequently visited place. Every day, masses of tourists rush in from the tourist centers of the Caribbean coast to Chichén Itzá. The administration of the site opens at 8 am. By 12 noon, however, it is almost impossible to stand on the site, because it is teeming with people.

Therefore, I recommend that the serious explorer should arrive early before (!) 8 a. m. in front of the entrance and buy his ticket. It's best to plan several visits because due to the size of the complex, you won't be able to visit all the buildings in one visit before the tourists set upon the ancient ruins.

Several times a day there are intercity buses that stop in Chichén Itzá from Tulum, Playa del Carmen, Cancún, Valladolid or Mérida. In the

Figure 29 - Chichén Itzá - Warriors and Eagles at the Tzompantli

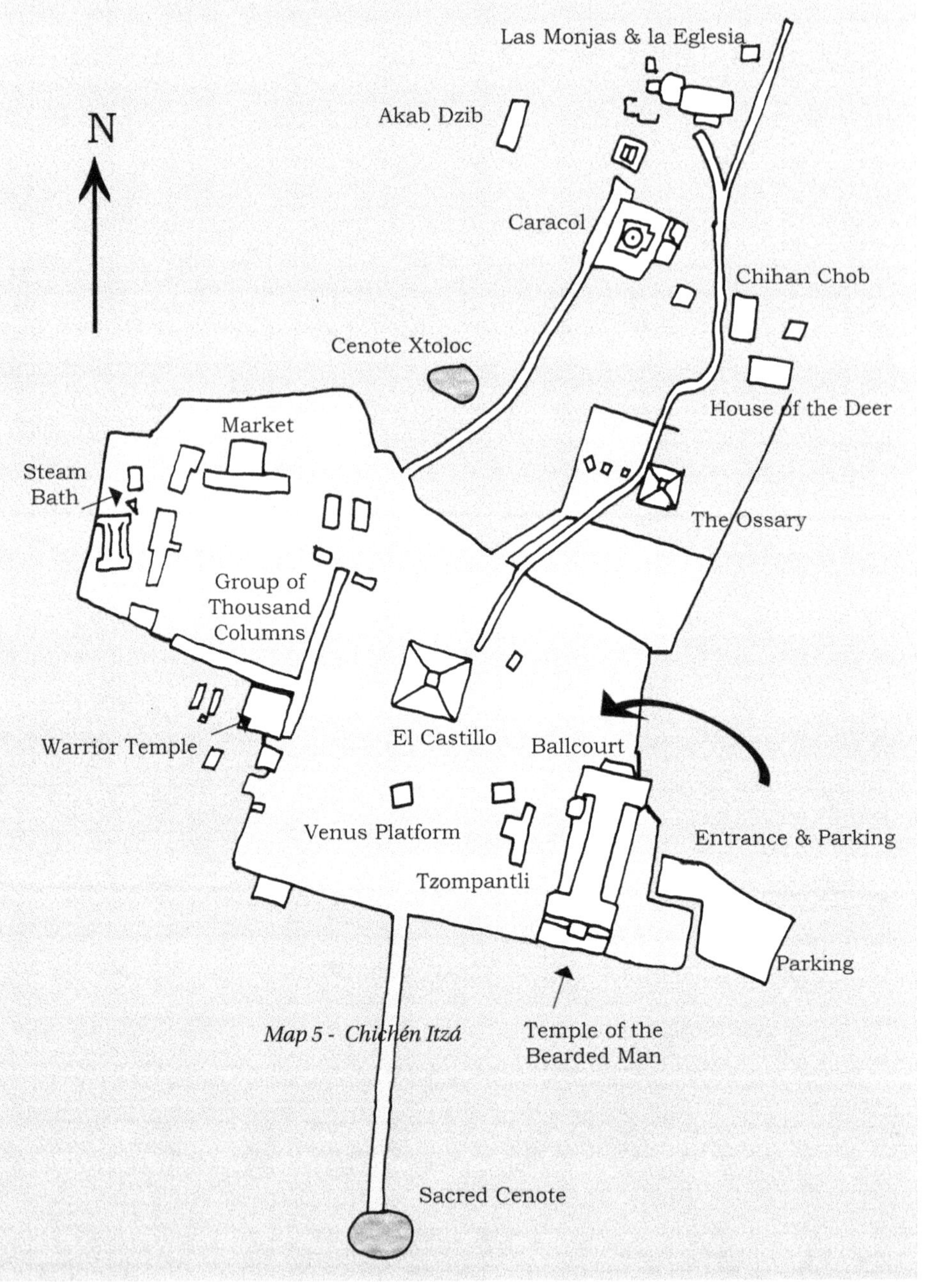

Map 5 - Chichén Itzá

entrance area of the Maya site, there is a ticket counter and luggage storage. In the small town of Piste, only five minutes away by car, restaurants and overnight accommodation are available.

Figure 30 - Izamal - KinichKak Moo - Top - Temple Pyramid >>>

IZAMAL - THE MAGIC CITY

Izamal is one of 35 locations in Mexico, which have been awarded by the Secretary of Tourism in Mexico to be called Magic City. This title was bestowed to somewhat unknown but exciting places of the country.

The small town of Izamal has just about 17000 inhabitants. The colonial-style village is located about 70km east of Mérida, the capital of the state Yucatán on the peninsula of identical name. Other names that are used for Izamal are Yellow City and the City of Hills. The first indicates that the facades of the city buildings are yellow colored. The

Figure 31 – Izamal - Kinich Kak Moo - Looking along the Side

latter term points to the presence of numerous ancient Maya ruins within the city limits. Izamal has a tremendous historical significance despite its low level of recognition and its small size.

The first traces of settling in Izamal can be traced back to the pre-classic period, but the actual development to a city center with more considerable importance for the Maya civilization and culture took place during the classical period. In this time, Izamal was possibly the most extensive Maya settlement of the northern Yucatán. Due to the large-area superstructure by the modern city, this fact is no longer visible. But at various points of the town, you can admire the remains of two gigantic pyramids. And "gigantic" is not an exaggeration...

Izamal housed sanctuaries which were dedicated to the creator god and the sun god. The most giant pyramid in Izamal covers an area of 8000m² and has a volume of 700,000m³. The name of this pyramid is KinichKak Moo. It was consecrated to the sun god of the Maya.

The surface of this pyramid, impressive per se, is so large that it provides enough space for another monument of the post-classical period. The corners of the upper pyramid are rounded, and it rises over ten levels.

The second of the great pyramids, called P'ap'hol Chaak, was

Figure 32 – Izamal - Kinich Kak Moo - Looking along the Side >>>>

dedicated to the god Itzamná. Itzamná was the creator of the world in the belief of the post-Classic Maya. One can see the importance of these two pyramids for the Maya culture from two facts. First, the name of the god Itzamná probably inspired the name of the city itself. The name Izamal can be easily derived from the name of the god Itzamná. Second, the Spanish conquerors demolished, precisely, this pyramid and built a Christian monastery on top of its surface. In this way, it was hoped to accelerate the Christianization of the Maya. This strategic approach of the Catholic Church is known since the Christianization of Europe. Churches were preferably built upon the fundaments of pre-Christian pagan temples.

The monastery complex, which still exists, was named after the saint San Antonio de Padua. It was completed in 1561. Because the underlying gigantic pyramid was used as a foundation for the construction, the monastery has a churchyard with an area that is only surpassed by the Vatican in Rome. Also, the inhabitants of the city have misused the pyramids as a quarry for the construction of the monastery and the surrounding buildings.

The first bishop of Yucatán had his episcopal in Izamal, and the fourth bishop Diego di Landa resided here as well.

Diego di Landa gained notoriety. After he had considered the papers and documents of the Maya as "heretical devil's work," he ordered the burning of all documents he was able to find. This "Autodafé" happened in 1562 in the town of Mani, south of Merida. Only four of the original

codices of the Maya were untroubled by this criminal act. One may visit them in European museums and in Mexico City. For his relentless activities, he was criticized by the colonial government of Mexico among others. They pressed charges against him, which ended with an acquittal. Probably as compensation, he wrote the book "Report on the Things in Yucatán," in which he recorded the history of the Maya. Today, this book is the oldest document describing the history of the Maya and their culture. It provided valuable indications to the decipherment of Maya hieroglyphs.

TRAVEL ADVICE

Izamal offers several accommodation options. You can comfortably make a stopover there. Izamal is best visited after Chichén Itzá on your way to Mérida. But this may be possible only with a car. Otherwise, you could make a day trip to Izamal while you reside in Merida using a public bus from there.

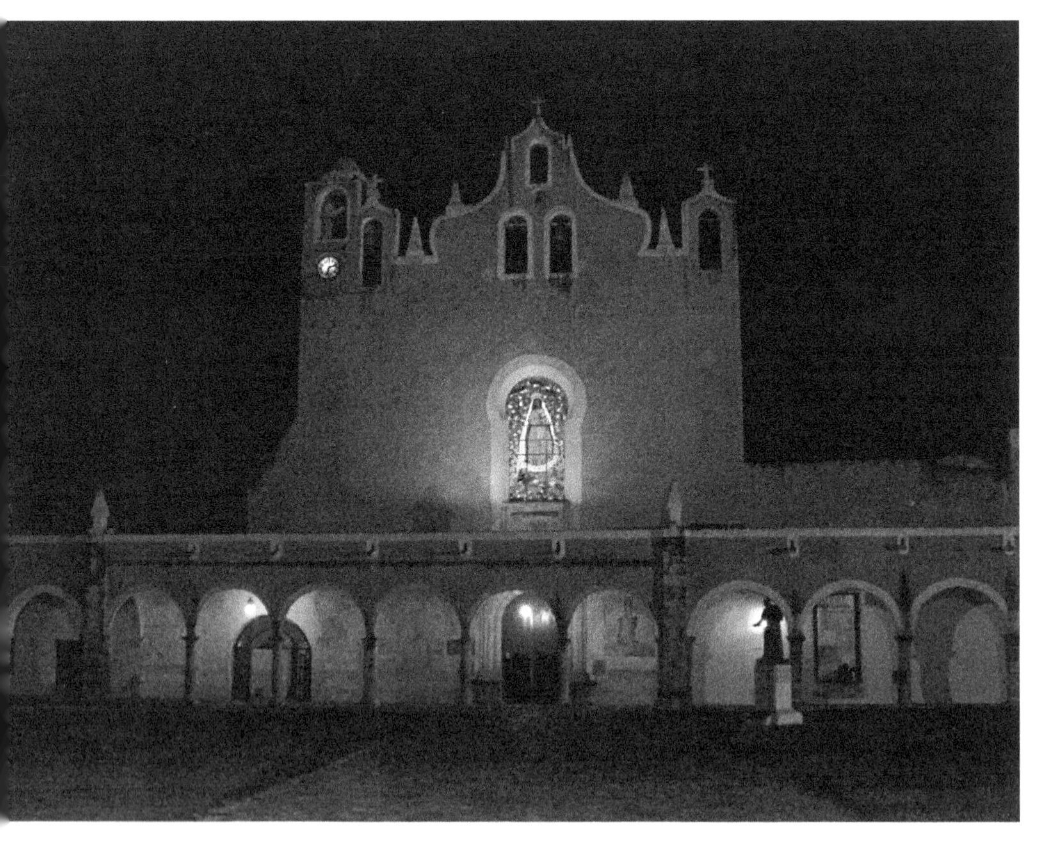

Figure 33 - Izamal - The Church of the Franciscan Monastery at Night, a statue of Diego de Landa on the right side

UXMAL - BUILT BY A MAGICIAN IN ONE NIGHT

The early history and beginnings of Uxmal are almost unknown. The city is located in the northwestern part of the Yucatán peninsula about 60km south of Mérida and can be reached by car in less than an hour. It is assumed that the name Uxmal is derived from the Mayan word "oxmal," which means as much as "three times built." The most striking building in Uxmal is the pyramid of the magician from the Late Classical period.

The most famous fable of the Maya locals about the mythological history of Uxmal was recorded by John L. Stephens, who visited the site around 1840. In his book Incidents of Travel in Central America, Chiapas and Yucatán, Stephens reproduces the fable of a magical dwarf. This dwarf had been challenged by the ruler of Uxmal to build a pyramid during a single night. He did this task without problems and created the Pyramid of the Magician.

The hill country area around Uxmal was already called Puuc by the ancient Maya. This name became characteristic of the architectural style, which prevails in Uxmal and is common in the whole Puuc area. Even outside the actual Puuc region, Uxmal influenced the architecture of Maya cities.

EXPLORATION AND HISTORY OF UXMAL

The first detailed report about Uxmal was written by the pen of a Spanish Franciscan monk or his secretary, who described the ruins in 1588. All prominent early explorers of the Maya world visited and

described the site. After von Waldeck, who arrived at the ruins in 1835, Stephens and Catherwood were the next explorers at Uxmal, while passing through the Yucatán Peninsula during their famous journey.

The earliest photos were taken by the world traveler and archaeologist Désiré Charnay, who lived here in 1859/60. In 1886, Teobert Maler reached the city during an extensive expedition across the peninsula and photographed the site. In 1907, Sylvanus Morley measured some of the buildings. The first detailed survey work was carried out by Frans Blom in 1930. Only a few surviving hieroglyphic inscriptions were found, so the details of the early history of Uxmal remain in the dark.

In addition to archaeological finds, Uxmal was mentioned in various documents which derive either from the post-classical or from the early colonial period. The oldest mention can be found in the books of the Chilam Balam of Chumayel:

> *The priests of Uxmal revered Chac,*
> *the priests of ancient time.*
> *And Hapai Can was taken to his boat.*
> *When he arrived, the walls of Uxmal*
> *were marked with blood.*

The Maya chronicles of the Chilam Balam say that Uxmal was founded at some time between 731 AD and 751 AD by the Maya dynasty of Xiu. This family originally came from the area of today's Tabasco and had migrated to the northern Yucatán at this time.

About the same time, there are indications of an immigration wave from the same area to Edzná in Campeche, which is located further south. However, the data found in the chronicles are not always precise. The period referred to, could have been 256 years later as well. But the archaeological finding would contradict this date.

With the arrival of the Xiu, the religious life changed. The central Mexican god Quetzalcoatl, known as Kukulkan by the Maya, was introduced into the priestly rites. Chaak, the rain god of the Maya, who had already been revered, still had a significant role even after this expansion of the Maya Pantheon.

The Spaniards met the Xiu family upon their arrival on the peninsula, though not in Uxmal, which had been left by this dynasty, but in the city of Mani, to the south, where the Xiu had their capital at this time. The Xiu formed an alliance with the Spaniards and supported them in the conquest of the peninsula.

Some family members helped Diego de Landa to write his book "Relación de las Cosas de Yucatán." The book was published in modern times in English language using the title "Yucatán before and after the conquest." This fact calls into question the objectivity of de Landa's report. At least as far as the historical events are concerned, one must assume that these were portrayed from the subjective perspective of the

<<< *Figure 34 - Uxmal - The Pyramid of the Magician*

Xiu dynasty.

However, the archaeological finds made in Uxmal, allow the observation that Uxmal was already populated centuries before the arrival of the Xiu. About 1000 AD, Uxmal was conquered by Toltecan invaders, whose origin was Central Mexico. By 1200 AD, construction activity ended. The city was not abandoned yet, but the Xiu settled, as mentioned before, in the small town of Mani, where Diego de Landa resided later.

When the Spaniards reached the area, Uxmal was still populated. Because the Spaniards did not build a colonial city here, Uxmal quickly lost its importance. Finally, the remaining inhabitants moved away and left the town to decay and to the ever-growing vegetation.

THE BUILDINGS

The main temple buildings, palaces, and pyramids of Uxmal have been restored and are in an excellent condition. They show a high development stage regarding construction and quality. The parts, which can be visited by tourists, all originate from the 9th or 10th century. Only a tiny part of the approximately 10 square kilometers, which make up the urban area, is accessible to tourists.

From the entrance, you first reach the Pyramid of the Magician. Basically, you reach its backside. The best way is to walk around the pyramid on the right side.

THE PYRAMID OF THE MAGICIAN

The most impressive building in Uxmal is undoubtedly this pyramid. It is a multi-layered step pyramid with rounded corners. With a height of 35 meters, it surpasses the other structures of the complex and dominates the view of the Maya site. During excavations, it has been found that the pyramid, which is visible today, contains several anteceding monuments in its interior.

In fact, the Pyramid of the Magician was constructed as a total of five nested structures, the newer one built on top of the older one. The phenomenon of overbuilt structures has also been found elsewhere, as in Chichén Itzá, and was common in the Maya world. Even the name Uxmal, the three times built, can be explained in this way.

The total construction period of the pyramid of the magician lasted over a period of 300 years. The beginning of the construction is seen by the archaeologists in the Late Classic period, around the time of 650 AD.

THE NUNNERY QUADRANGLE - CUADRÁNGULO DE LAS MONJAS

Right next to the Pyramid of the Magician is the location of the Nuns Square or Nunnery Quadrangle. These are several buildings. Grouped

<<<< *Figure 35 - Uxmal - Detail of the Nunnery Quadrangle*

Figure 36 - Uxmal - The Nuns Square

Figure 37 - Uxmal - The Turtle Temple

together they surround a central courtyard. The side length of the platform on which the group was erected measures 120 meters. The buildings have a large number of rooms that open onto the courtyard. Because of its architectural similarity with Christian monastic buildings, the first visitors had given the name Nuns Square to it. In fact, it seems they were wrong, and the Nuns Square served as a palace building inhabited by the ruling dynasty. The last inscription in Uxmal can be found here as a painting on a vaulted cornerstone, mentioning the year 907 AD. Another one with a date inscription is just one year older. These inscriptions are also the last ones made in the Puuc region. By the way, the latest date inscribed at all by the Maya and recorded in the manner of the "Long Count" is an inscription in Tonina, which dates back to the year 909 AD, just 2 years later.

THE GOVERNOR'S PALACE

The narrow building is nearly 100 meters long and stands on a slightly larger platform. On the west side, there is a staircase about 40 meters wide. The governor palace was built around 900 AD by a ruler named Chaac.

Figure 38- Uxmal - The Governor's Palace and two-headed jaguar throne in front

The upper part of the exterior walls is richly decorated, while the lower part is smooth and lacks the ornaments.

Accurate surveys have shown that the building edges are aligned with the northern extremes of Venus as the evening star. Venus as the supernatural avatar of the god Chaac marks the beginning of the rainy season at this position. In this way, the ruler and constructor Chaac demonstrated his agreement with the divine power.

In front of the staircase on a small platform is a sculpture representing a double-headed jaguar. It was initially used as a throne. A painting in Palenque, meanwhile gone lost, showed a similar throne.

THE HOUSE OF TURTLES

This temple is located on the same platform as the Governor's Palace. You can reach it by leaving the Square of the Nuns to the west and crossing the ball court. Figures of turtles have been applied to the upper part of the walls and gave the name to this building.

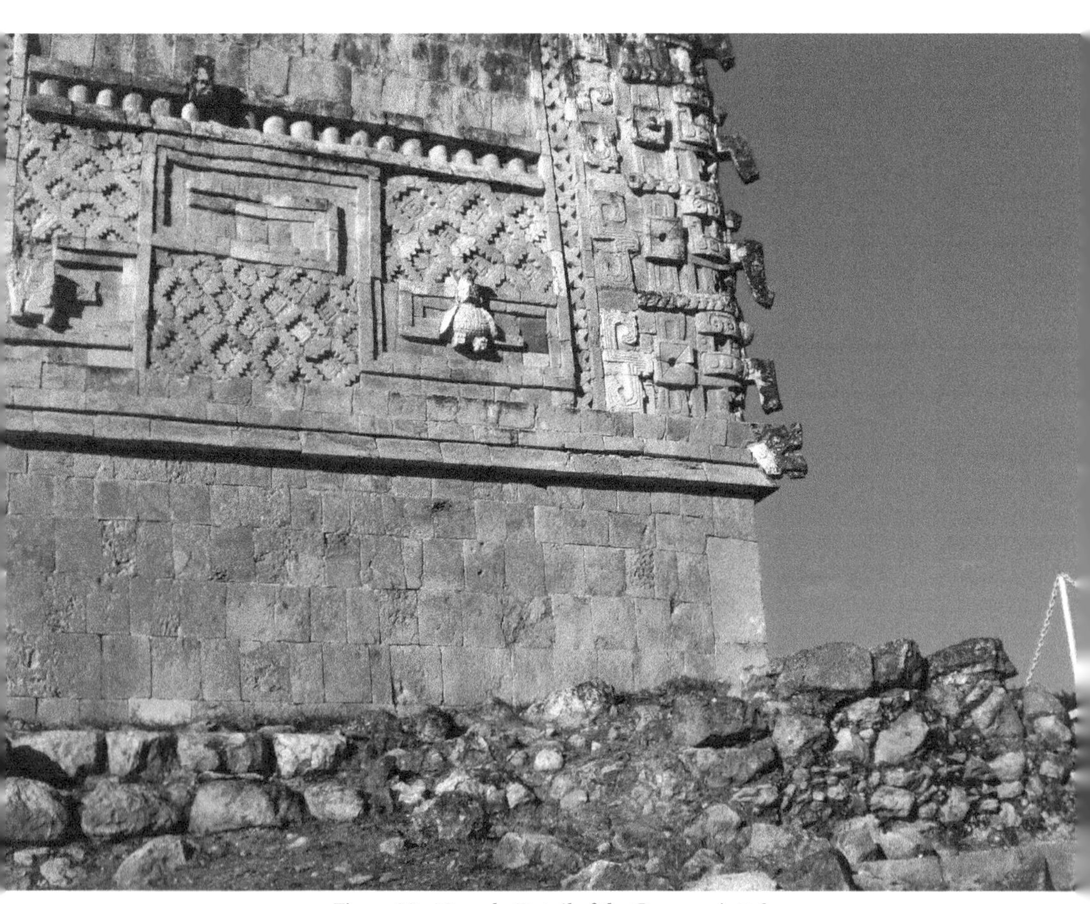

Figure 39 - Uxmal - Detail of the Governor's Palace

THE GREAT PYRAMID - PIRÁMIDE MAYOR

Passing the back of the Governor's Palace, continuing westwards, you reach the Great Pyramid. It resembles the pyramid of the magician. A staircase leads up to the upper platform on its east side. From there you have an excellent view of the entire area.

THE HOUSE OF THE PIGEONS

The House of the Pigeons got its name because of numerous slit-shaped openings in the roof comb of the building. It belongs to the complex of the same name, which is located in the west of the site.

TRAVEL TIP

It is best to visit Uxmal with a stay in Merida, the capital of the state of Yucatán. This not only allows you to enjoy the city life of Merida but to use this city as a central point for visiting other interesting Maya sites, such as Mayapan or Izamal.

It takes about an hour by car to reach Uxmal. The ancient Maya site is located about 60km south of Merida. A ride by public transport is also possible. Local tourist offices in Merida offer the possibility to book tours to different locations in the area.

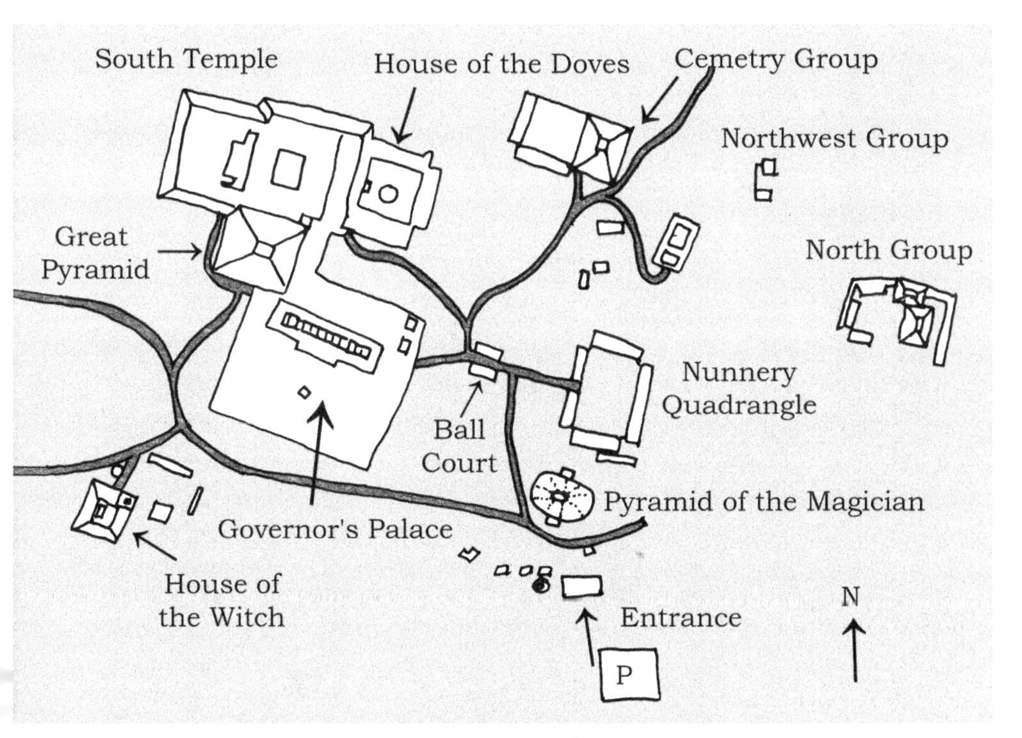

Map 6 - Uxmal

Region: Chiapas and Campeche

EDZNÁ - THE HOUSE OF THE ITZÁ

Have you ever visited the ruins of Edzná in Campeche? The answer should be "no" because only a few people find their way to this superbly preserved site of the Maya.

The city is about an hour's drive from Campeche, the capital of the Mexican state of the same name. From Mérida, you can reach Edzná in about three hours. The Maya ruins of Edzná are located inland, about 40 kilometers from the Gulf coast in the west of the Yucatán Peninsula.

The name Edzná comes from the language of the Yucatecan Maya, called Mayathan. It means the house of the Itzá, which would point to a possible connection between Edzná and Chichén Itzá. The city was once the capital of a relatively large state area. Their influence extended in the north to the Puuc region, in the south-west, it bordered on the sphere of influence of Calakmul. The town area recognized to date has a size of approximately 25 square kilometers. 25,000 people could have lived here.

HISTORY

Several huge buildings have been erected during the classic period of Maya history. But the beginning of Edzná dates back to the pre-classical period. About 400 BC to 1450 AD, the area was inhabited over a period of more than 2000 years.

During the excavations in Edzná, 32 steles and 2 hieroglyphic stairways have been discovered. Thanks to the inscriptions, it was possible to create a list of ten dynastic rulers that reaches from 633 AD to

869 AD. A close relationship to Calakmul seems to have existed. It is assumed that in the seventh century, Yuknoom Cheen II, also known as "the Great," who was a prominent ruler of the Kaan kingdom based in Calakmul, was simultaneously the ruler of Edzná.

A remarkable event, worth to be noted in the inscriptions, was the arrival of a female ruler or princess from the Maya city of Petexbatun in the southern lowland in today's Guatemala, also in the 7th century.

During this time the influence of Edzná grew far north to the Puuc region.

Towards the end of the 7th century, the forces of Calakmul were defeated in the war against Tikal. Calakmul did not recover from the defeat and lost his pre-eminence in the Maya world. After a series of wars, presumably against Cobá on the east coast of the peninsula and his allies, Edzná had to accept a temporary loss of its power and influence.

In the 8th century, the city experienced the arrival of a group of people from today's Tabasco, which was probably the Itzá group. The last "Long Count" inscription dates from the year 810 AD. Edzná was not abandoned at the end of the classic period as it happened to the classical cities of the South. It was still inhabited in the post-classic era and was

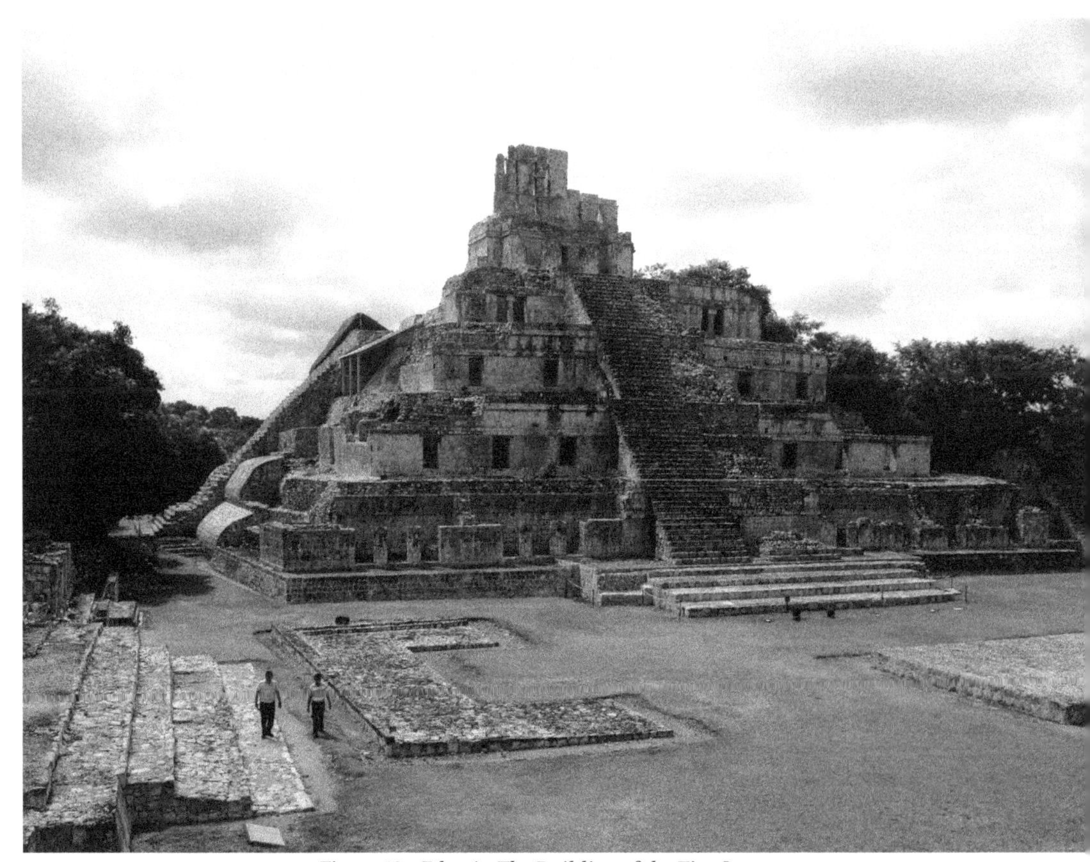

Figure 40 - Edzná - The Building of the Five Stores

Figure 41 - Edzná - The Building of the Five Stores - Side View

an essential center of the region. It was only at the end of the post-classical period between 1450 and 1500 that Edzná was abandoned.

The ancient ruins were rediscovered in 1907. Organized excavations began in 1958. Since the 1980's, considerable efforts have been made to restore the buildings.

BUILDINGS

The entrance, through which one enters the site, is located in the north of the area.

THE BIG SQUARE

In the center of Edzná, you will reach "the big square," to the east of which is the Acropolis located. In the north, the square is bordered by the platform of knives, to the east is "The Big House,"" Nohochná," which is thought to have served administrative purposes. To the south of the square are the South Temple, a ball court and the Temple of Masks. From the stairs to the great Acropolis, two "sacred streets" - Sacbeob - lead to the two corners of the Great House "Nohochná."

THE GREAT ACROPOLIS

There are numerous temples and palace buildings on a square platform, which can be reached via the west-facing long straight stair. The whole complex is called "The great Acropolis." The largest of the buildings is the temple of the five stories with its central staircase. It raises about 40 meters above the environment using five steps. This pyramid has very unusual door openings on its front that lead to rooms with cobbled vault. It is, therefore, to be assumed that the monument not only had a ceremonial character, but also served as a palace, and thus a place of residence.

On the north side of the Great Acropolis, you will find the Northern Temple. The last structural change of this building is from the post-classical era. Just beside is a structure named "Patio Puuc" with a limited inner courtyard, which initially contained a steam bath. The name derives from the design elements of the Puuc style found in this structure.

At the southern end of the Great Acropolis, just opposite the northern temple, stands the Temple of the Moon, which, with its front stairs, faces the Northern Temple.

THE SMALL ACROPOLIS

The Small Acropolis is another platform that is located south of the Great Acropolis. On it is the Temple of the Steps situated.

Figure 42 - Edzná - Temple of the Masks

THE TEMPLE OF THE MASKS

The Temple of the Masks is rather small but nevertheless interesting. It is located west of the small Acropolis. There you will find two big stone masks, which presumably represent the sun god of the Maya. They are in a perfect state of preservation.

THE OLD WITCH - LA VIEJA HECHICERA

About 800 meters from the center, in the north-western direction, is another significant structure, the Old Witch - La Vieja Hechicera.

WATER MANAGEMENT

The area around Campeche is the least rainy in the Maya area during the dry winter months. Accordingly, the vegetation on the north-eastern Gulf coast is also characterized by dry forests that change to shrubland or savanna further north.

But during the rainy season, from July to September, the daily average rainfall reaches 180mm per day, making the area the wettest region in the northern lowlands. The relatively impermeable subsoil can quickly lead to flooding. This was a big problem for the Maya in classical times, but they have solved it masterfully.

Remains of a complex system for water management can be seen at various points on the site. The primary purpose of this water system

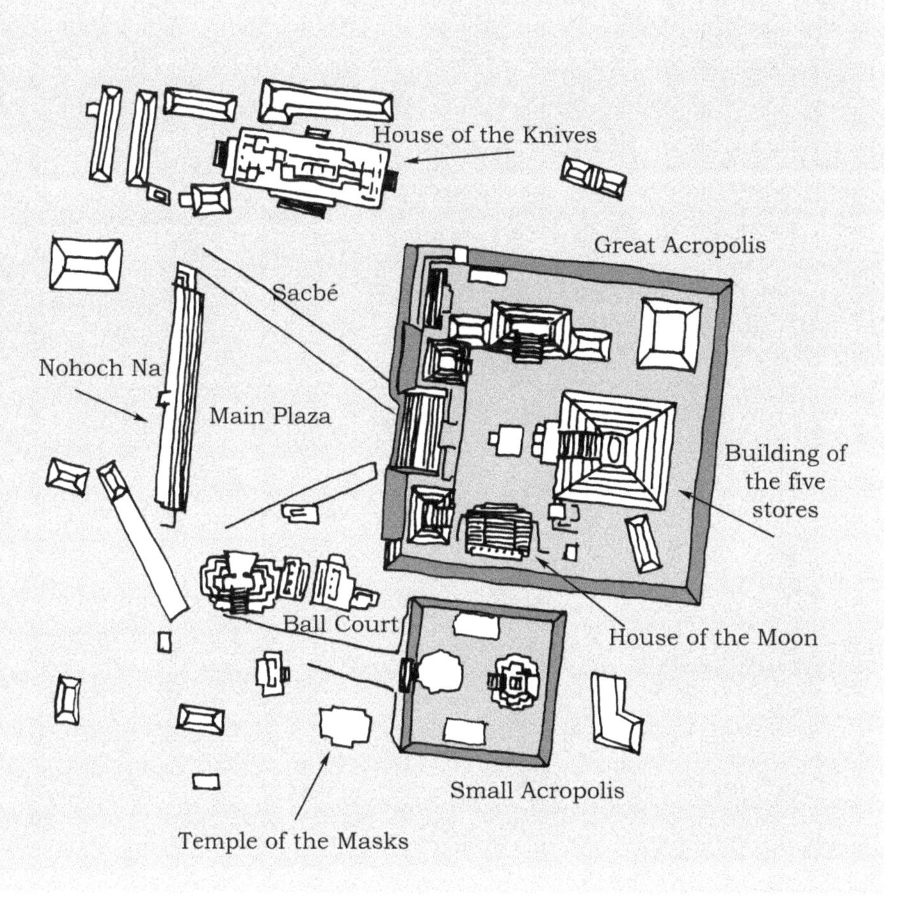

Map 7 – Edzná

could have been the rapid drainage of the municipal area after heavy rainfall. The length of the channels used for this purpose was up to 6 kilometers. Several of them lead to a nearby lake. In addition to the outflow, canals were also used as transport routes and, of course, for irrigation of the fields. Additionally, they might have been served as a defense facility. Also, they helped to enrich the selection of food using fish farming.

TRAVEL ADVICE

To visit Edzná, it is recommended to stay in Campeche. Around Edzná there are no significant options for accommodation. The public bus runs from Campeche only once or twice a day. That is why I rented a taxi for a day to visit Edzná. It is more favorable if you join with others or book an organized tour. In the central square in Campeche, you will find local

Image 43 - Edzna - Stele 21

Figure 44 - Campeche - Colonial Houses

travel agents that will arrange this trip. The hotels can also help you with the organization of such an excursion.

Since 1999, Campeche has been a UNESCO World Heritage Site. The city of 250,000 inhabitants was founded in 1540 by the Spanish conquerors.

Over the centuries Campeche was attacked by pirates several times, sometimes even conquered and all its inhabitants sold into slavery. A museum devoted to the theme of "pirates," as well as the nightly performances on the old city walls, keep up the memory of these events. The mighty fortifications with their rusted cannons are well preserved and can be visited.

The city center has been able to preserve the old style of the colonial period, with much less tourism than the smaller San Cristobal de las Casas in Chiapas.

Although numerous travel guides especially highlight the fresh seafood offer right here on the Gulf Coast, I would strongly advise to only eat cooked food.

After the visit of Campeche, I recommend continuing to Palenque. The bus takes about four hours for the route.

PALENQUE - MYSTICISM IN THE MIST OF THE RAINFOREST

High temperatures and unusually high humidity will be your companion when visiting Palenque. The ruins of this once important Maya city were covered by the jungle for more than 1,000 years. When the hobby archaeologist and US diplomat John L. Stephens visited Palenque in 1841, he had to hack his way with a machete through the jungle. Nowadays, it is easy to get there.

If you have not followed the recommended route arriving from Campeche, you may have taken the air-conditioned night bus from the Riviera Maya, or flown in by plane to the airport.

Palenque is located in the lowlands of Chiapas, not far from the Rio Usumacinta, which marks the border with Guatemala in the south of Mexico. The Maya built the city in a hilly landscape, on the northern edge of the highland of Chiapas. For some of the temple constructions, they used the natural structure of these hills.

The name of Palenque in the classical period was Lakamha, which means as much as "Large Water." Presumably, the city got its name because of the many springs and streams that are found in the urban area. The state structure, whose capital Lakamha was during the Classical period, was called B'akaal - the place of bones. Today, the Maya call Palenque Bàak.

Throughout the Maya area, the region around Palenque is the one with the most rainfall. At the peak of the rainy season in September, an average of 440mm of raindrop per square meter is recorded, over the year it is more than 2000mm. In comparison, a total of 570mm fall in Berlin in Germany and just 70mm in the rainiest month of June, despite the fact that Berlin is a rain-laden Central European city.

No wonder the vegetation around Palenque is in full bloom all year round. The surrounding tropical rain forest is very impressive, as the ancient Palenque is part of a relatively large nature reserve. Sometimes, misty veils stand out from the hills behind the temple buildings, giving a mystic-mysterious touch to the scenery in combination with the ancient

<<<< *Figure 45 - Palenque - Palace*

temples. The eerie cries of howler monkeys, sounding from the green of the forest increase the mysterious atmosphere.

In Palenque and the surrounding area, you will also find a large number of more spiritually oriented tourists. Druids, shamans, new-age supporters, UFO-believers, hippies, and seekers of all kinds can be found here, especially at the astronomically significant days. They arrive from all around the world to absorb the particular aura and the magical vibrations that supposedly goes out from the place. By the way! Smoking, even if you use spiritually stimulating substances, is prohibited in the ruins area - that's true for all Maya sites, not only for Palenque.

I strongly advise against the magic mushrooms offered in this region. First of all, you have no idea how good the mycological knowledge of the mushroom gatherer really is, and on the other hand, you have to eat the things raw. This will become a job for your travel pharmacy, to which you hopefully have packaged some anti-diarrhea pills. In the best case, you will lose a day of your travel time! In case of diarrheal symptoms, it will take a few more days.

EARLY EXPLORATION

The first report of Palenque was noted by a monk. In 1567 Fray Pedro Lorenzo de la Nada came to the city, which he called Palenque.

Figure 46 - Palenque - Temple of Inscriptions

The first official expedition to Palenque was initiated by the Spanish king at the end of the 18th century, but the report was not published for more than 20 years. It was not until 1822 that a translation appeared in London.

The first explorer who visited Palenque and spent several years here was the adventurer and artist Johann Friedrich von Waldeck in the 19th century. The Frenchman made numerous drawings of buildings and inscriptions but was not very accurate. Many of the hieroglyphs drawn by him are entirely misrepresented. Convinced that he was dealing with the remnants of a Phoenician-Egyptian culture, Waldeck did not shrink from including elephants and other objects borrowed from the Egyptian hieroglyphs in his illustrations. A certain charm, however, cannot be denied to his paintings.

Stevens and Catherwood were the next researchers shortly after that. They visited the ruins during their wanderings through Central America. Catherwood's drawings and Stephen's written report are the first serious testimonies about Palenque.

From 1940 on, the systematic investigation began with excavations and the subsequent restoration of numerous buildings, which can be visited today.

The Maya site of Palenque is a foundation from the classical period, so relatively late. The first settlement traces discovered so far date from the

Figure 47 - Palenque - Temple of the Sun

Figure 48 - Palenque - Temple of the Foliated Cross

time 400 AD. At that time, the pre-classical cities of the lowlands, such as El Mirador had already perished. Others, such as Tikal, who had survived the collapse at the end of the Late Pre-Classical period, were just about to reach their classical flowering.

Palenque was a new foundation and inhabited for about 400 years, from 400 AD to 800 AD. In the meantime, however, inscriptions have also been discovered pointing to a time before 900 BC, but no one knows the exact meaning of this inscription. One should be aware that only about 6% of the ruins have been scientifically investigated so far. In the next few years, numerous, breathtaking discoveries are likely to be made.

Like most cities of the classical period, Palenque was abandoned by its inhabitants around 800 AD.

The Monuments

Only a small part of the former city area is open to visitors. The most famous structures in Palenque are the Temple of the Inscriptions, the Palace, and the Cross Group.

THE PALACE

The Palace is located approximately in the middle of the accessible area, thus forming the center of the site. A small tower, which may have served astronomical observations, rises on one of its sides. The complex consists of numerous interconnected rooms and courtyards. Baths and saunas were discovered. An aqueduct supplied the facilities with running water. Within the building, well-preserved reliefs can be seen in various places. With almost 7000 square feet of floor space, the palace is the most massive building in Palenque. The construction period lasted over the entire 400 years that Palenque was inhabited.

THE TEMPLE OF THE INSCRIPTIONS

The building known as the Temple of the Inscriptions was called B'olon Yej Te'Naah in the classical period of the Maya. This means House of the Nine Sharpened Spears. The construction work is expected to have begun at 675 AD. The structure was named "Temple of Inscriptions" due to the second longest inscription of the Maya world ever discovered. It was found inside the temple shrine. This temple on top of the building has 5 door openings, which are bounded by pillars each decorated with reliefs, which contain the representation of persons and inscriptions. Originally, these graphical representations were painted in color. Even if it is not allowed to mount the pyramid, you can at least see the images on the pillars from below.

The 8-stage base pyramid has a height of 27 meters. The temple above has a height of 11.4 meters.

The building contains the famous burial chamber in which Pakal the Great, whose real name was K'inich Janaab Pakal I. was buried. The access to the burial chamber was discovered in 1952 by the Mexican archaeologist Alberto Ruz Lhuillier.

The stone slab on its sarcophagus represents the ruler when he descends into the underworld Xibalbá. The plate weighs 5.5 tons; the monolithic sarcophagus itself weighs 15 tons.

This picture became famous due to Erich von Daniken, who undoubtedly recognized an astronaut at the start of a vehicle. This is a discovery that the local Maya are still laughing at when asked about. The burial chamber inside the temple is not accessible to visitors.

THE CROSS GROUP

This group of buildings, to be found in the south-east of the public complex, consists of three temple pyramids: the cross-temple, the leaf-cross temple and the temple of the sun.

The whole complex was built during the late classical period by K'inich Kan-Bahlum, son of Pakal. He reigned as successor to Pakal the Great from 684 AD To 702 AD. The group stands on a base platform and consists of three impressive temple pyramids. The mountain behind the group of crosses is called YehmalK'uk 'LakamWitz, meaning "The great mountain of the descending Quetzal."

The common explanation that the Cross group got its name due to the arrangement of the three temples in the form of a cross is misleading. In fact, the three temples form an equal-sided triangle. The name of the cross-group is derived from a relief depicting the cruciform representation of the life tree. This sculpture was found inside the cross-temple, gave it its name and thus also the entire group. The buildings were erected in commemoration of the coronation of K'inich Kan-Bahlum.

The temples of the cross group are all built similarly. Temples with a roof comb were erected on a basic step pyramid. All three temple shrines on the upper platforms have a three-part relief with long inscriptions inside at the back wall.

It is believed that the temples in their totality served the worship of three local but unknown gods.

THE TEMPLE OF THE COUNT

This structure is located in the north of the site. It received its name in honor of the already mentioned Johann Friedrich von Waldeck, who lived here for several years. Von Waldeck was a dazzling personality and had the peculiarity of calling himself sometimes a count, a baron, or a duke. He also changed the information about his nationality from time to time.

THE LION TEMPLE

The Lion Temple is located in the southern part of the complex. It got its name from a relief that was unfortunately destroyed. A ruler, sitting on a throne in the form of a double jaguar head, was depicted.

THE SKULL TEMPLE AND TEMPLE 13

These two temples are to the right of the temple of inscriptions. The Skull Head temple is the first structure on the right, reached when you enter the site from the entrance. It was named after the relief of a skull

Figure 49 - Palenque - Cross Group

found on one of its pillars. It could be a mixture, partly man, partly hare. Some people also see a deer.

In 1994, Arnoldo Gonzales Cruz of the INAH discovered the "Tomb of the Red Queen" inside of temple 13. The remains of a female corpse were covered by red cinnabar dust. The grave was equipped with rich grave goods, which resembled the tomb of Pakal. The body could be of Tz'ak-bu Ajaw, the wife of Pakal. Genetic investigations have shown that there was no familiar relationship with Pakal so that one can rule out Pakal's mother, who was also relevant in Palenque's history.

Figure 50 - Palenque - Temple of the Skull

THE AQUEDUCT AND THE RIO OTOLUM

It was only recently detected that the Piedras Bolas Aqueduct, which served the water supply, was able to press the transported water so much that it must have been possible to produce a six-foot high fountain. This discovery, of course, allows all sorts of speculation, and one can ask whether the original name of the city, Lakamha - Great Water, is due to the presence of such a fountain. The portrayals of the life-tree in the crucifixes also resemble such a water column.

Lovely is the brook in the north of the site, which flows over several cascades downhill towards the exit. Outside the venue, between the modern Palenque and the ruins, there is a museum with findings of the site, built in 1960.

HISTORY

Thanks to the well-preserved inscriptions found in various places in Palenque, it was possible to gain extraordinarily detailed insight into the history of this Maya city.

The early time of Palenque, however, is in the dark. It is assumed that about 100 BC the first people settled in the city area and enjoyed a simple, agricultural life.

During the early Classical period (200 - 600 AD) the population increased rapidly.

A series of rulers is named in the inscriptions, of which I mention here only those who are of particular importance. It is interesting to note that at least twice during the classical period queens got the power of government.

583 AD Yohl Ik' Al, a king's daughter, succeeded her father on the throne. During her reign, Palenque was attacked and defeated by Calakmul in 599, but then she ruled further until 605 AD.

605 AD her son Ajen Yohl Mat followed her to the throne. In 611 AD, he too was attacked by Calakmul and defeated. He died a year later.

For the year 612 AD two rulers are mentioned: Kanahb Pakal, who ruled only in 612 AD and SakK'uk, who followed him in the same year.

Sak K'uk' was the mother of Pakal the Great and committed the throne to her son in 615 AD.

Pakal the Great ruled over the city from 615 to 683 for nearly 70 years. K'inich Kan-Bahlum, son of Pakal, ruled from 684 AD to 702 AD. The most extensive construction activity in Palenque fell in the time of these two rulers. The majority of today's buildings were built during this period.

702 AD the grandson of Pakal, K'inich K'an Joy Chitam II was the next heir to the throne of this dynasty. It appears that he was captured in an attack by Toniná in 711 AD. The winners took him to their hometown in the valley of Ocosingo but did not sacrifice him. Instead, Toniná put a governor on the throne of Palenque. By this trick, Palenque had to wait

Figure 51 - Palenque - Waterfall of the Rio Otolum - North of the site - It is called "El bagno de la reigna" ---the bath of the queen.

until 721 AD when the captured king died naturally in Toniná. Then they were able to put their own king on the throne again.

Another significant event described in the inscriptions was the marriage of a Princess of Palenque with a ruler of Copan. This event took place in 742 AD. It shows how far-reaching the relations of the Maya cities were. As you might remember, Copan and Palenque are located at two extreme points in the west and east of the classic Maya area.

799 AD is the date of the last inscription recorded in Palenque. It describes the accession of Janaab Pakal III who is also the last known ruler of Palenque.

As one of the first city-states in the Maya area, Palenque fell victim to the mysterious “collapse.” The reasons are puzzling. In the case of Palenque, there are considerations as to whether the invasion of hostile forces coming along the Rio Usumacinta might have led to the destruction of the city. Section 3 of this book contains a chapter describing what we know about it so far.

Map 8 - Palenque >>>>

TRAVEL TIP:

From the modern Palenque, some eight kilometers away from the ruins, several colectivo-taxis travel to the ruins during the day. These vehicles are clearly recognizable by the signature "Ruinas" - written on a piece of cardboard and clamped behind the windshield. Usually, a wink is enough to stop the bus. Opposite the big bus station, on the other side of the road is an excellent place to wait for one of them. To visit the ruins, you have to pay twice. When you access the nature reserve, you have to pay for a day ticket. A second time, a fee has to be paid at the gates of the ruins.

If night drumming, music making and the encounter with a lot of spiritually oriented travel people do not disturb you, then you might prefer, to stay overnight in Panchan during your time in Palenque. With some luck, you will also meet one of the archaeologists involved in the excavations. The wooded area offers various accommodation, mini-hotels, camping and even individual cottages, at very reasonable prices. There are also two restaurants where you can enjoy the local cuisine. One

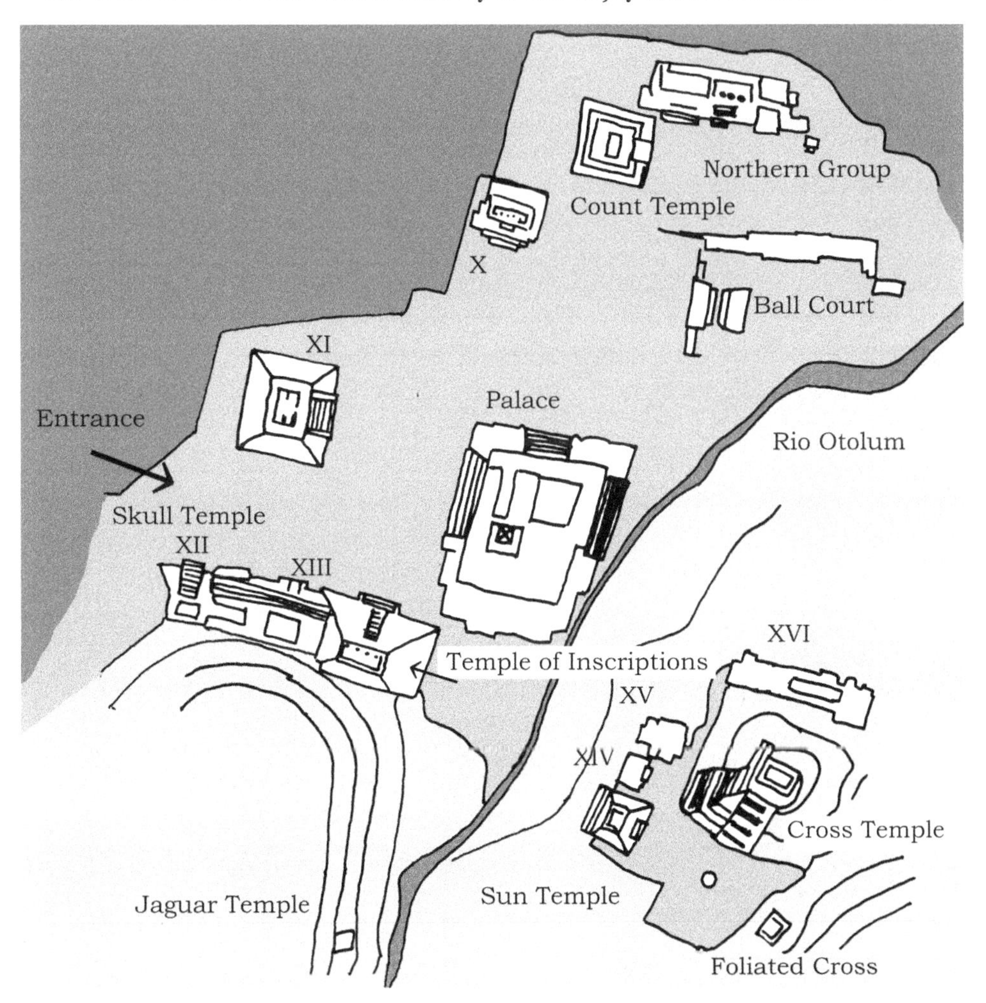

of them, the more rustic Mono Blanco is my favorite. Panchan, in the local language of the Maya, means paradise or heaven. It is just at the entrance of the nature reserve, halfway between Palenque City and the ruins.

From Palenque, big overland buses run in many directions. Overnight, one reaches the Riviera Maya, on the other hand, one can go to Mexico City or Oaxaca in one hop. Palenque is also an excellent place to plan a trip to Guatemala!

Beginning in Palenque, you can visit several other sights in short trips. For Bonampak and Yaxchilán in combination, one needs two days. Toniná near Ocosingo and the La Venta Museum Park in Villahermosa can be completed in one day each. A trip to San Cristobal de las Casas is worth to spend at least 5 days.

Also, two other world-famous attractions can be admired near Palenque: the waterfall of Misol-Há and the blue cascades of Agua Azul. Both together can be visited in a combined one-day-trip. The visit of the sites, Bonampak and Yaxchilán, is offered by local travel agencies as a stopover on the way to Flores in Guatemala. The journey to Flores, which is otherwise done within a day, takes two or three days longer, depending on how much time you want to spend on the two Maya sites situated in the vicinity of the Rio Usumacinta.

Tip Catazajá: Actually tourists usually never get to this place, which is designated with "Playa" on the tables of the colectivos. Catazajá is the correct name for this village, some 20km from Palenque. Its name means "valley covered by water." Apparently, a beach is not to be found there, but a large lake, the Laguna of Catazajá. During the rainy season, when the plain at the mouth of the Rio Usumacinta is flooded, the water level rises here so much that several small islands are flooded. Then there are hundreds of cranes, storks and other large, exotic water-birds, along with some very rare orange-colored iguanas, on the branches and in the tops of the vegetation.

It is also possible that manatees - from the Gulf Coast reach through the flood channels to the lagoon, at least the legend says so. At the harbor, where the statue of a manatee recalls this rare event, you can rent a fishing boat and then slip between the trees. Again, it is cheaper to do this as a group. The ship costs the same amount, regardless of whether you sit alone or with ten others in it. There is also an excellent fish restaurant at the harbor.

THE OLMEC - LA VENTA PARC MUSEUM IN VILLAHERMOSA

At this point, I would like to insert a small side trip, both geographically and ethnic-historically. We will deal temporarily with the ancient culture of the Olmec and the La Venta Museum Park in Villahermosa in Tabasco.

Figure 52 - Olmec - Massive Stone Head of the Olmec culture in the La Venta Parc musuem in Villahermosa

The original site of La Venta was one of the leading ceremonial centers of the Olmec. These historical Mesoamerican people are believed to be the precursor of the Maya culture. The Olmec already cultivated maize, knew a calendar system and used a kind of hieroglyphic writing. La Venta was located on an island in the marshes of the estuary of the Rio Tonalá, not far from the Gulf Coast. During the construction of an oil refinery and an airport, large parts of the historic site of La Venta were unfortunately destroyed or built over.

The very impressive artifacts that have been found in La Venta were saved and brought to Villahermosa, where you can marvel at them in the La Venta Museum Parc. It might be that the Olmec culture began on the Pacific coast of Guatemala, where archaeologists found the oldest, pottery of Central America dated about 1800 BC, at the sites of the Monte Alto culture.

Following this theory, the Olmec culture spread initially along the coastline northward into what is now Mexico and to reach the Gulf of Mexico then after crossing the Isthmus of Tehuantepec. It seems that the Olmec preferred wet and swampy lowlands for their settlements.

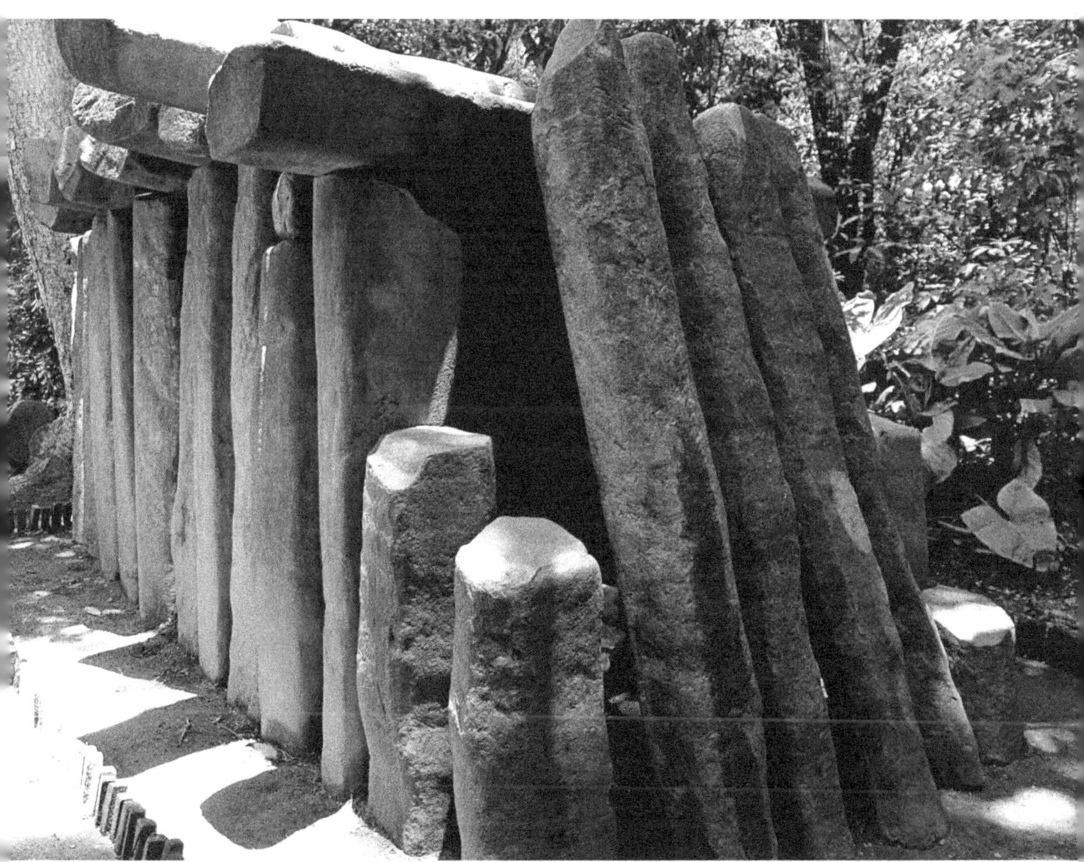

Figure 54 - Olmec - Monlithic Structures found in La Venta

<<<< *Figure 53 - Olmec - Stone Figure of the Olmec culture*

But not alone, the skill of producing ceramics spread in this way. It seems that specific techniques for stone processing also followed this path. Also, the archaeologists found colossal stone heads, similar to those of La Venta and Mounds, hills of earth and clay, in La Blanca, a site of the Monte Alto culture.

La Venta consisted of several pyramids, which were constructed as "Mounds." Clay from the surrounding area was used as construction material.

The heyday of La Venta began around 1200 BC. 800 years later by 400 BC, the place was abandoned. La Venta is famous mainly for the monumental stone figures that were found there. Among them are the world-famous gigantic stone heads.

It was the Mexican poet Carlos Pellicer Cámara, who initiated the creation of this open-air museum. Established in 1952, it is so far the only museum of its kind in Mexico.

A total of 36 megalithic stone structures have been discovered in La Venta and were re-erected in the Parc Museum. Part of the Parc is a small zoo, which presents some of the native wildlife. The highlight of the zoo is a black Jaguar.

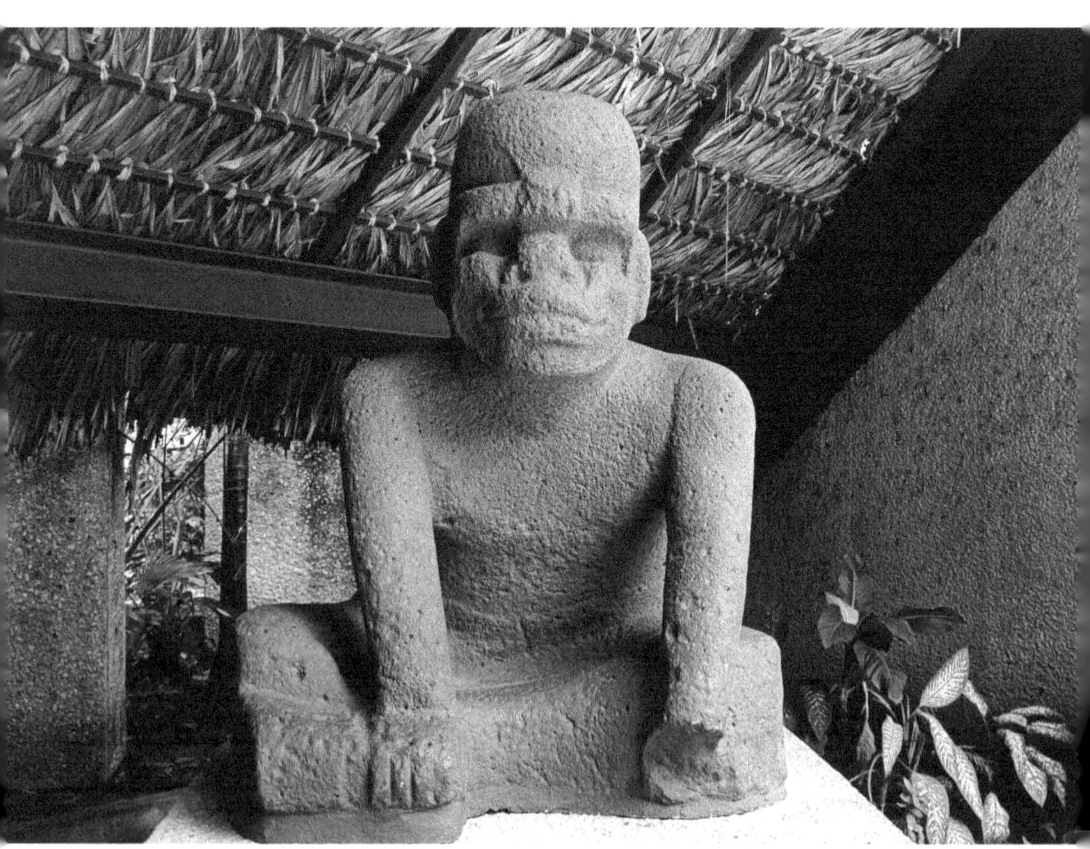

Figure 55 - Olmec - Stone Figure of the Olmec culture in the La Venta Parc museum

Figure 56 - Impression from Villahermosa - The Blue House

TRAVEL ADVICE:

Starting from Palenque, it is straightforward to get there. The regular bus service from Palenque to Villahermosa takes about two hours for the journey. From the bus station in Villahermosa, you can use a taxi to get to the La Venta Park Museum.

Villahermosa is the capital of the Mexican state of Tabasco. It is located approximately midway between Cancún and Mexico City about 1000 km from both cities.

It is worth to include the city of Villahermosa for a visit. It is not only a pleasant city to go out at night and enjoy the local cuisine in one of the restaurants. One can also just admire the city's architecture or take the opportunity for a shopping tour in an almost tourist-free environment. The restaurant “Rock n 'Roll” in the city center offers an excellent shrimp cup.

Figure 57 - Toniná - Looking from the pyramid across the Valley

Figure 58 - Toniná – Area of the Zapatista movement - in the background, the pyramid >>>:

TONINÁ - IN THE OCOSINGO VALLEY

Seen from a distance, Toniná seems to own the largest Maya pyramid that you have ever seen. The gigantic building rises at least 71m wide over the ball court in front of it. Various temple buildings are located on the seven levels that make up the underlying structure.

Actually, it is a natural mountain which was covered using carved stones to create this imposing structure.

The city was inhabited between 400 BC and 900 AD and belongs to the classical period. The people who lived in Toniná seem to have been exceptionally bellicose predisposed. Inscriptions, which were found on the spot, speak of several conflicts with other cities in which Toniná was

Figure 59 - Toniná - Restoration of Wall Paintings

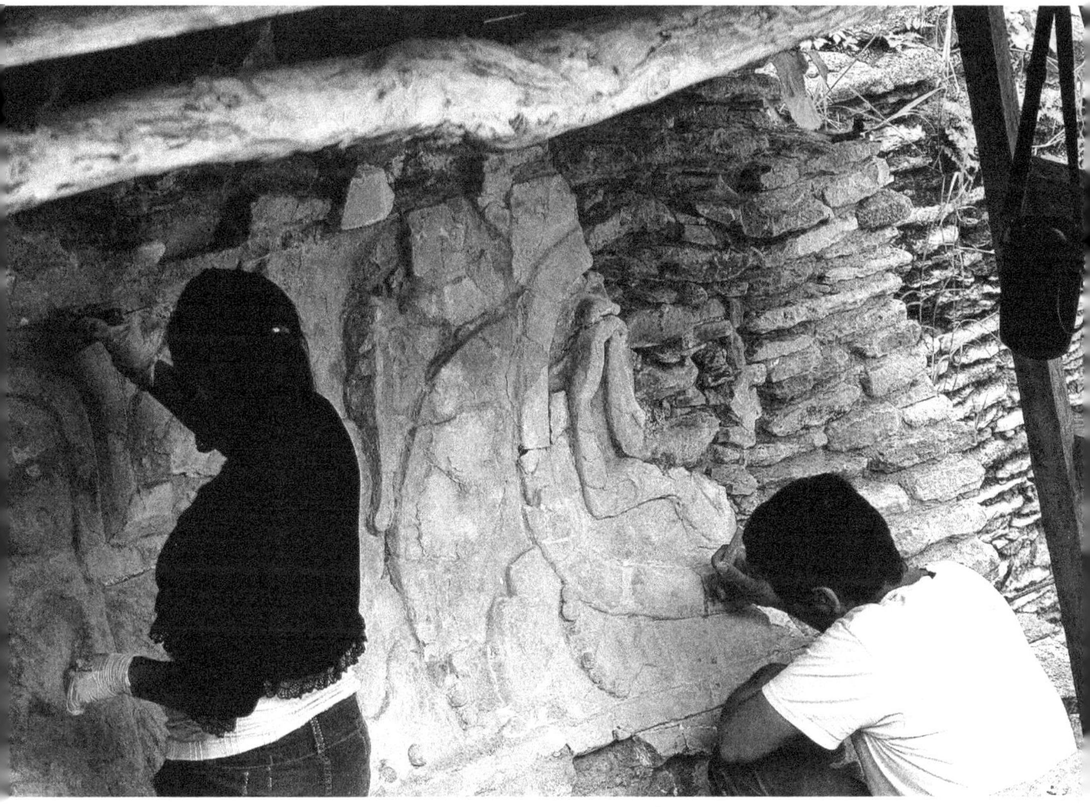

Figure 60 - Toniná - Restoration Works

involved. One can safely describe the standard behavior of Toniná as aggressive.

During a war against the neighboring Palenque, the force of Toniná succeeded in conquering Palenque and capturing its ruler K'inich K'an Joy Chitam II. The timing of this event is known. It was in the year AD 711. A short look to Europe, just to compare: In the same year Islamic troops did land in Gibraltar, defeated the Visigoths and started to conquer Spain.

Back to Mesoamerica: Finally, the aggressive foreign policy of Toniná didn't provide benefits. Shortly after AD 900, the city was abandoned and the inhabitants disappeared.

A number of stucco reliefs, murals, and sculptures have been found in Toniná. Many of them can be seen in the museum next to the entrance or directly in the remains of the buildings at the various levels of the pyramid.

Interestingly, the last calendar inscription of the classical period in the Maya world has been found here, dating to the year AD 909.

The name Toniná means "House of Stones" in the Mayan dialect

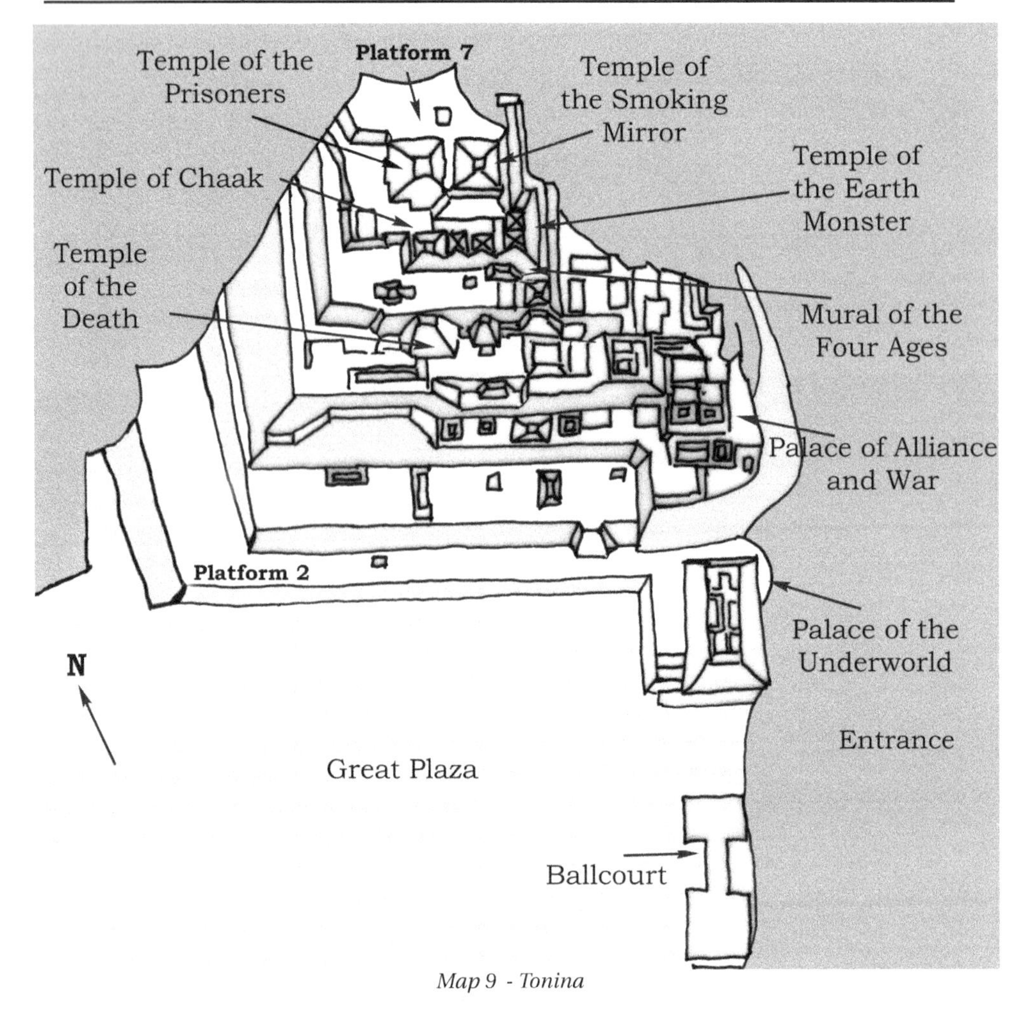

Map 9 - Tonina

Tzotzil, spoken by the indigenous population in the highlands of Chiapas. Historians believe that in ancient times the city was named "Popo."

TRAVEL ADVICE

Toniná is about 30 minutes' drive away from Ocosingo. This town in the Valley of Ocosingo is lined with tall mountain ranges overgrown with evergreen conifers. It is located approximately halfway between Palenque and San Cristobal de las Casas in the highland of Chiapas.

You can visit Toniná and Ocosingo easily during a day trip from Palenque. This involves taking the regular bus from Palenque to San Cristobal. In Ocosingo you have to jump out of the bus. You best take a Taxi then from the bus station to the market or go directly to Toniná.

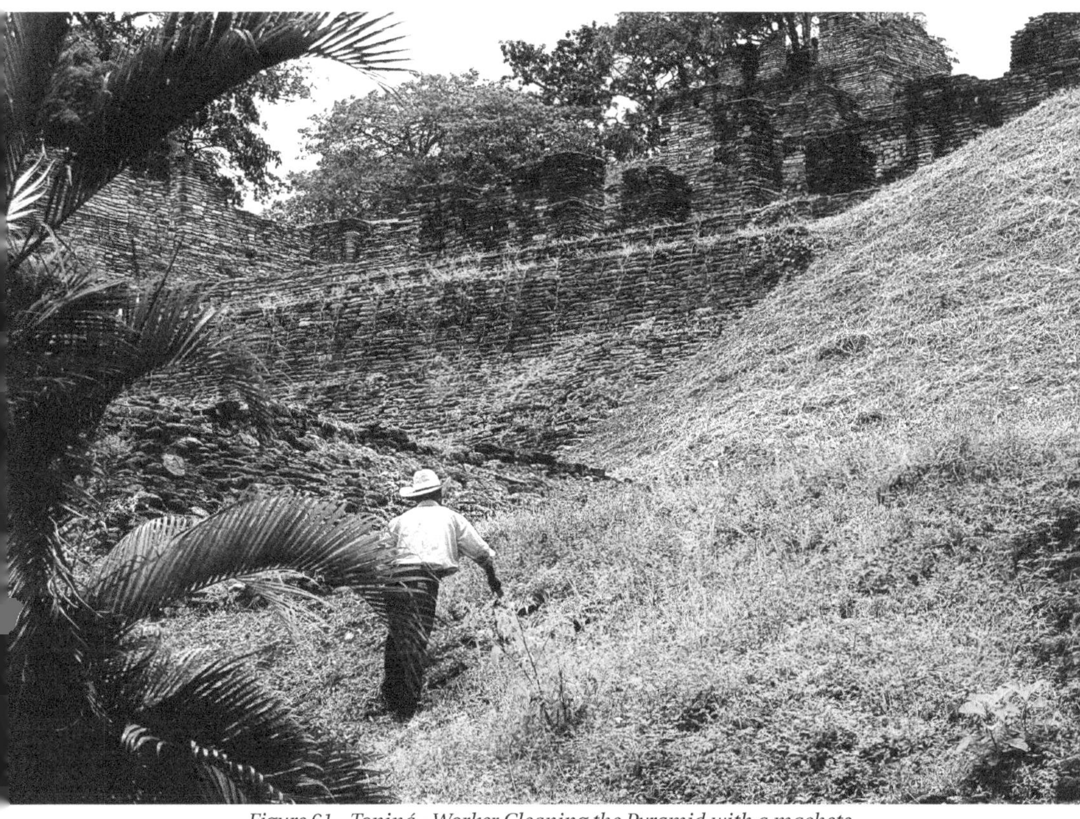

Figure 61 - Toniná - Worker Cleaning the Pyramid with a machete
Figure 62 - Toniná - Tamales from the Market in Ocosingo

Colectivos starting at the market drive past the ruins. With luck, you can jump on one of the roofless pickups, from which you can watch the pyramid from far and have a very direct impression of the surrounding landscape.

The market of Ocosingo is a typical indigenous farmers' market where the products of the area are offered colorfully. The people are friendly, albeit timidly, as tourists rarely show up here. Some reluctance from the explorer is advised!

Several stalls on the market offer tamales, corn cakes with a filling cooked in corn leaves. Must try!

Do not forget to take enough water with you. I consumed 1.5-liter water during the ascent and spent a good hour until I arrived at the top. The central staircase leads upwards over 260 extraordinarily narrow and very high steps. And there is no shade!

But from the top level, you will have a breathtaking view over the Ocosingo Valley with its green pastures and the forested mountains of the highlands.

Figure 63 - Yaxchilán - On the Rio Usumacinta

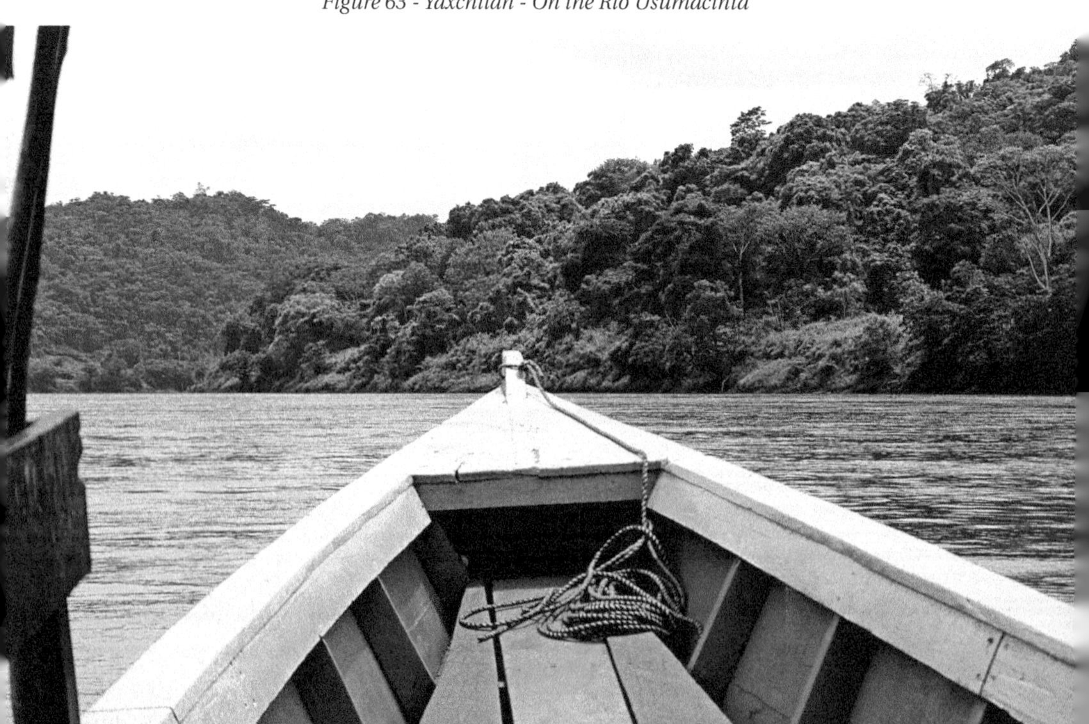

YAXCHILÁN - ON THE BANKS OF THE RÍO USUMACINTA

Yaxchilán is a Maya site in southern Mexico in Chiapas. It is located right on the river banks of the Río Usumacinta in a river loop on Mexican territory. The Rio Usumacinta forms the natural border between Guatemala and Mexico over a long distance and is lined by dense rainforest.

Some facts of the history of Yaxchilán are known today due to the successful deciphering of historical inscriptions.

The area was occupied between the years 359 BC and AD 800, a time period ranging from the pre-classic to the classic period. Yaxchilán had numerous military conflicts with other Maya cities, Palenque, Toniná and Piedra Negras to mention a few.

Archaeologists believe that the Maya had constructed a suspension bridge with a length of approximately 100m here, to allow pedestrians to cross the river. If so, it would have been the longest bridge in the pre-Columbian Americas.

Figure 64 - Yaxchilán - Temple 33

Figure 66 - Yaxchilán - The small Acropolis

Figure 67 - Yaxchilán - The Labyrinth

<<<< *Figure 65 - Yaxchilán - At the end of the stairway is the top of Temple 33*

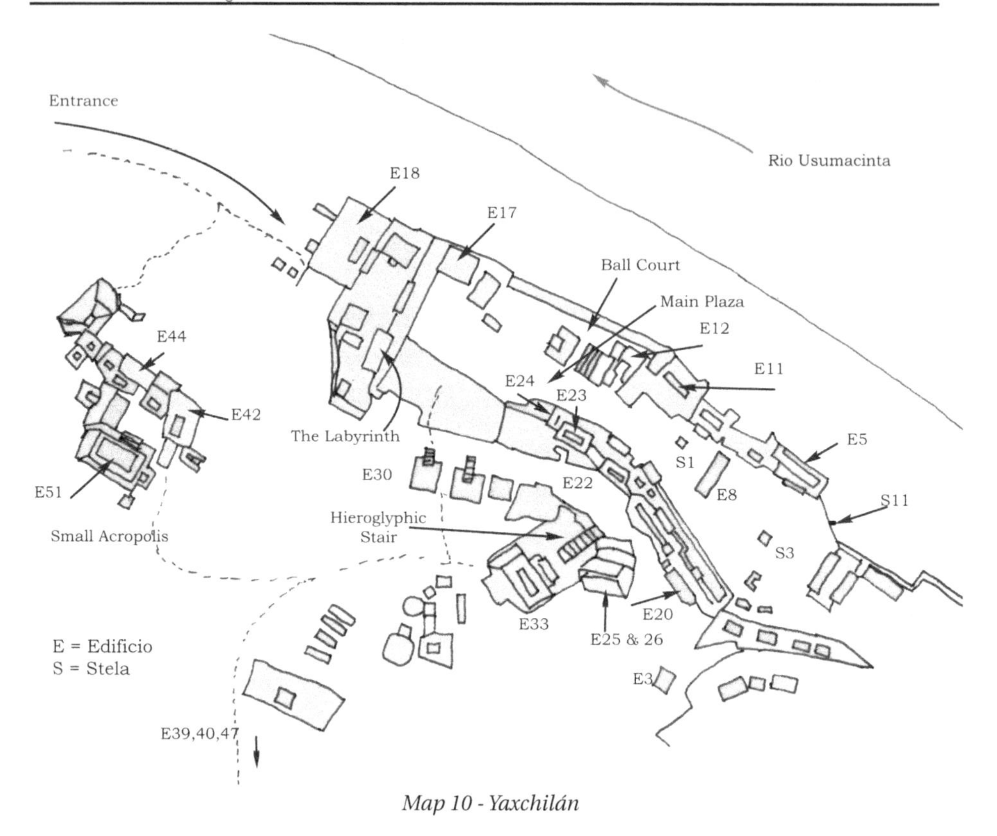

Map 10 - Yaxchilán

Several large structures, temple pyramids, and temple buildings can be visited on these premises. Yaxchilán is famous for the numerous sculptures of the Maya culture that have been found here. Unfortunately, most of them were removed. You can examine them in various museums around the world.

Yaxchilán does not offer the same kind of broad open space that features many other sites. The jungle extends right up to the buildings, and often you will walk under the dense foliage of the forest. This gives you the opportunity for very close observation of nature. Tropical birds, butterflies, and howler monkeys have to be mentioned.

A bit of luck is necessary if one wants to see a crocodile in the river or at its banks. Only a few of them remain along the Río Usumacinta and in its tributaries. Sometimes, even nowadays, members of the Maya tribe of the Lacandon visit Yaxchilán to worship their ancient gods here.

You should also expect to encounter snakes. Trousers and sturdy shoes are strongly recommended for this trip.

TRAVEL ADVICE:

Due to the absence of a road, it is not possible to access Yaxchilán directly by car. There is only the possibility of a boat ride from the Mexican border town Frontera Corozal on the Río Usumacinta.

This trip takes about half an hour. From Palenque, you drive an estimated three hours until you reach Frontera Corozal.

It is recommended to combine a visit of Yaxchilán with a trip to the neighboring Bonampak and to plan two days for the entire tour. For this, you can stay in the village Lacanja inhabited by Lacandon. They are prepared for the arrival of tourists with several accommodations.

Some travel agencies in Palenque offer such a two-day trip. Some tours include even the onward journey to Flores in Guatemala. Traveling in the opposite direction, coming from Flores in Guatemala, you can book the reverse trip there, to visit Yaxchilán and Bonampak including the later continuation of the drive to Palenque.

I strongly recommend leaving the organization of this trip into the Selva Lacandon to one of the travel agencies in Palenque or Flores. This is by far more efficient than to do this on your own since the connections whether boat, taxi or bus and further shipments are less expensive to perform in this manner and can be handled without loss of time.

The price of a boat is independent of the number of its occupants, whether one, five or twelve. The prize is the same. This also applies to taxis. A group is also recommended because the border area is not necessarily the most secure area around here.

Figure 68 - Yaxchilán - Relief and inscriptions at the plaza

BONAMPAK - MURALS IN THE SELVA LACANDON

Bonampak is a very exotic destination for the average tourist. This famous Maya site is located in the Selva Lacandona, the forest of the Lacandons. It is located west of the Usumacinta River, about 30 kilometers from Yaxchilán in the lowlands of Chiapas and close to the Guatemalan border.

HISTORY

Bonampak was founded around 250 AD during the early classical period of the Maya culture. In the beginning, the city seems to have been independent of other city-states. Around 400 AD, after several wars, it lost this status and came under the influence of Yaxchilán.
When Yaxchilán was defeated by Piedras Negras 100 years later in 514

Figure 69 - Bonampak - Murals

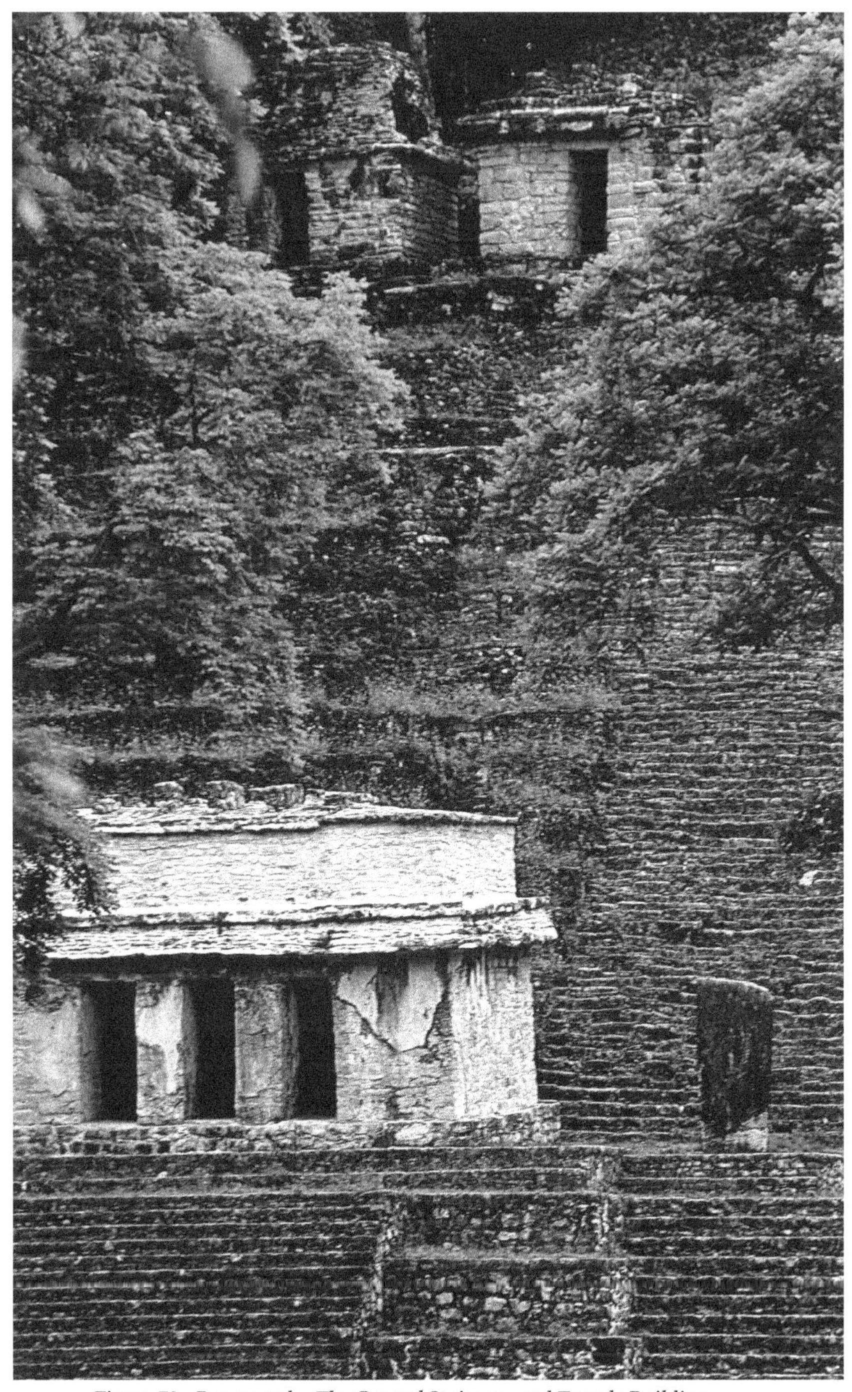

Figure 70 - Bonampak - The Central Staircase and Temple Buildings

AD, Bonampak also suffered. And in 526 A.D. there is the talk of the capture of numerous nobles.

700 A.D. a ruler named Yajaw Chan Muwaan I. ascended the throne of Bonampak. Under his reign, the construction of the Acropolis began.

One of his presumed descendants, Chan Muwaan II, had the temples built and the murals painted. These were completed around 800 AD.

When Yaxchilán perished at the beginning of the 9th century, this also meant the end for Bonampak.

MONUMENTS

Only a small part of the entire ruin site is accessible to the public. If you enter the complex from the entrance, you are already standing directly on the Plaza Principal, the large square. One then looks directly at the Large Acropolis with the various temple buildings.

Many of the buildings are geographically oriented towards the neighboring Yaxchilán. The peninsula surrounded by the Rio Usumacinta, on which Yaxchilán is about 30 kilometers away, opens up precisely in the direction of Bonampak. This is also astonishing because a ground elevation between the cities does not allow a direct line of sight at all.

Bonampak became famous for its well-preserved mural paintings, the

Figure 71 - Bonampak – On the Top

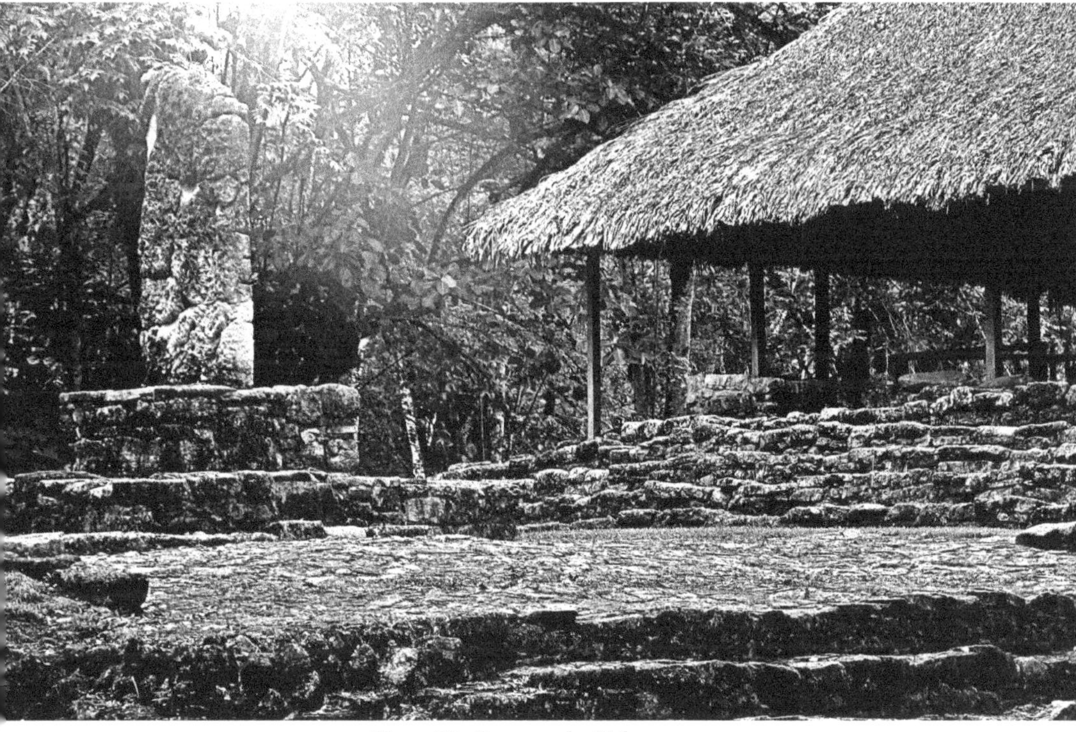

Figure 72 - Bonampak - Stela

so-called "Murales." Bonampak was not discovered for research until 1946, although the site was already known to the Lacandons living here.

The Temple of the Murals is one of several small temple buildings located on the Great Acropolis. It has three separate rooms, the walls of which are covered with pictures.

The interpretation of the images found in the Temple of the Murals is not always clear and is, therefore, the subject of various speculations. Among other things, one sees the representation of a procession of dancing priests or musicians, war scenes and a courtyard with prisoners of war. The scenes are very detailed and unique in their quality.

The Temple of the Murals is the only temple in Bonampak that consists of several rooms. The paintings were created around 790 AD.

Excellently preserved stelae with relief illustrations of rulers and inscriptions have been placed in various places.

The accessibility of the three rooms with the paintings is not always given. During my visit, restoration work was underway in one of them, the other rooms were accessible. In any case, photography is only permitted without a flash.

To this day, the temples of Bonampak are used by the nearby Lacandons, a Maya tribe living in the forest nearby, for religious reasons during their ceremonies. They also manage the Maya site and the local information center.

TRAVEL ADVICE

The nearby village of Lacanja is the administrative center for the remaining Lacandons. It is assumed that the tribe has only about 500 members. There are also a few hotels to spend the night.

Colectivo taxis drive from Palenque to Frontera Corozal. To get to Bonampak, you have to get off at the appropriate junction. The best thing to do is to visit Yaxchilán first, then take a taxi to Lacanja, spend the night there and visit Bonampak the next morning. Afterward, you return to Palenque. As I already wrote in the chapter about Yaxchilán, I recommend booking this section of the trip with the help of one of the tourist offices in Palenque. This saves time-consuming waits for taxis or colectivos, and the hotel room will be organized.

In Lacanja there is the possibility to visit the famous waterfall of the Lacandons and other ruins hidden in the rainforest during a hike through the jungle. Also, one should then calculate an additional day.

If you are particularly interested in the culture of the Lacandons, a visit to the Lacandon Museum in San Cristobal de las Casas is highly recommended.

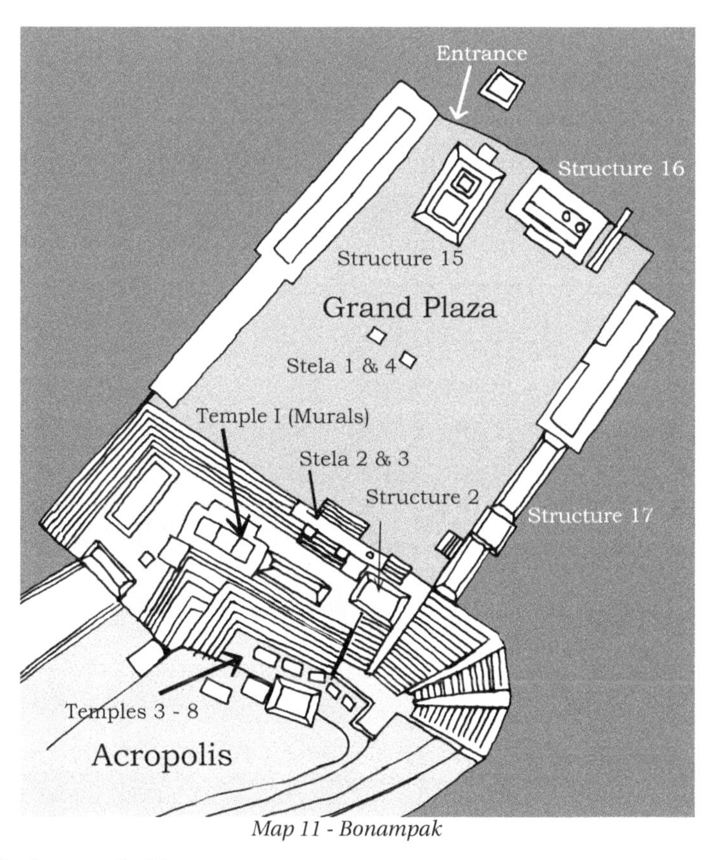

Map 11 - Bonampak

<<<< *Figure 73 - Bonampak - Masonry*

Figure 74 - Tikal - Temple II

Region: Petén in Guatemala

TIKAL

The Maya city of Tikal is only about 60km northwest of Florés, located on Lago Petén. It is situated in the middle of a vast nature reserve stretching from the north to the Mexican border. The dense rainforest that surrounds the Maya site is typical for the southern lowlands of the Maya region and uniquely characterizes it. With a bit of luck, you can watch numerous animal and plant species during a visit to the site. For a good reason, then, Tikal has been granted both, the UNESCO World Heritage and World Heritage status by UNESCO.

On the road to this probably best explored Maya city in Guatemala, one gets an impression of the lush nature, because the asphalted street leads through dense jungle over long distances. The treetops meet above, giving the idea of driving through a green tunnel. Every now and then, exotic traffic signs warn that snakes, coatis or jaguars could cross the road.

The original name in the Mayan language for Tikal was Yax Mutal. The researchers do not yet agree on the original meaning of the word. The emblem of Tikal contains the stylized image of a bundle tied together. Several different purposes have been discovered for the word stem “Mut”: omen, bird, braided plait or hair knot. The suffix -al was often used for places. Yax, in turn, means "first" and emphasizes the importance of Tikal in the ancient Maya world.

The word Tikal, on the other hand, is of modern origin. It was given to the place by rubber collectors. It might mean "place with a waterhole."

The settlement of Tikal began in the pre-Classical phase around 900 BC.

Figure 75 - Tikal - Coati in the tree

The first architectural traces date from this period and go back to 200 BC. This phase also marks the city's first period of prosperity, which lasted until around 200 AD.

Tikal did not escape the general decay, which set in at the end of the pre-Classic period. But it survived the time and swelled to new heights during the classical period, while many other pre-Classic Maya cities were already wholly abandoned by their former inhabitants.

In this second heyday during the Classic period, the area controlled by Tikal might have provided living space for a total of 200,000 people, while the city itself and its immediate vicinity are thought to have been home to about 60,000 people. The actual detected urban area covers the footprint of 65km². So far, 6000 buildings have been identified. However, it is believed that more than 10,000 buildings are still waiting to be discovered. Using LiDAR technology, a type of 3-D laser scanning, scientists have detected thousands of ancient structures in the jungles of Guatemala and Mexico that have been unknown before.

Around 900 AD, at the end of the classical period, Tikal met the same fate as the other cities of the southern lowlands. The inhabitants abandoned the town and left it to decay.

FIRST EXPEDITIONS TO TIKAL

The first expedition to Tikal was carried out in 1848 by Modesto Mendez, governor of the province of Petén at this time, under the leadership of Ambrosio Tut. A written account of this expedition was published five years later as a German translation in a publication of the Akademie der Wissenschaften in Berlin. The next news of a traveler was announced by a Swiss doctor named Carl Gustav Bernoulli. He visited the ruins in 1877 and took some wooden door lintels, which he had found on site, with him to Switzerland. They can be seen in Basel today. Subsequently, Alfred Percival Maudslay (1881) and Teoberto Maler (1895 and 1904) visited the site and examined it more closely for the first time. After a visit by Alfred Tozzer and Raymond Merwin in 1910, silence returned to the jungle for a long time. It took until the 1950s when the regular inspection and restoration of the ruins began.

SITE DESCRIPTION

From the entrance of the site, after about 1.3km you reach the centrally located Gran Plaza. Several of the famous buildings are grouped along the four sides of this large square. Temples I and II are located on the east or west side of the square and are aligned with each other. North of the square is the Northern Acropolis, on the south, you find the Central Acropolis. The Central Acropolis probably served as a palace-like residence of the ruling family, while in the Northern Acropolis several graves with burial objects have been discovered and therefore it is believed that this building served as a burial place.

SACBEOB - CEREMONIAL ROADS

Four dams built by the Maya were found in the area of Tikal, called Sacbéob. Sacbeob is the majority of the Mayan word Sacbé, which translates as "white road." They probably originated in the late classical period, but some of them date back to earlier times and connect several ceremonial centers with each other.

Three of the four Sacbéob, which are named after the famous first-time visitors, lead from the center for peripheral monuments. The fourth Sacbeob connects two of these groups.

CALZADA MENDEZ

The Sacbé called Calzada Mendez leads, from the Plaza del Oriente behind Temple I, over a distance of 1.3km, past the buildings of Group G to the southeast to Temple VI, the temple of inscriptions.

CALZADA TOZZER

Behind Temple II, begins the Calzada Tozzer. It leads westwards past Temple III to Temple IV, about 500 meters away.

Figure 76 - Tikal – Temple I (right), Temple II (left)

CALZADA MALER

The Calzada Maler directs from the Plaza del Oriente to the north, past the complexes R and Q, and reaches the complexes H and P. The distance is about 800 meters.

CALZADA MAUDSLAY

The fourth road, the Calzada Maudslay, connects Temple IV and the complexes H and P. It has a length of about 800 meters.

THE TEMPLES AND GROUPS OF BUILDINGS

The temple pyramids are usually numbered. However, some of them have specific proper names because of unique illustrations or inscriptions found there.

TEMPLE I - THE TEMPLE OF THE JAGUAR

This temple pyramid, located at the Gran Plaza, is basically Tikal's landmark and, next to the Kukulkan pyramid of Chichén Itzá, it is probably the most famous pyramid of Mesoamerica.

It is 47 meters high and served as a burial place for a vital ruler of Tikal, Jasaw Chan K'awiil I, who ruled over the territory of Tikal in 682-734. The building is realized as a regular pyramid with nine levels. It is assumed that the construction was completed around 732 AD. The front staircase has precisely 100 steps.

TEMPLE II - THE TEMPLE OF THE MASKS

This three-stage pyramid reaches a height of 38 meters. It stands opposite the Jaguar Temple on Gran Plaza. It is believed that this building was erected by Jasaw Chan K'awiil I as a tomb for his wife Kalajuun Une' Mo'. The architecture of the building is similar to other buildings from the early classical period, but of course, it was constructed at about the same time as the jaguar temple.

TEMPLE III - THE JAGUAR PRIEST'S TEMPLE

Temple III was completed around 810 AD, during the late classical period. As the only one of the pyramids in Tikal, the actual temple shrine on top has only two instead of the usual three rooms, as have been found in the other temple pyramids in the city. The height of the structure is 55 meters.

The monument was erected during the rulership of a king whose real name is unknown. Due to the hieroglyphic inscriptions found there, archaeologists call him "Dark Sun." He ruled during the time in which the pyramid was built.

TEMPLE IV - THE TEMPLE OF THE TWO-HEADED SNAKE

At 65 meters, Temple IV is the tallest building in Tikal. His builder is Yik' in Chan K'awiil, who possibly ruled from 734 AD to 766 AD. Inside the temple pyramid, the tomb of this ruler is believed to be located, but an excavation into the interior has not yet taken place. The building was completed around 741 AD. From the upper platform of the pyramid, a scene for the movie "Star Wars - Episode IV" was filmed in 1977 and shows the temples at the Gran Plaza that protrudes above the surrounding jungle.

THE ASTRONOMICAL SIGNIFICANCE OF TEMPLE IV

But the view of Temple IV was not only interesting for George Lucas. The Maya also knew how to use the elevated location for their purposes. The alignment of Temple IV to Temple I took place according to astronomical aspects. From Temple IV you can see the rising sun on February 12th, and October 30th in the ridge of Temple I. The two dates are essential for the Tzolkin calendar, a calendar used by the Maya. The distance between the two days is exactly 260 days, which corresponds to the length of the Tzolkin calendar. The calendar system of the Maya is described later in this book.

TEMPLE V

This temple is the second highest of Tikal's temples, 57 meters high. The construction time is assumed in the late classical period during the 7th century. Possibly, it was built during the reign of Nuun Ujol Chaak, who ruled from 650 - 679. On its left-hand side, an almost 50-meter-high extremely steep wooden staircase leads to the upper platform. The view is breathtaking, but so is the ascent. And when you then stand on the stairs again to climb down, it will catch your breath again. You should definitely be free of vertigo, especially since there are no barriers on the platform.

TEMPLE VI - THE TEMPLE OF THE INSCRIPTIONS

The Temple of the Inscriptions is believed to have been a palace building rather than a temple. It got its name from a series of engraved hieroglyphic texts on the sides and the back wall. The dates recorded in these inscriptions date back to the pre-Classical period and refer to a possibly mythical city founder of Tikal. His name was White-Owl-Jaguar with an accompanying date of 1143 BC. The construction period dates back to the first half of the 8th century, probably under Jasaw Chan K'awiil I. The monument was built in the middle of the 8th century. A stele found in front of the temple describes his son Yik'in Chan K'awiil ascent to the throne.

THE NORTHERN ACROPOLIS

The Northern Acropolis on the north side of the Plaza Major is one of Tikal's oldest structures. Around 350 B. C., towards the end of the Middle Pre-Classicism, the first construction works for the base on which the northern Acropolis was built were documented.

However, finds indicate that this place was used for ceremonies as early as 800 BC. At the end of the pre-Classical period, during the 1st century AD, the first burial took place. It is assumed that this is the grave of the dynasty founder YaxEhb' Xook, who ruled around 90 AD.

Later graves of Tikal's rulers date from the classical period. A total of 43 stelae and 30 altars were found in Tikal, many of them with inscriptions that allow the individual graves to be assigned to specific rulers.

One can see that the Northern Acropolis was used as a necropolis or graveyard for the ruling dynasty.

The Northern Acropolis measures about 100 by 80 meters at its base. Its surface, 12 meters above the Plaza Major, can be reached via several stairs on the south side. In the following centuries, numerous temples which were often used as burial places were built on the platform. Unfortunately, many of them were plundered by grave robbers, an activity that started soon after Tikal's demise. Some of these smaller temples still reach impressive heights, such as Temple 33 at 33 meters.

THE CENTRAL ACROPOLIS

The Central Acropolis is located on the south side of the Plaza Major. As for the Northern Acropolis, construction activities began around 350 BC in the pre-Classical phase. The older buildings were partly over-built in later times. The function of the central acropolis differs markedly from that of the northern one. It served the aristocratic ruling families as their residence. A total of 43 structures have been identified in the area. Among some of them, burial traces could be found. In many cases, it was common for family members to be buried under the floor of their own home. Where these burials are missing, it is assumed that the structure in question has not been used as a residence but as an administrative building.

Maler's Palace - a building structure, also called 5D-46, was probably the residence of the king. It was built around 350 AD.

GROUP H

Located on the north-eastern periphery, Group H can be reached via the Calzadas Maudslay and Maler. In both cases, the distance is about 800m. So there and back add up easily to 1.6km, without taking into account the walking around temples and other structures. The building structures you can see there date back to the late classical era.

GROUP G

Walking along the Calzada Mendez in the direction of Temple VI, you will pass Group G, which is located to the right of the path. This is a significant palace district. There are inner courtyards and two-story residential buildings. A total of 29 vaulted chambers have been discovered here.

MUNDO PERDIDO - THE LOST WORLD

The Square of the Seven Temples and the Mundo Perdido group of buildings are located south-west of the Gran Plaza in a short distance and are not connected to the center by a Sacbé.

With a footprint of 60,000sqm, this is one of the most massive structures in Tikal. The name “Mundo Perdido - The lost World” was given to it by the archaeologists of the University of Pennsylvania, who

SUBIR

conducted the first investigations here.

There have been six construction phases. The beginnings of building activities date back to 700 BC during the pre-Classical period. In later times, the complex was extended and built over again and again. Works that took place between the 4th and 6th centuries clearly show the influence of Teotihuacan, a Meso-American culture in the high valley of Mexico, which at times had a significant impact on the Maya territory. The architectural peculiarity of this influence is the Talud-Tablero style, known from Teotihuacan. During the gradual construction of the pyramid structure, vertical sections (tablero = board) alternate with inclined sections (talud = slope). The temple, numbered 5C-49, is an example of this construction method and at the same time the second most significant structure of the group.

The center of the Mundo Perdido complex is "The Great Pyramid" or "Lost World Pyramid." It is 31 meters high. At its base, it measures almost 70 meters and is thus the most extensive construction project ever to have taken place in Tikal. A total of 5 superstructures have been found. The beginnings here also date back to the pre-Classical phase.

The Skull Temple or Templo de las Calaveras is the third largest structure of the Mundo Perdido complex. Here too, several superstructures have been found. Numerous graves detected in this complex indicate that for a long time, Mundo Perdido served as a necropolis for the ruling class as the northern Acropolis.

SQUARE OF THE SEVEN TEMPLES - PLAZA DE LOS SIETE TEMPLOS

West of the central Acropolis and south of Temple III, is the Square of the seven temples - Plaza de Los Siete Templos. There are some smaller temples on the eastern side of the square. The area has an area of 25000sqm, which makes it the third largest square in Tikal. Construction work began in the Pre-Classic period during the 7th century BC.

TWIN PYRAMIDS

A total of nine twin pyramid complexes have been discovered in Tikal. These are small pyramids with a platform that can be reached via four stairs on each of the four sides corresponding to the cardinal points. Two of these pyramids are arranged on the east and west side of a square respectively. Due to inscriptions, we know the years in which each of these pyramids was erected. Each couple of twin pyramids was named with a letter, as Group M, N, O, P, Q, and R.

It is noticeable that these data are exactly 20 years apart and mark the change of the Katun at that time. Apparently, they were built on the occasion of this change for ceremonial reasons. The twin pyramids can be found in different places in Tikal's urban area.

<<<< *Figure 77 - Tikal - Temple IV*

Group	Date	Long Count
Group M	692 AD	9.13.0.0.0
Group N	711 AD	9.14.0.0.0
Group O	731 AD	9.15.0.0.0
Group P	751 AD	9.16.0.0.0
Group Q	771 AD	9.17.0.0.0
Group R	790 AD	9.18.0.0.0

Table 1 - Twin pyramid groups in Tikal with date and long count date

Similar twin pyramids have been detected in only three other places. One of them in Yaxhá, one in Ixlu, at the bottleneck between Lago Petén and Lago Salpeten near El Remate and two others in Zacpetén, on a peninsula in Lago Salpeten. No twin pyramids have been found yet outside this area near Tikal.

HISTORY OF TIKAL

Thanks to numerous well-preserved inscriptions on stone tablets, we are better informed about the classical phase of Tikal than of other ancient Maya cities. This is true especially for the Classic phase during which the inscriptions were created. For the time before or after this period archaeologists have to rely on spade finds to get at least a rough overview.

PRE-CLASSICAL PERIOD

The first agricultural activities were found in the Middle Pre-Classic, around 1000 BC. Ceramic remains found among the oldest buildings date back to 800 BC. Construction work on the oldest structures in Tikal began very early, approximately 650 BC, as it is assumed for the Square of the Seven Temples and the Mundo Perdido Group.

At that time, Tikal's influence in the region was still small, and its importance was overshadowed by the power and splendor of El Mirador and Nakbe, which were the power centers of the Maya area during the pre-Classical phase.

CLASSICAL PERIOD

A total of 33 rulers were found in Tikal. They reigned and steered the fate of the city for 1800 years. The dynasty founder was probably Yax Ehb

Xook, whose reign fell into the late pre-Classical period, the 1st century AD.

The first centuries of the early classical period were marked by warlike activities, which involved not only Tikal but also Uaxactun, Caracol, Calakmul, and Naranjo.

In 378 AD, an invasion by an army of Teotihuacan in Tikal took place. The current 14th ruler "Jaguar claw" Chak TokIch' aak I was deposed by the foreign military power and probably executed immediately. In his place "The first crocodile" – Yax Nuun Ahiin I took the throne. Apparently, the crocodile was a son of the ruler of Teotihuacan, Atlatl Cauac, which means "the owl that strikes" and which historians call the "spear-chucking owl," too.

The following rulers were able to expand their sphere of influence. Uaxactun was incorporated into the kingdom, Rio Azul was conquered, and other towns on Lago Petén became politically dependent on Tikal.

At the end of the 5th century, the power of Tikal even reached into the present-day border area of Guatemala and Honduras. Not only the foundation of Copan but also the beginning of a ruling dynasty there can be traced back to Tikal's initiative under the influence of Teotihuacan. At the same time, the city of Quirigua was founded near Copan.

In the 6th century, a long-lasting war with Calakmul began. Around 562 AD, an alliance between Calakmul and Caracol Tikal succeeded in conquering and killing the reigning king. This date marks a time which is called “Hiatus of Tikal” by historians. Characteristic of the Hiatus is that during about 120 years no new inscriptions were created.

Figure 78 - Tikal - The Northern Acropolis and Temple II

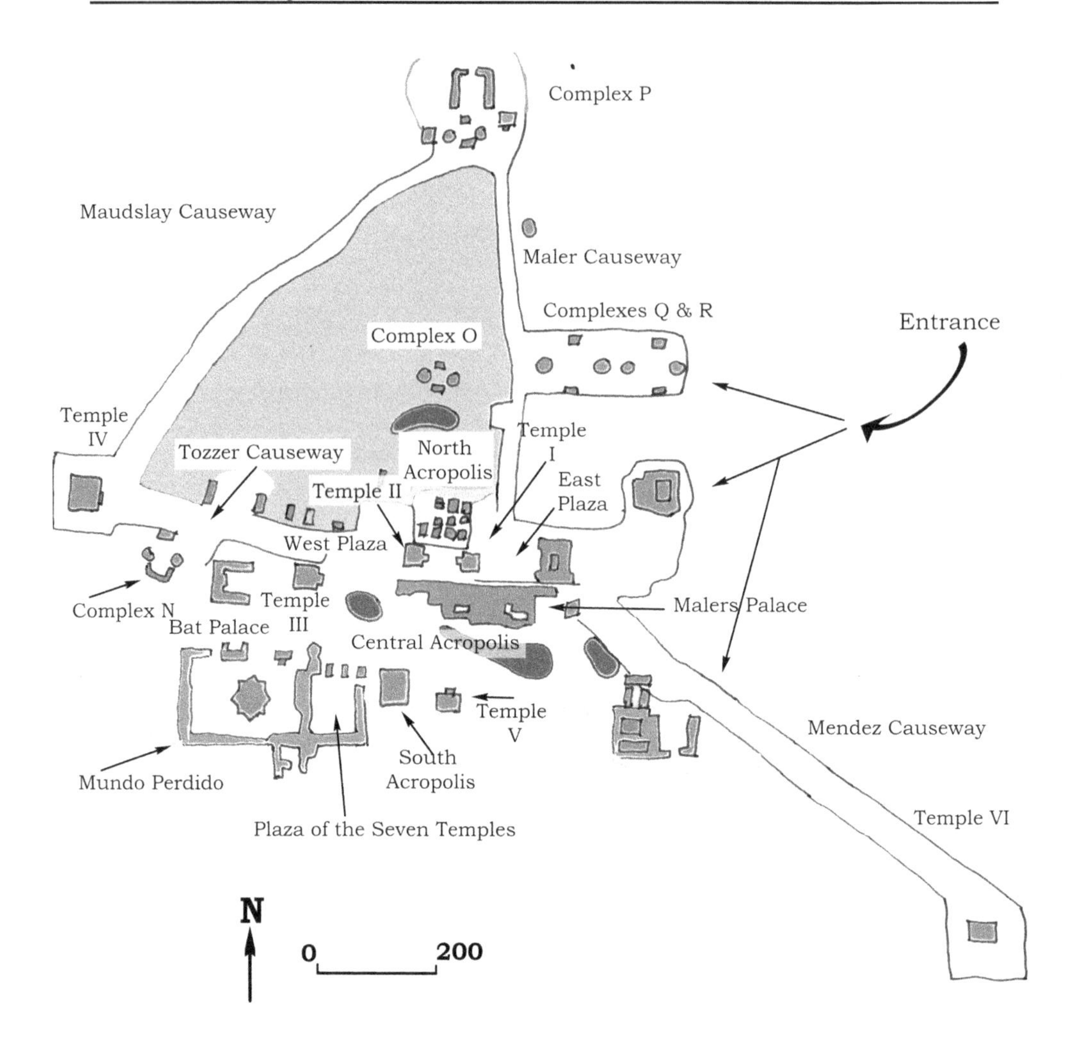

Map 12 - Tikal

Part of Tikal's ruling class seems to have succeeded in saving themselves at the court of Palenque.

However, Calakmul's control of Tikal was incomplete and only temporary. Although Tikal's power was initially broken and his sphere of influence was significantly reduced, it was not extinguished.

About 70 years after the defeat in 629 AD, Tikal founded the military outpost of Dos Pilas, thus gaining control of the critical trade route along the Pasíon River. Dos Pilas was apparently a thorn in Calakmul's side. After 30 years, in 657 AD, it was conquered by Tikal's rival. The king of Dos Pilas, who descended from the dynasty of Tikal, changed sides, joined Calakmul and launched an attack, which was almost fatal for Tikal. But the subsequent counterattack by Tikal led to the expulsion of the ruling king.

After the break of 120 years, the next inscription in Tikal was made in 682 AD. Jasaw Chan K'awiil I., who had built the temples I and II at the Gran Plaza, finally succeeded in defeating Calakmul in 695 AD and captured its ruler. Calakmul was stricken in a way that the decline of this once mighty city was sealed. After this defeat, there were no more inscriptions in Calakmul. Until then, the war had lasted for almost 150 years and thus covered the entire Hiatus period.

During this time, Teotihuacan's influence on Tikal and the rest of the Maya region gradually diminished and eventually ended completely. The city in the high valley of Mexico, which had been influential for many centuries, was destroyed around 700 AD and abandoned by its inhabitants. The exact reasons for the sinking of Teotihuacan have not yet been clarified, but the cause is believed to be a people‘s uprising.

The 8th century saw some construction activity in Tikal, but the number of inscriptions gradually decreased.

869 AD, the last inscription was finally written. The population number steadily melted away and around 950 AD the city was mostly abandoned.

TRAVEL TIP

From the bus station in Flores/St. Elena, you can quickly reach Tikal by public transport. The journey in the colectivo takes about one hour. You should have good shoes and enough drinking water with you to visit this Maya city. The routes within the area are relatively long. It is 1.3km from the entrance to the Plaza Major. If you plan to see all the famous temples, then you have to cover almost 6 km. Consider that some of the pyramids and temples can also be climbed, so that it is easy to add 100 meters of altitude to the hike.

YAXHÁ

Yaxhá is a Maya city whose heyday was during the early classical period between 250 and 600 AD. It is located in the lowlands of Guatemala in the state of Petén. The name Yaxhá means "blue-green" water in the Mayan language. The border to the neighboring country Belize is only a few kilometers away. From Flores on Lake Petén, the distance measures about 60km.

The city was built on the shores of the Laguna Yaxhá. It is surrounded by the original subtropical rainforest of a vast nature reserve, the Parque Nacional de Yaxhá-Nakum-Naranjo. The area of this reserve is 371.6km², which corresponds to approximately 37000ha. The park is adjacent to other nature reserves and is part of the "Biosphera Maya," a cross-border sanctuary that connects the countries of Mexico, Belize, and Guatemala.

Following Tikal and El Mirador, Yaxhá was the third largest Maya settlement in Guatemala. The first report about the city originates from Teobert Maler, who visited the site in 1904.

Restoration work began in the 80s of the last century. Nine, of the more than five hundred identified structures, are temple pyramids. About 40 stelae, some with inscriptions, have been discovered here.

DESCRIPTION OF THE MAYA SITE

Four Sacbeob have been found in Yaxhá, connecting the primary centers of the city. It is good to know the location and the direction of these ancient processional streets, as they still form the connecting routes between the individual groups of buildings.

CALZADA DEL LAGO

This is the oldest of the Sacbeob. It starts at the lakeside of Lago Yaxhá and runs northwards into the center of the city. The Calzada del Lago was already built in the late pre-Classic and was renewed several times. The extension of this causeway is then called Via 5. It is believed that this Sacbé was initially the official city entrance running from a pier at the lake up into the city.

<<<< *Figure 79 - Yaxhá - Structures of the Maler Group*

Figure 80 - Yaxhá – Eastern Acropolis, Building 216 – View over the Lake

CALZADA BLOM

North of the city center begins a Sacbé called Calzada Blom, which leads from here to the Maler group in the north. Franz Blom was a researcher who studied the small folklore of the Lacandon Maya from the 1930s on. His home in San Cristobal de las Casas in the highlands of Chiapas was transformed into a museum about this ethnic group.

CALZADA GALINDO

The Sacbé named after a Central American researcher and officer runs in a north-south direction. It starts in the north at the Eastern Acropolis and ends in the south at Plaza C.

CALZADA LINCOLN

The Calzada Lincoln is the first Sacbé to encounter from the entrance of the site. It runs from Plaza C to the northwest and meets Plaza D, on the edge of the city center.

GETTING AROUND

Coming from the entrance, you first reach the Plaza C. Here is a so-called E-group, which was used for astronomical purposes.

E-GROUPS

E-group complexes are commonly found in Maya sites. The term E-group has to do with the fact that the first complex of this type, which was identified in Uaxactun, north of Tikal, was given the designation "Group E." It is the oldest type of architectural complex whose appearance can be seen from the middle pre-classical period on. E groups served the Maya as tools for astronomical observation and calendar determination. Several structures were arranged so that one could determine or observe the sunset on the equinoxes and on the solstices from an eastern observation platform. This was done by targeting various structures built west of the platform.

The path forks behind Plaza C. On the left, Calzada Lincoln leads to Plaza D and the city center. On the right, a massive wooden staircase leads up to Plaza B. The latter way is the one my site description follows.

Once you have reached Plaza B, you see the embankment of the Eastern Acropolis on the right side. Going on and keeping to the right, another wooden staircase leads up to the square in front of Temple 216.

Figure 81 - Yaxhá - Structure of the Acropolis North

<<<< *Figure 82 - Yaxhá - Stela with Central-Mexican Style Elements*

From here, another wooden staircase leads up to the top platform of this temple.
Temple 216 is the highest point of the city. From here you have an excellent view of the lagoon. Other ancient buildings stand out from the jungle.

The construction work on the eastern acropolis began already in the middle pre-classic phase on a limestone hill. The old components, initially designed in a triadic way, were extended continuously and several times overbuilt, until the end of the classical period. The pyramidal substructure of Temple 216, including the upper temple building, is 30 meters high and the tallest structure to be found in Yaxhá. In addition to Temple 216, there are several palace buildings on the Eastern Acropolis.

When you descend the stairs of Temple 216 and the Eastern Acropolis again and turn to the north, you will find Plaza A. Here you will see the remains of a twin pyramid complex. Otherwise, this kind of compounds is known only from Tikal and its immediate surroundings. In Tikal, twin pyramids were built every 20 years to celebrate the change of the Katun, a 20-year period, in the calendar cycle. More details about the twin pyramids can be found in the chapter about Tikal.

After passing between the still unrestored twin pyramids, the path turns left in western direction. After passing additional unrestored structures, you reach the ball court. There you turn right to the also not restored Acropolis Noreste and continue walking until you reach the Acropolis Norte.

The pyramids of the Acropolis form a triad and were part of an E-complex too. The pyramids were built in the late pre-classical period and later overbuilt, which can be seen on a shaft dug into one of the monuments.

To the right, passing the middle of the pyramids to the north, you finally reach the Maler group. This group consists of several well-restored pyramid temples. Particularly interesting is that, at least during my visit, a colony of Montezuma Oropendola birds lived on the edge of the Plaza Maler. These songbirds belonging to the family of the Icterid birds build hanging nests similar to the weaver birds.

From the Plaza Maler, walk southwards on the Calzada Blom to get back to the city center. At the end of the Sacbé, you come across a barely exposed but rather tall structure, which you can climb over a wooden staircase. Again, this gives you a beautiful panoramic view over the jungle. After you walk around this structure on the right side, you can continue southwards along Via A to the Acropolis Sur.

If you still have some power, you can go down the Calzada del Lago until you reach the lake and of course later then, back up to the Acropolis Sur again. South of the Acropolis Sur, the path leads to the east. If you come back from the lake, you have to go right in front of the Acropolis.

Finally, you get to Calzada Lincoln, which leads you back south to Plaza C and thus to the entrance.

The entire route covers an estimated 5 to 6km. Also, there are about 100 vertical meters, because of the pyramids and the lagoon. Having a bottle of water with you is appropriate. Also, firm shoes and long pants, as protection against bites of all kinds, are recommended.

Historical Overview

From 600 BC to 900 AD, during 1600 years, Yaxhá was inhabited.

PRE-CLASSIC

Yaxhá had already reached a remarkable size in the pre-classical period. The strategic location on one of the leading trade routes between the Caribbean and the Petén area is likely to have encouraged this development.

EARLY CLASSIC (250 AD - 600 AD)

After the conquest of neighboring Tikal by troops of the Central Mexican Teotihuacan, Yaxhá seems to have been influenced by this Mexican state. At the end of the early classical period, earthquakes in the Yaxhá region seem to have led to significant destruction.

LATE CLASSIC (600 AD - 900 AD)

Of course, the war between Tikal and Calakmul going on during this period also affected Yaxhá, which was allied with Tikal. Naranjo, allied with Calakmul, defeated Yaxhá around 710 AD only to be beaten then by Tikal. Despite numerous conflicts, the time of the late Classic was also a time of increased construction activity.

POST-CLASSIC

Unlike other lowland locations, Yaxhá's existence did not end abruptly, but rather slowly. Findings from the post-classical time are proven but may be remains of visitors from Topoxté, a small post-classical settlement on an island in Lake Yaxhá, which was inhabited until 1450.

Nature reserve

In addition to the monuments, the surrounding nature in Yaxhá is also imposing. About 200km² includes the nature reserve in which Yaxhá is located.

Between the buildings you move in a park-like cleaned forest area, which gradually turns into the primeval forest, the further you walk away

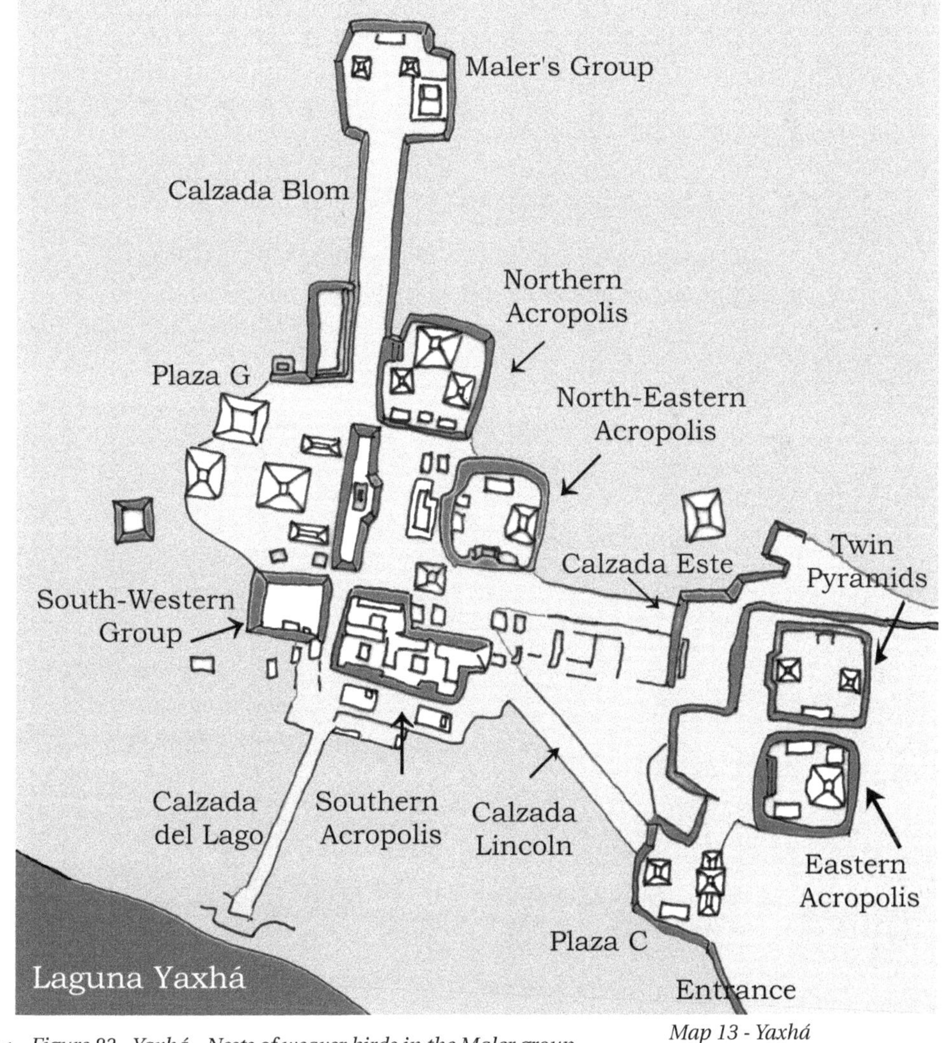

Map 13 - Yaxhá

<<< *Figure 83 - Yaxhá - Nests of weaver birds in the Maler group*

from the edifices.
In addition to exotic plants, orchids, bromeliads and tillandsia, you can see and observe different species of tropical birds, reptiles, mammals and of course insects in their natural environment. The lake is home to some crocodiles, so you should do without swimming activities. As mentioned before, at the Maler group you may see Montezuma birds and their hanging nests. If it keeps rustling in the treetops, then you probably have to deal with a horde of howler monkeys.

Travel Tip

Few tourists find their way to Yaxhá. Therefore, the infrastructure is not developed to the same extent as it is the case with Tikal. It is recommended to book the trip there via one of the tourist offices in Flores. I found it very useful to meet Dieter Richter in Flores, who runs a small restaurant called Café Yax-Háthere. Dieter, a German architect, was involved in the investigation and restoration of the ruins of Yaxhá and, provided he is on the spot, can give the interested explorer valuable tips on visiting this and other Maya cities. He and his team also organize tours to the various Maya sites in the surrounding area.

If you are traveling in a group, then it can make sense to rent a taxi together. Yaxhá is challenging to reach by public transport. From the main road leading to the Belize border near Melchior, one would have to walk several kilometers of gravel road, before entering the Maya site.

EL MIRADOR - THE JUNGLE ADVENTURE

El Mirador in Guatemala is featured as a place of superlatives due to the highest pyramid, and the most massive ruins of the Maya ever discovered. And El Mirador is also regarded as the most adventurous destination for those explorers interested in the Maya culture.

No roads, only winding, jungle cutting mule trails lead to this enchanting place.

Hidden in the subtropical rainforest for centuries, only jaguars and howler monkeys knew of the existence of the gigantic stone monuments between the forest trees, waiting for their rediscovery. Originally pre-Classic pyramids before nature swallowed and transformed them into hills, overgrown by tropical plants. The few "Chicleros," rubber collectors, who reached this place, called it El Mirador – the viewpoint.

The ancient buildings, still covered by nature to a big extent, tower impressive above the surrounding forest, thus allowing a broad panoramic view over the canopy of the Petén even across the border to Mexico, about 20km north of El Mirador.

El Mirador has a considerable expansion. It is larger than any other Maya city, even Tikal, Palenque or Yaxchilán. Most probably El Mirador was founded before 600 BC, in the middle of the pre-classic period of the Maya culture. During its heyday, El Mirador might have been inhabited by more than 100,000 people. Like all cities of this area, El Mirador was finally abandoned around AD 900. At this time it had existed for 1500 years.

The three main pyramids of El Mirador are called El Tigre, Los Monos, and La Danta. All three were built in several huge layers. Each of them has a group of three smaller temple pyramids at the top level. The total

<<<< Figure 84 - El Mirador - Sunrise - View of La Danta from El Tigre

Figure 85 – El Mirador - Temple Pyramid on the Top Level of La Danta

Figure 86 - El Mirador - Restoration Work at La Danta

Figure 87 - El Mirador - Workers climbing up El Tigre

altitude of La Danta is 70 meters, El Tigre reaches 55 meters and Los Monos after all, still 48 meters. Due to its massive volume of 2.8 million cubic meters, La Danta is one of the largest pyramids in the world. For comparison, the Great Pyramid in Egypt reaches the double height with 138 meters, but its volume is only 2.5 million cubic meters. That is less than La Danta.

To get there, you have no choice but to go hiking. Sometimes you can also rent mules and cover the track mounted. But as a pedestrian, you are faster, and you also have the advantage of looking more closely at the nature around you. The one-way length of the route is 37km. Back and forth sum up to 74km, therefore.

Because of the distances that you have to cover during the visit of El Mirador, you will have to accomplish a minimum of 80 to 90 km during the trip. The terrain is mostly flat and occasionally swampy.

It is a five-day march to El Mirador and back. You should not attempt to try this on your own - see my remark at the end of the chapter.

DAY 1

The first day starts with a drive to Carmelita, 45 km north of Lago Petén. The route follows a dirt road. Carmelita is the last village before the jungle begins. Power supply for the residents does not exist. Only the administration building receives power from a generator.

Here is the beginning point for the hike to El Mirador. A guide and a Mula besides a muleteer will accompany you. The mules are required to transport food, water, and luggage. You will carry a water bottle and your photo equipment only on your own, and perhaps some toilet paper for emergencies.

At the end of the first day, you will reach the small location Tintal. Tintal is an ancient Maya settlement with temple pyramids, but less important than El Mirador and still poorly discovered. There, you will find a picnic area with some roofs, fireplaces, a stove and a pit latrine.

Just a few workers, who keep the location free of vegetation and occasionally some archaeologists investigating the ancient site live there.

DAY 2

After a beautiful night with a campfire, mosquitoes and exotic jungle sound, you will continue your journey the next day. From here on, the trail leads you through a few flat valleys and can sometimes be very muddy. The jungle becomes denser, the trees are more abundant now. You might see monkeys, snakes, frogs, birds and you will be fascinated by the fact that there are very painfully biting ants in the area. On the evening of the second day, you will reach the final destination: El Mirador.

<<<< *Figure 88 - El Mirador - The Mula*

Figure 89 - El Mirador - Prickly on the Path

Figure 90 - El Mirador - Waterhole in Tintal

DAY 3

After the second night, you should get up as soon as possible and climb up the pyramid El Tigre to see the sunrise, covering the jungle in a fantastic light. Thus, this third day is used for observation and exploration.

About 300 workers and a handful of archaeologists live in El Mirador. If you're lucky, you can talk to some of the archaeologists about their doing or watch them at work.

In any case, you should climb the three great pyramids La Danta, Los Monos and El Tigre. But El Mirador has much more to see. Overall, it will be a time-consuming program.

After all, La Danta and El Tigre are about three kilometers distant to each other so that the walking performance of this day should not be underestimated. You should expect to walk additional ten kilometers while on site.

DAY 4 AND 5

On the fourth morning, you'll leave El Mirador, and after another night in the jungle, you will arrive exhausted but happy in Carmelita, where you are picked up and transported back to Flores.

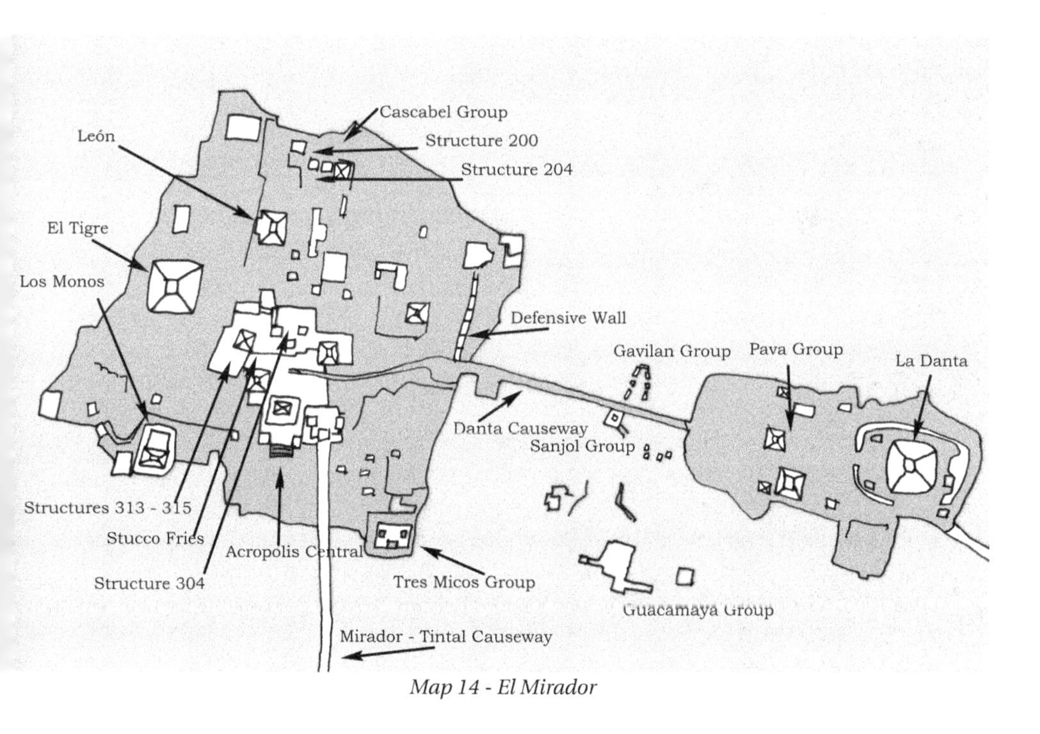

Map 14 - El Mirador

<<<< *Figure 91 - El Mirador - Jungle Cooking - Stove and Tortilla in Tintal*

TRAVEL ADVICE:

Good shoes: If you're not used to it, then do not under any circumstances walk the route in rubber boots like the locals do it. I was there during the rainy season and found that the condition of the path even in this season was good enough for regular walking boots.

Clothing: You should wear long pants and a long-sleeved shirt. There are snakes, tarantulas, scorpions and mosquitoes waiting just for you.

Yes, just for you!

Hygiene: Water is limited. Do not expect that you have the opportunity to take a shower. Teeth brushing should be possible, but a shower with fresh water is unthinkable. After three days, you're going to have the subtle scent of an old buffalo. This makes you unattractive not only for your comrades but for the mosquitoes as well.

Insect protection: Take adequate amounts of insect repellant with you. Expect massive mosquito attacks during day and night. In San Jose, north of Lake Petén, there is an organization that produces traditional Maya medicine. They also sell an ointment against mosquitoes. The advantage of this greasy salve is that it is not washed off by sweat and rain, such as the sprays commercially available. I had a pot of the Maya salve with me and used it during the five days. After I had used it for three days, the mosquitoes lost any interest in me.

Light is attractive: It's not a bad idea to carry a torch with you, especially, if you have to go to the bathroom at night. But do not use it under any circumstances while sitting together with your fellow travelers near the campfire when taking dinner after dark.
Are you afraid that an insect might fall in your soup? Don't mind, you cannot change it anyway! But if you should try to illuminate your plate to control its content, then indeed one thing will happen: You'll attract myriads of insects, whose only desire seems to be to hop into your vegetarian Spaghetti Bolognese. It is far more intelligent to eat in the dark and to allow the small insects, to hop in the soup of your fellow travelers while they illuminate their own bowl.

Safety: Under no circumstances try to make this trip on your own. It is dangerous! People have walked into this jungle and were never seen again. And you never know who you will meet in the forest. If anything wrong should happen, then civilization is a two-day march away. It is much better and secure to ask at a local tourist office in Flores. They organize guides, meals, and mules for the trip, take you to Carmelita and pick you up again.

Have fun!

Section 3
–
History and Culture of the Maya

THE HOMELAND OF THE ANCIENT MAYA - THE MAYAB

When the Maya culture flourished during the classical period, the area inhabited by them stretched from the north coast of the Yucatán peninsula to the Pacific coast of Guatemala in the south. In the east, the Isthmus of Tehuantepec, the bottleneck between the Gulf of Mexico and the Pacific Ocean, limited the settlement area. In the west, it extended into today's Honduras and to El Salvador. Mayab' is the name that the Maya gave to the northern part of the area.

The word Ma' ya' ab, which derives from the Yucatec Maya, literally means "not many" and in a metaphorical sense, the "place where only a few people live." It remains to be seen whether this is a good explanation. The conquistadors called the peninsula Yucatán, probably

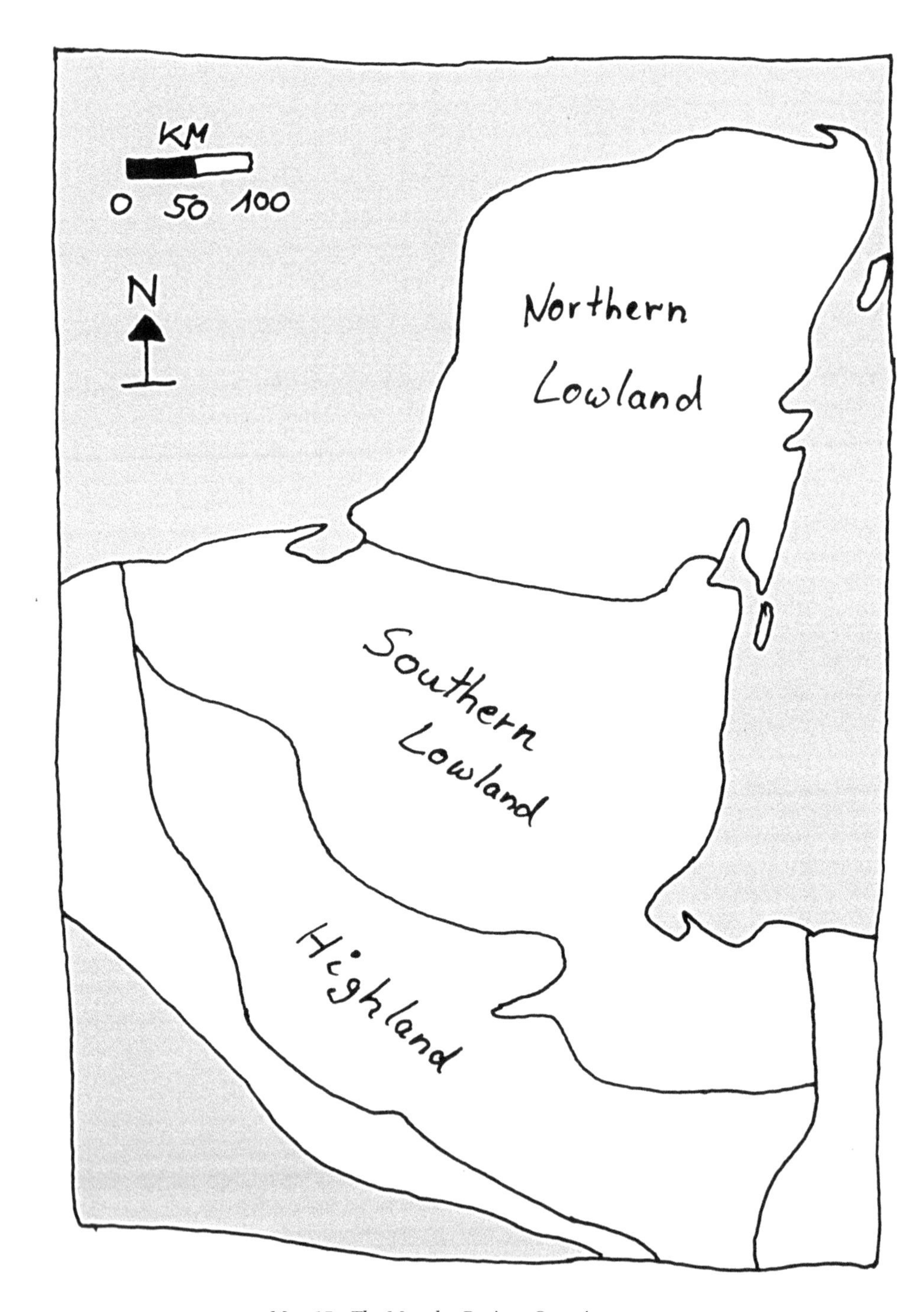

Map 15 - The Mayab - Regions Overview

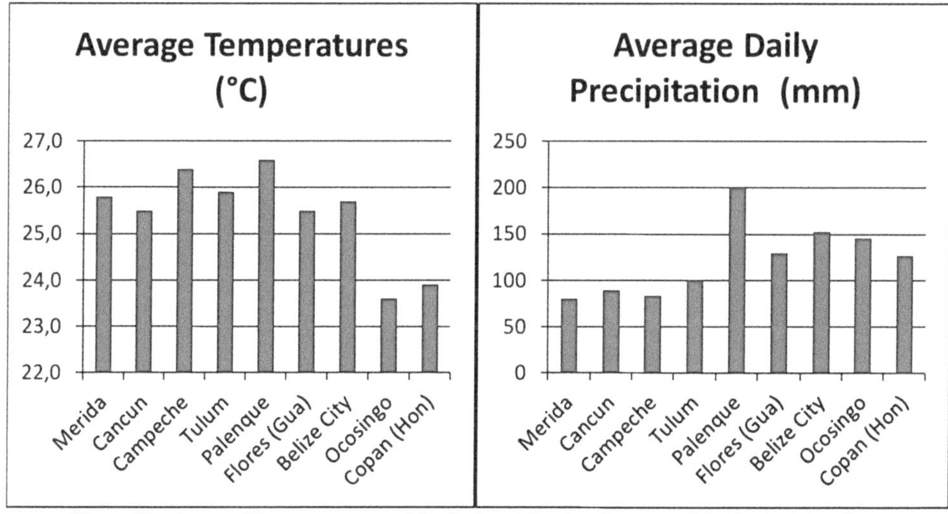

Figure 92 - Average Temperatures and Daily Precipitation for some cities in the Mayab area

because of a communication problem. Cortez reports that the name came up because a group of Indians had answered the question about the name of the country with "Yuk akkatán" – "I do not understand." Today, it is proposed to designate the entire area inhabited by Maya as Mayab.

The Mayab is a part of the region also known as Mesoamerica. This is the zone in Central America which is characterized by discoveries of ancient civilizations. It stretches from the central high valley from Mexico to the south to Honduras and El Salvador.

Just the Maya region has approximately the same area and diameter as Germany or Montana. The distance from the northern Gulf coast to the Pacific Ocean is 700 kilometers. The Mayab extends by the same amount from east to west at its widest points.

LANDSCAPE

The landscape can be divided into three roughly equal parts: The northern and the southern lowlands, and the highlands. The great city-states of the classical Maya civilization arose mainly in the flat landscape of today's Guatemala. But at the time of the Spanish conquest, only in the northern lowlands larger settlements and cities with a state character remained.

The northern lowlands include the Mexican state of Yucatán and the North of Campeche and Quintana Roo. The southern lowlands cover the South of these states, the Petén in Guatemala and parts of Chiapas. It reaches up to the ascending mountain ranges of the Sierra Madre in Chiapas and Guatemala. Here is where the highlands of Chiapas and

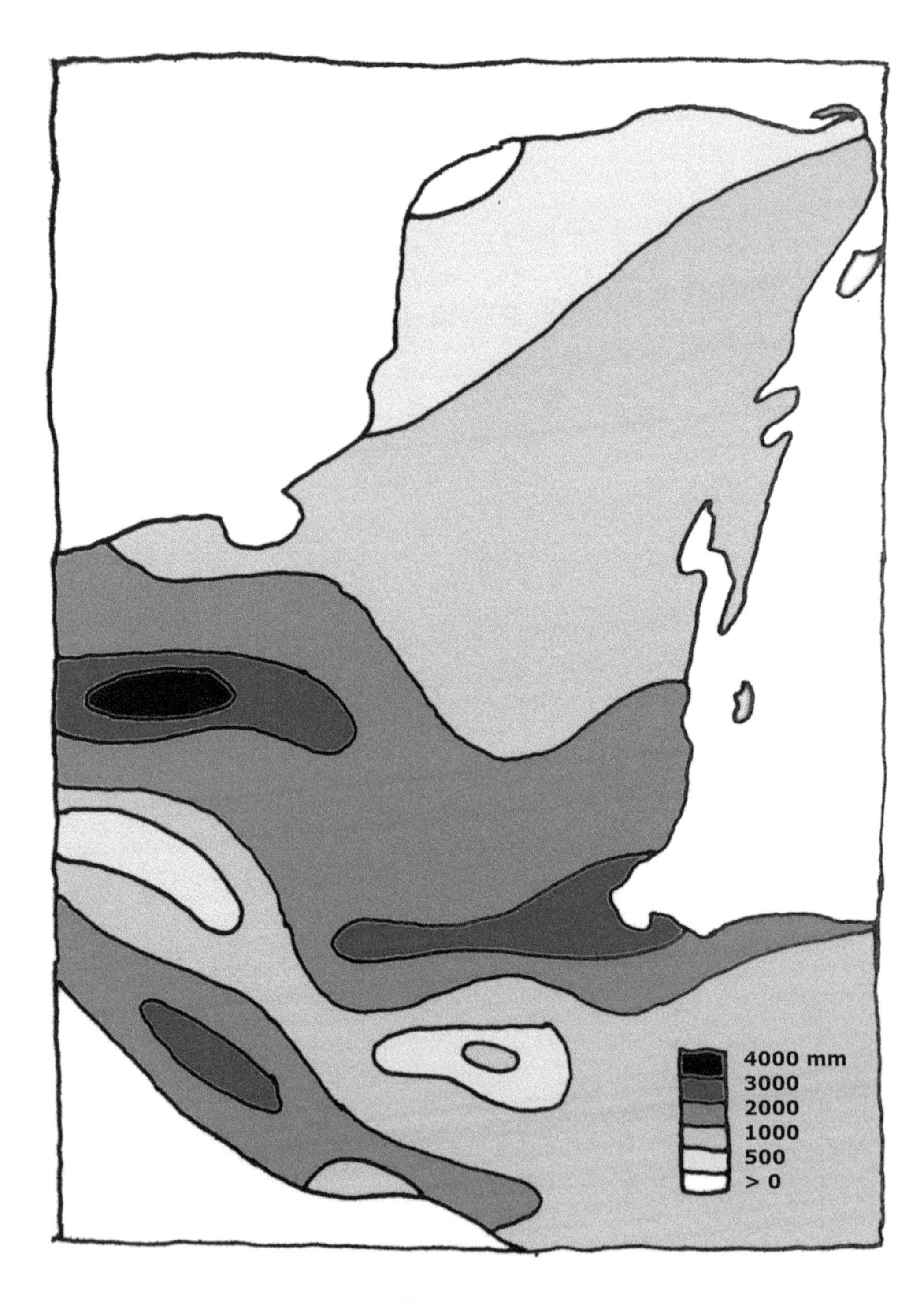

Map 17 - The Mayab - Precipitation

Guatemala start. These highlands are crisscrossed by volcanic chains and high valleys and can reach an altitude of more than 4000 meters. Further to the south, the landscape lowers abruptly. After a narrow, swampy coastal strip, which is mostly bordered by mangrove forests, you reach the Pacific Ocean. There are also brackish shallow water lagoons, wetlands and mangrove forests on the coasts of the Caribbean and the Gulf Coast.

There are no rivers in the northern lowlands. The karstic nature of the subsoil causes rainwater to seep away immediately and forms a hidden freshwater reservoir at a depth of about ten meters. Deep below the surface, an underground river system has formed in this way. At some point, the ceiling of these caves collapsed and so creating what we know as cenotes. These holes, filled with freshwater have been used by ancient Maya and are still used by modern Maya for drinking water supply. Since the cenotes are located on a spatially limited semicircular line, geologists have developed the theory that their formation is due to the impact of a large meteorite in the Gulf of Mexico.

The shockwave that emanated from this impact changed the composition of the limestone layer, thus favoring the formation of cenotes. In this way, the cenotes trace the distortions at the edge of the crater. The meteorite impact occurred about 65 million years ago. It got its name Chicxulub after the place Chi'ik Xulub, which means something like "Devil's flea" or "demon's tick." A fitting name, because the impact of the Chicxulub meteorite at the end of the Cretaceous period was also the trigger for the extinction of the dinosaurs.

Several separate river systems shape the character of the southern lowlands. The most extensive of these systems is the Rio Usumacinta. The river, including its two spring rivers La Pasíon and Rio Salinas in Guatemala, is almost 1000 kilometers long and forms the border between Guatemala and Mexico over long distances. Hondo River, Belize River, Rio Mopan, Rio Candelaria, Rio Champoton, Rio Motagua and Rio Lancantun are other rivers that either drain into the Caribbean or flow into the Gulf of Mexico. They extend far into the heartland. At the time of the Maya, these rivers were the main routes for transporting goods.

CLIMATE

Throughout the lowlands, temperatures are relatively constant. Towards the south, they rise only slightly. The average temperature is 26 degrees Celsius. In the southern highlands, they become significantly lower again.

Things are entirely different with the rainfall. Here, the northern and southern lowlands differ to a significant extent. To the south, precipitation increases considerably. Mérida in the north-west of the peninsula receives an average rainfall of 80mm - less than half the amount of rain falling on Palenque. On average there are 200mm per

	Jan	Feb	Mar	Apr	May	Jun	Jul	Aug	Sep	Okt	Nov	Dec	Average	
Merida	22,70	23,40	25,60	27,20	27,70	27,80	27,30	27,50	27,20	25,80	24,00	22,80	**25,75**	°C
Merida	33,00	26,00	18,00	22,00	72,00	143,00	142,00	152,00	175,00	98,00	42,00	36,00	**79,92**	mm
Cancun	22,70	22,90	24,50	25,90	26,80	27,30	27,50	27,70	27,30	26,00	24,20	23,00	**25,48**	°C
Cancun	76,00	51,00	29,00	38,00	80,00	144,00	71,00	72,00	160,00	194,00	77,00	79,00	**89,25**	mm
Campeche	23,20	24,10	26,20	28,10	28,80	28,70	28,00	28,00	27,70	26,30	24,40	23,40	**26,41**	°C
Campeche	23,00	12,00	19,00	15,00	57,00	143,00	181,00	187,00	190,00	92,00	46,00	34,00	**83,25**	mm
Tulum	23,20	23,60	25,30	26,70	27,50	27,60	27,50	27,50	27,40	26,30	24,70	23,50	**25,90**	°C
Tulum	65,00	49,00	37,00	39,00	105,00	167,00	100,00	113,00	184,00	186,00	80,00	75,00	**100,00**	mm
Palenque	22,60	25,30	26,40	27,70	29,50	28,80	28,00	28,00	27,50	26,40	25,10	23,90	**26,60**	°C
Palenque	127,00	89,00	76,00	72,00	148,00	270,00	217,00	302,00	**444,00**	322,00	183,00	144,00	**199,50**	mm
Flores (Guat)	22,80	23,30	24,70	26,30	28,10	28,40	27,10	27,20	26,80	25,20	23,40	22,50	**25,48**	°C
Flores (Guat)	66,00	55,00	43,00	34,00	136,00	209,00	187,00	183,00	227,00	208,00	115,00	87,00	**129,17**	mm
Belize City	22,90	23,60	24,80	26,50	27,30	27,70	27,00	27,10	27,10	26,40	24,40	23,20	**25,67**	°C
Belize City	126,00	61,00	53,00	43,00	99,00	216,00	186,00	164,00	237,00	278,00	216,00	162,00	**153,42**	mm
Ocosingo	20,80	21,40	23,30	24,60	25,40	24,90	24,70	24,60	25,10	24,10	22,30	21,50	**23,56**	°C
Ocosingo	46,00	37,00	43,00	69,00	147,00	263,00	234,00	220,00	325,00	225,00	87,00	54,00	**145,83**	mm
Copan (Hon)	22,00	23,00	24,70	25,70	25,80	24,70	24,40	24,50	24,20	23,50	22,50	21,90	**23,91**	°C
Copan (Hon)	31,00	20,00	23,00	33,00	127,00	302,00	221,00	220,00	269,00	156,00	74,00	52,00	**127,33**	mm

Table 2 - Temperature and Precipitation on the Yucatán Peninsula

month.

September is the month in which the most precipitation occurs. The months of greatest drought are March and April.

The differences in the amount of rainwater, combined with the composition of the subsoil, have a significant influence on the prevailing vegetation and thus on the living conditions of the people in these areas.

Dry scrublands characterize the landscape in the far north-west of the peninsula. Towards the southeast, these gradually merge into dry broadleaf forests and later into rain forests. The broadleaf forest types are only leafy during the rainy season. During the dry periods, the trees shed their leaves. Finally, evergreen rainforest dominates the southern lowlands.

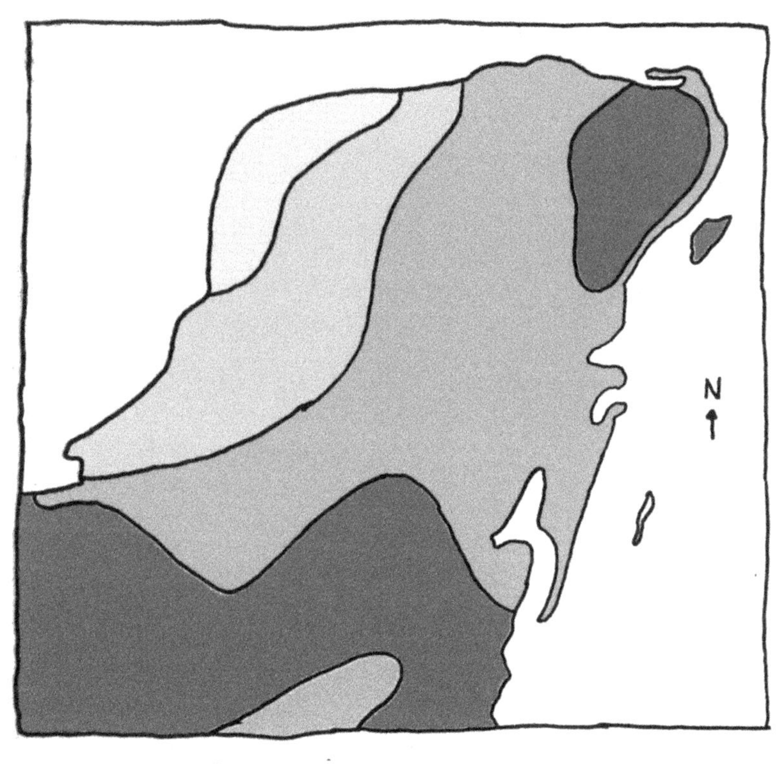

Scrubland / Savanna
Dry Forest
Wet Forest
Rain Forest

Map 18 - Vegetation Zones in the Mayab

NATURAL RESOURCES IN THE ANCIENT MAYA WORLD

Climate and geology are the determining factors for agriculture. For a long time, it was assumed that the Maya used only a simple slash-and-burn method to open up new agricultural areas. This form of farming is still in use today in large areas of the Maya region. In the meantime, however, archaeologists have discovered that the Maya also used other techniques. Terraces were laid out in mountainous areas, and raised beds were used in swampy areas. In Edzná, Campeche, a drainage system has been discovered, and in Tikal, a dam was found to supply water.

The main foods; corn, beans, and pumpkin were grown using the methods of a milpa. Milpa is a word derived from the language of the Aztecs, the Nahuatl, and means "cornfield." The method is still in use today. On the field intended for cultivation, first, the trees are cut and left to dry. One year later, the bushes are cut off. After clearing the field and after removing the rootstocks, the remaining plant parts are burned. The ashes add minerals to the soil. After the field has been prepared, a method known as the "Three Sisters" is used. Corn, beans, and pumpkins are planted at the same time by planting several seeds of each of these plants in the same seed hole. The use of these three plant species is perfectly coordinated. The corn provides support to the bean tendrils, the pumpkin plants shade the soil, and the beans contribute to this symbiosis by releasing nitrogen into the ground. After the field has been intensively used several times in this way, the area is left fallow again.

In addition to these basic foods produced by slash-and-burn, the Maya also had "home gardens" in which they cultivated fruit, vegetables, and herbs. Manioc, tomatoes, chili, avocados, guavas, pineapple, papaya and sweet potatoes enriched the menu. This list is just a small part of the plants that have already been used as food by the Maya in classical times. On the website of the "Foundation for Latin American Anthropological Research FLAAR.", you can find an excellent overview of the plants used by the Maya in ancient time until today (see Appendix).

The Maya had two kinds of domesticated animals – turkey and dog - on arrival of the Spaniards. Both were part of the classic Maya cuisine. Wild game was also popular. The prey was mainly deer, but also other animals such as possum, manatee or tapir found a place in the cooking pots if the hunters could get hold of them. Near the coast, of course, fish and seafood were common foods.

I addition to the directly consumed foodstuffs, there were also those that grew not uniformly everywhere but had to be traded over very long distances.

Cocoa cultivation played a significant role. Cocoa was so coveted and valuable that cocoa beans have been in use as a means of payment. Cocoa was also crucial as a drink in a cultic context.

Plant juices and resins may not be underestimated as sources for several products. Copal, chicle, and gum have been obtained by making incisions to trees and sampling the leaking juice. Copal was and is still part of ceremonies as incense. It can also be used to drive away mosquitoes. Chicle has already been harvested from the Maya and processed in many different ways. It still forms the basis of chewing gum today. Rubber was not only the material from which the Maya made the balls for the ball game. They also used it to seal containers waterproof or for garments.

Salt extraction could be proven at various stretches of coastline, but there were also such sites inland. Salt was probably the most important of all commodities. Vast quantities of salt were needed not only for seasoning but also to preserve food. It is assumed that the amount of 140 tons of salt was consumed just in Tikal per year.

Large quantities of salt were produced on the coasts of the northern lowlands. Cotton was also grown there in what is now the state of Yucatán. Beekeepers gathered honey whose natural sweetness was used to produce alcoholic beverages.

The sites where Obsidian and Jade was found had been located in the highlands of Guatemala. Obsidian was extremely important for the Maya, as they didn't know metalworking yet. It was used to make tools and weapons. Jade served as jewelry and was highly regarded by the ruling class. Bird feathers especially the feathers of Quetzal, a bird that is mainly native to the mountain forests of Guatemala and Chiapas, were widely traded products too.

The Maya also had a high demand for cinnabar, which was used in funeral ceremonies. The origin of the cinnabar used in this process has not yet been clarified. Substantial deposits and mines dating back to ancient times were discovered near Las Ranas, north of Mexico City in the state of Queretaro. The amount used for funerals was enormous.

The unequal distribution of goods, combined with a steady demand for many products, meant that the Maya territory was covered by a dense trading network.

However, the picture of the Indian traders dragging loads is only partly accurate. The Maya hadn't yet discovered the wheel for themselves and therefore had no particular need for roads, apart from some processional roads. The long-distance goods traffic was by waterways. The rivers mentioned above allowed the Maya to reach far into the interior of the peninsula without having to walk. In places that were impassable due to natural barriers, rapids or waterfalls, the canoes were unloaded merely, transported over land and then put back into the water, as is also known from the portages of the Indians in Canada.

Trade was also conducted along the coasts. The long reef, which stretches from Belize to the north along the coastline and breaks the waves coming from the open sea, made it possible to sail with small vehicles. Columbus already reported that the Maya also owned large seaworthy canoes. On his first voyage, he met a Maya canoe which was 2.5 meters wide at its widest point and which had a crew of more than 20 men.

The importance of trade and trade routes is shown by the fact that the location of many Maya cities was based on the geography of the large rivers. Cities that were located favorably for trade were of course in better conditions, prospered and gained importance.

Many of the warlike conflicts recorded in the Maya inscriptions may have their origins in the fact that the ruling houses of the city-states tried to contest each other's control of the trade routes. I guess it was no different than it was in other cultures and times – until today. After all, the Maya were just humans as we are.

THE HISTORY OF THE MAYA CIVILIZATION

Of course, there were already people on the Yucatán peninsula and in the surrounding areas long before the Maya stepped out of the darkness into the limelight of history. After individual hordes of hunters had crossed the Bering Strait from Asia at least 13000 years ago, it did not take long until the first humans arrived in Mesoamerica.

Archaeologists and historians have divided the time period from the first settlement of America to modern times into numerous phases, which are characterized by the commonality of specific characteristics respectively. However, as there have been many new discoveries over and over again, especially in recent years, the limits of these phases have shifted again and again, so that in recent works about the Maya, time phase descriptions are found that differ significantly from older classifications.

This is made even more complicated by the fact that each mayanist, archaeologist or mesoamericanist seems to maintain his own epochal classification and organizes the phases as it comes to his mind. Some people put additional periods in between, and of course, each of them thinks of specific criteria with which the respective classification can be justified. However, since not all researchers consider all these criteria to be equally plausible, the phenomenon arises that when looking at different textbooks in the field of Ancient American Studies, one can find just as many different epochal classifications as books about the subject. Even in Wikipedia, which can be updated quite quickly, you can see three completely different systems for the phases.

On the whole, I did not follow this custom but decided to make a classification, which is similar to that of Michael D. Coe. Only for the names of the epochs did I borrow from other authors.

The presence of human beings in America is already evident in the prehistoric and archaic periods. During the Prehistoric period, these people were just hunters. In the Archaic period, many people became sedentary farmers. From this point on, after these first traces of civilization, the time until the arrival of the Spaniards has been divided into three phases: Pre-Classic, Classic and Post-Classic.

All these phases are characterized by specific peculiarities that justify this classification. However, it should not be forgotten that these phases are not strictly delimited, but that the boundaries are subject to flow. Since there are often new finds in the Maya region, the edges can shift from time to time. So it is no wonder that there is not only the one classification I am presenting here.

The first two of these three epochs, Pre-classic and Classic, are both divided into three sub epochs. Roughly speaking, these are phases whose main characteristics are ascent, flowering, and decline. They are designated with the attributes early, medium and late. For the Post-classic period, just two subclassifications have been chosen. As I said before, one can subdivide these phases once more. Some authors thus state an "early late-classic" or "late, early pre-classic," but I will forego this.

Until the “discovery” of America by Columbus, iron was unknown on the entire continent. (Yes, I know, the Vikings forgot a sword somewhere...) In metallurgy, the indigenous peoples of the continent had previously only discovered the processing of gold for themselves. This material was used for cult objects and jewelry. Copper had already been used slightly. The stuff from which weapons and tools were made in large quantities was obsidian, a vitreous stone of volcanic origin. It was mainly used because it allows producing extremely sharp blades. But ordinary flint was in use as well.

PREHISTORIC - UNTIL 8000 BC

The exact time for the early settlement of America is controversial among scientists. Isolated finds made in both South and North America actually suggests that the American continent was invaded by the first humans as early as 20,000 to 30,000 years ago. However, since the archaeological evidence for this early period is sparse and measurement errors in the determination of age cannot be ruled out, the majority of historians believe that this period started about 13,000 years ago, beginning with the appearance of the first humans in North America. The seizure of the continent then took place at breakneck speed. Almost simultaneously, the first people appeared in Mexico. These were roaming hunter hordes that had to change their location frequently in search of new hunting grounds. If the group became too large or the food reserves too scarce, individual family associations had to split off and try their luck on their own.

ARCHAIC 8000 BC - 1500 BC

These first humans were hunters and gatherers. Significant stocks of provisions could not be built up while wandering around. The diversity of species and abundance of game in the immediate surroundings determined the limits for population growth. In the search for lucrative hunting grounds, these people had to dismantle and relocate their camps again and again. But already in 8000 BC, a new development started. People began to grow crops and stay in stable settlements.

This phase, in which agriculture came up and finally became the dominant way of life, is the archaic period. Craftsmanship such as weaving and pottery also developed during this period. Decisive for the further progress was the use and breeding of the maize plant. From the original Teosinte, a primordial form of maize, farmers have grown the corn variety that we know today as a foodstuff over the years. As a result, far more people could be fed in the same area than it would have been possible through sheer hunting and gathering. The dwindling food supply was probably the main reason why people in America, just like in the old world, changed from hunting to the sweaty activity of farming.

It is remarkable that this development in the ancient American "way of life" cannot be attributed to external influences from outside the continent. Agriculture, pottery, and weaving were developed on the American continent independently of the other cultures that had already taken this step. The fact that the development here in America started later was probably because the hunting grounds in America had been sufficient as a food source for such a long time. The independent discovery of the cultivation of one type of grasses (Poaceae), because nothing else is maize, reveals something else. Around the world, people of the early days seem to have had grass seeds on their menu. In those areas where rice, millet, and other cereals were cultivated, they were also bred from members of the Poaceae group of plants.

Around 2500 BC, the ancestors of the Maya settled down in the area which they later inhabited.

The era of the archaic period ends around 1500 BC. The time period after that until the arrival of the Spaniards is divided into three phases: the pre-Classic, the actual Classic and the post-Classic.

PRE-CLASSIC 1500 BC - 200 AD

The pre-Classical phase, as you can imagine, precedes the later classical period. Sometimes, it is divided into two or three subsections. These are called early and late, and sometimes additionally middle pre-Classic.

Another term for the pre-Classic is "formative phase" because in this phase, all the characteristics that are typical for the following classical period gradually emerged." However, the original inventors were not the Maya, but the Olmecs and Zapotecs, who thus became precursors of the Maya culture. In addition to human sacrifices, writing, calendar system, corporate structures such as ceremonial centers, cities and city-states - monumental stone architecture, sculptural art and the construction of step pyramids are some of the noteworthy new features and achievements of this epoch. The origins of the Gods' Pantheon of the Maya can also be traced back to this time.

In the old world, the Bronze Age came to an end at the same time. The new kingdom of Egypt, Babylon, Assur, the Hittites, and Minoans determined history in the Near East. At that time the Israelites left Egypt and conquered Canaan.

Let us look at the sub-phases of the pre-Classic period in detail:

Early Pre-Classic 1500 BC - 700 BC

When the early pre-Classical period began, agriculture based on maize cultivation had finally been established as a way of life throughout Mesoamerica. The Olmecs formed the first cities or city-states. The first temples were built, such as La Venta in Tabasco and Tres Zapotes in Veracruz. The possibility of processing gold was discovered.

In Europe
On the other side of the Atlantic, on the Italian peninsula in the Mediterranean, Romulus, and Remus, twins raised by a wolf, founded the city of Rome towards the end of this period in 753 BC.

Middle Pre-Classic 700 BC - 300 BC

During the middle pre-Classical period, the culture of the Zapotecs was born in Monte Alban, Oaxaca. The Olmec town of La Venta was destroyed and abandoned around 700 BC.

Gradually, the Maya become tangible. First of all on the Pacific coast in Guatemala, where the Izapa culture, strongly influenced by the Olmecs, created first sculptures typical for the Maya. Almost at the same time, huge cities emerged in the southern lowlands, in the Mirador Basin in Petén.

El Mirador, the largest of these settlements, dates back to 600 BC. The two most famous pyramids in El Mirador are "La Danta," which reaches a height of 72 meters, and "El Tigre," which towers 55 meters above the forest floor. La Danta is one of the highest buildings in Mesoamerica. Due to its volume, it is also one of the most massive ancient buildings in the world.

In addition to El Mirador, other well-known Maya cities in the Mirador basin were established in the Middle Pre-Classic: Tikal, Uaxactun, Edzná, Piedras Negras and some more.

And in Europe? During this period, Rome's transformation from a kingdom to a republic took place. The Romans began to build the Roman Empire.

Late Pre-Classic 300 BC - 200 AD

The Maya city of El Mirador reached the peak of its development at that time. Up to 250,000 people probably lived in the urban area. Up to 20 kilometers of connecting roads to neighboring cities on high dams could be detected. One of them can even be seen on Google Maps' satellite image as a thin line just south of El Mirador. It presumably leads to the village of Tintal, which is passed on the walking trail to El Mirador.

Around 200 BC, outside the Maya region, the rise and prosperity of the central Mexican city of Teotihuacán near Mexico City began. The oldest buildings in the city date from this period. Teotihuacán had a significant influence on the further development of the Maya.

In the southern lowlands, there was a dramatic decline in development from 100 AD onwards. In El Mirador, fortifications with walls up to eight meters high were built. Nevertheless, the city was abandoned around 150 AD.

Findings indicate that the city was conquered by an army with the help of a command from the north, possibly from Teotihuacán, and the upper class of the city's population was massacred.

Whatever the reason was, at the end of the pre-Classic era, the first destruction of the Maya culture occurred: the pre-Classical collapse. Many of the pre-Classical cities were abandoned. Within a short time, they were overgrown by the jungle. However, this does not apply to all cities in the lowlands. Some of them, such as Tikal, recovered again during the following 150 years.

In Europe: The Roman Empire had changed from a republic to an empire meanwhile and had reached its most significant extent in 117 AD in the year of the death of Emperor Trajan. The city of Rome had up to 1.5 million inhabitants during this period.

CLASSIC PERIOD - 200 AD - 900 AD

The Classical period of the Maya is a phase during which several new city-states were founded in the lowlands. The large cities of this area were in full bloom, and various alliances were formed between the royal houses of remote settlements. The rulers united by marriage or fought wars against each other. The outstanding conflict between Calakmul and Tikal lasted for nearly 500 years and ended with the conquest of Calakmul by the Tikal forces.

During this phase, stelae were erected throughout the lowlands, or inscriptions were placed on buildings that told of the kings' heroic acts. They testified birth or death of a king, the ascension to the throne, or merely the fact that a ruler performed a special ceremony on a specific day. Basically, the existence of inscriptions with data from the Long Count marks precisely the period of time of the classical period. Earlier engravings that used the Long Count are known, but they are isolated findings. In Corso de Chiapas, a plaque with the date 36 BC was found. However, there is a lack of related historical information, so that we do not know to what purpose the recording of this date served. Section 4 of this book explains the Maya Calendar and how the Long Count was used in the inscriptions.

The first dating of the classical period took place in Tikal in 292 AD. On stele 29 that was found there, this date is shown next to the figure of a ruler.

The classical period is also divided into early, medium and late classics. As mentioned before, there seems to be no agreement in the world of Mayanists about how to divide this phase into sub-phases. Depending on whether the neighboring Meso-American cultures are included in the classification or whether the authors consider specific unique features to be particularly important, the time limits are pushed back and forth.

Early Classical period 200 AD - 500 AD

This period saw the creation of a large number of cities in the southern lowlands, including Palenque, Yaxchilán, and Copan in Honduras. In many cities, some stelae tell of the first dynasties, some of which are mythical inventions that may have been pushed into the past. Others actually mark the beginning of royal houses.

Outside the Maya region in Central Mexico, Teotihuacán reached the zenith of its development around 200 AD. 125,000 inhabitants could have lived in the city north-west of Mexico City at that time. Many finds from the Maya region suggest that Teotihuacán did not only have a cultural influence on the Maya. Militarily, however, the Maya had little to oppose the armies of Teotihuacan.

Towards the end of the Early Classical period, most of the Maya cities in the southern lowlands were under the control of Teotihuacán. Teotihuacan established its own rulers in some towns and gained control over essential trade routes.

In Europe, the peoples began to move. From the steppes of Asia, the Huns pushed west and caused a domino effect. Entire nations fled from the hordes of horsemen and thus urged other groups further west to set themselves in motion as well. The Roman Empire, unable to secure its borders, fell apart more and more.

Germanic tribes raided Italy, moved through Gaul and Spain to North Africa, establishing various kingdoms, the most powerful of which was to become the Franconian Empire. Almost unnoticed by world history, a group of Suebes, who had crossed the Rhine together with the Vandals and Alans in 406 AD and later invaded Spain, founded a kingdom in the northwestern tip of the Iberian Peninsula.

It corresponds approximately to present-day Galicia and the northern part of Portugal. In 476 AD, the Thuringian Odoacer in Rome deposed the last Roman emperor and marked the fall of the Roman Empire.

Middle Classical period 500 AD - 700 AD

During this phase, the classical cities reached the peak of their growth. During this period, satellite cities such as Bonampak, which had a close connection to Yaxchilán, were founded. Numerous conflicts and changing alliances shook the city-states of the lowlands. Of particular note is the conflict between Calakmul and Tikal, which led to the conquest of Calakmul, ending the kingdom of Kan.

New cities were founded in the northern lowlands. Uxmal, Chichén Itzá and Ek Balam developed to power centers.

At the same time, the decline of Teotihuacán began and around 600 AD the city was abandoned by its inhabitants. For the further course of history, also in the Maya region, it is important to note that part of the population, the so-called Toltecs, moved away from Teotihuacán and founded the city of Tula about 60 kilometers north of Mexico City in the state of Hidalgo.

In Europe, the Christianization of the Germans began in this period. Visigoth Theoderich the Great ruled in Italy, the Merovingians ruled the Franconian Empire. In Arabia, Mohammed wrote the Koran, and the expansion of Islam in North Africa began.

The weather anomaly LALIA (Late Antique Little Ice Age), which was well documented in Europe, is also interesting. As a result of this anomaly, the "Justinian plague" occurred, which presumably claimed up to 50 percent of the population of Europe, the Near East, and Africa at that time. The causes of the weather anomaly are controversial. Two substantial meteorite impacts north of Australia and two major volcanic eruptions, one in Indonesia and the second in El Salvador, have been detected. In northern Spain, the kingdom of the Suebes was annexed by the Visigoths.

Late Classical period 700 AD - 900 AD

The late Classical Period was above all a time of decline in the southern lowlands. At the same time, a phase of increased activity began in the northern regions. The downturn can be seen from the fact that no inscriptions were made with the Long Count. 799 AD is the last recorded date in Palenque, 822 in Copan, 879 in Tikal. Tonina, in the highlands of Chiapas, stayed longest. There, the final inscription dates from the year 909 AD. Also in Uxmal in the north of the peninsula, an endmost Long Count-inscription from the year 909 AD was discovered.

The reasons for the decline that archaeologists call the "classical collapse" are still mysterious. It seems there are as many theories for this as there are Maya researchers. Over the past few years, there have been growing signs that a prolonged drought could be the trigger for the downfall of classical Maya civilization. Failure of harvests could have led to famine, epidemics, social unrest and armed conflict, resulting in a further deterioration of people's livelihoods, which could have led to the collapse of trade and the decline of the ruling dynasties. The central region of the Maya area was depopulated within a short period of time.

At the same time Tula, the seat of the Toltecs in Central Mexico, developed.

In Europe, the Islamic expansion reached its maximum extent around 750 AD with the founding of the Emirate of Cordoba, after the Visigothic Empire had been broken up in Spain. Only the north of the Iberian Peninsula remained in Christian hands as the Kingdom of Asturias. In 800 AD, the Pope crowned Charlemagne, King of the Franks and Emperor of the Holy Roman Empire. In England, the raids of the Vikings forced the Anglo-Saxon kingdoms to unite under King Alfred the Great.

POST-CLASSIC 900 AD - 1540 AD

In the post-classic period, the center of activity shifted northwards, and new actors from Central Mexico entered the stage of the Maya country: the Toltec.

Early post-Classic 900 AD - 1200 AD

Tula had just reached its climax when the 14th Toltec ruler, Ce Acatl Topiltzin, was forced to leave the city. This Toltec ruler was named Kukulcán by the Maya. According to Aztec sources, this happened around 900 AD. He crossed the Gulf of Mexico and conquered Uxmal and Chichén Itzá. Around 930, the northern part of the Yucatán peninsula was in Toltec hands. But already around 970 the Maya gained the upper hand again and pushed back the Toltec influence.

The short interlude had a significant impact on art and architecture. The temple of warriors and the thousand-pillar hall in Chichén Itzá are copies of buildings in Tula. The representations of the warriors on the columns of the warrior temple are also based on Toltec models. Diego de Landa tells us that the temple of Kukulcán was named after this Toltec ruler.

In 1168, Tula was destroyed, and the empire of the Toltec fell apart.

Europe: From 1000 AD onwards, conflicts between Berbers and Arabs in Spain began to weaken the Caliphate of Cordoba, which had been founded in the meantime, until it disintegrated into several small states. In 1085, Alfonso VI the Brave, King of Leon, Castile, and Galicia succeeded in reconquering Toledo, in the center of the Iberian Peninsula, from the Arabs. Thus the Reconquista of the Iberian Peninsula was in full swing.

Late post-Classic 1200 AD - 1540 AD

Around 1200 AD, Chichén Itzá was conquered by a ruler from the Cocom family and lost his supremacy in the north. From 1250 to 1450, Mayapán was the city with the most considerable influence in Yucatán. The city planners took Chichén Itzá as a model for the construction of Mayapán. The town appears to be a scaled-down copy of Chichén Itzá.

In 1461, Mayapán was finally destroyed by the Xiu dynasty based in Mani, and this city became the capital of this last state of the northern peninsula. Mani himself was finally conquered by the Spanish.

In Central Mexico, in 1427, the Aztecs founded their empire in Tenochtitlan, in the center of a lake, overbuilt meanwhile by present-day Mexico City.

Europe: In 1347, the bubonic plague broke out in Europe and spread across the continent. In 1492, the last Muslim bastion on the Iberian Peninsula was conquered with Granada, the Reconquista in Spain was completed.

In the same year 1492, Christopher Columbus crossed the Atlantic Ocean and rediscovered America. And it took two years for Vasco de Gama, who sailed around the southern tip of Africa in 1497 and found the sea route to India.

The Colonial Period

Colonial times shall not be the subject of this treatise. Nevertheless, I would like to mention three important dates at the edge of this period.

From 1517 on, several Spanish expeditions had landed in Yucatán. But the conquest of the Maya lands took place between 1528 and 1542.

On 12 July 1562, Diego de Landa had burned all the books and images of the Maya gods, which he was able to seize, at an inquisitorial court of law, an "autodafé," in Mani, south of Merida.

The last independent state of the Maya was the city of Tayasal on Lago Petén in Guatemala. It was finally conquered by the Spanish in 1697. After that, the Maya no longer had any political independence.

THE COLLAPSE OF THE CLASSICAL CENTERS

After the empires of the Maya had grown in the southern lowlands for almost 700 years, the event that the Maya researchers call "collapse" occurred at the beginning of the post-classical period.

Usually, one understands a collapse as something that occurs suddenly and abruptly. In contrast, meanwhile, it is known that the decline of the Maya world had gradually taken place. And basically, it was limited to the southern lowlands.

It took more than a hundred years after the first prosperous city had sunk into silence until a Maya scholar carved the final Long Count date into stone for the last time in world history.

First, construction work and inscriptions ceased. A little later, people disappeared. And finally, nature took its rightful place and devoured the deserted cities.

The decline began at the end of the 8th century in the west of the Maya region. This development can be seen from the fact that no new steles have been erected after this time. People continued to live in the villages for a specific period of time. However, the numbers then declined quickly.

Palenque, Bonampak and Piedras Negras began, closely followed by Yaxchilán. After that, the fatality jumped over to the eastern border. Life in Quirigua and Copan ended. In Calakmul, the capital of the snake kingdom of Kaan, the last inscription was written in 810 AD, but it was still mentioned in 849 AD in an inscription in Seibal. It can, therefore, be assumed that the darkness did not descend over this once most powerful empire of the Maya until a time when its long-time ally, Caracol, sank into the dust. In 889 AD, the great Tikal in the center of the southern lowlands was overtaken by its fate. After 1500 years of existence, life in this former metropolis of the Maya disappeared within a concise time. And a little later, Uxmal in the north and Toniná in the highlands of Chiapas were the next in line. In the year 909 A. D., the use of the long count calendar finally ceased. The population had left the last of the classical cities and disappeared. The southern lowlands were depopulated, and the rainforest took possession of the ceremonial centers. At those places where for more than 1000 years the songs and drums of the priests had been sung for the dance of splendidly dressed kings, now only the creepy sounds of the howling monkeys and the mourning call of tropical birds resounded in the dense green. The classical period of the Maya came to an end, and the post-classic phase of the Maya began in the north of the Yucatán peninsula.

792 AD	Bonampak
795 AD	Piedras Negras
799 AD	Palenque
808 AD	Yaxchilán
810 AD	Quiriguá
822 AD	Copán
810/849 AD	Calakmul
859 AD	Caracol
889 AD	Tikal
907 AD	Uxmal
909 AD	Toniná

Table 3 – Dates of the last inscriptions

The reasons for the decline of the classical state structures seem to be complicated. But from the increasing number of mosaic tiles that emerge during exploration and research, however, it gets easier to draw the picture of the transition from the classical to the post-classical period.

Initially, the Maya had optimized the performance of their agricultural production. They were probably able to do this thanks to the elaborate organization that emanated from the royal houses in the cities. The surpluses not only allowed them to keep on in population growth but also allowed them to release forces to build great temple pyramids, palaces, streets and irrigation systems.

It is possible that the Maya had reached the maximum limits of agriculture during the 8th century at the beginning of the late classical period and the fertile soils became scarcer. It is also believed that at this time only remains of the original forest of the region were left.

For this period, the beginning of several centuries of extreme drought in the region has been proven. Harvest failures were the inevitable consequence and in their wake hunger, illness and death.

Initially, this seems to have led to local unrest. Dynasties disintegrated, other families, unstable and short-lived, followed. The political alliances between the cities collapsed, and in the struggle for survival, they began to wage war against each other. This is shown by fortifications that were

built more often during this period.
At the end of the 8th century, millions of people must have settled in the southern lowlands. In addition to hunger and disease, it is also possible to assume an increased infant mortality rate. All in all, this should have led to a decimation of the population within a concise time.

Finally, there were migratory movements. It can be assumed that parts of the population moved south into the highlands, hoping to find new settlement opportunities there. Other groups, however, seem to have migrated northwards to the northern lowlands, where it is possible to prove for the 10th century at the beginning of the post-classic that the cities began to grow extraordinarily strong. For some regions, such as Uxmal and Edzná, the arrival of foreign population groups is recorded partly in inscriptions and partly in the later records of Chilam Balam.

Unfortunately, one does not know much about this post-classical period. The use of stone inscriptions was out of fashion in the Post-classic period. Paper seems to have been the medium on which the Maya scribes now used to record their concerns. At first glance, this is also much more practical than laboriously carving a text into an inscription. Unfortunately, the disadvantage is obvious. Not only is paper much more fragile when exposed to the high humidity in this area, but it is also more volatile. Paper also burns easily, a circumstance that the Spanish conquerors took advantage of. By inflaming all the Maya books they could get hold of, they erased the Maya's memory of their own high culture and past.

Finally, there is still hope that the Spaniards were not really victorious regarding the written heritage of the Maya and that, in addition to the five well-known Maya codices that have survived to this day, there is still a place somewhere in the Mayab where a large number of ancient books are kept. Well-hidden and preserved at best, they wait there for the discovery by a lucky archaeologist...

SOCIETY AND EVERYDAY LIFE OF THE CLASSICAL MAYA

The Maya society was structured hierarchically. So much can be seen from the inscriptions and archaeological finds. A large number of peasants were faced with an educated upper class, from whose ranks the rulers and priests emerged. Opinions differ as to whether priests and kings had different ministries, or whether these offices were held simultaneously by the same person. It is inevitable that the society was patrilineal. The kings were mostly men, although there were some exceptions where a woman could hold this highest position in society.

In addition to the title for the king "Ahau," which is also simply translated as "Lord," other titles have been identified in the inscriptions. Unfortunately, for many of them, it is unknown what their level of importance was. The inscriptions do not provide any information about the priests' lives. When religious ceremonies are the object of the content, they describe the king's performance.

Maya spent a lot of time on warfare. It seems doubtful that wars were only fought to take prisoners. It was more about territorial claims and trade routes. Wars served to increase power and income through the use of violence. Nevertheless, the number of prisoners was meaningful for the dignity of the commanders. In the inscriptions, this number was preceded by the name of the military leaders as an award.

The prisoners were treated similarly to the old world. The working lower class was added to the winner's sphere of influence while the upper class was put to the "sword." The executions of the prisoners described by the Mayanists make us, present people, shudder. Especially since they are also seen as sacrifices to the gods, which increases the scary factor.

Tearing out the heart on the altar of sacrifice is the first thing that comes to mind when you think of the human sacrifices of the Maya. But it was also common to be maltreated, i. e. skinning the prisoner while alive. Other prisoners were merely tied up and laced with bars and arrows. There are also representations where the fingernails were ripped out of the prisoner's fingers, possibly as a way to punish the scribes. Others were drowned, and finally, some Maya experts conclude from the hieroglyphs of the head signs, in which the lower jaw is replaced by a hand, that there was a ritual in the Maya in which the lower jaw of the victim was removed.

Some of this kind of treatment was also known in the old world. The unpleasant procedure of flaying has been carried out on nasty people since the time of the Assyrians, in Roman antiquity, in the European Middle Ages and even until modern times (Balkan war). In these cases, however, the process is called execution and not human sacrifice, which is only relative to its choice of words and makes the Maya look particularly cruel. The victims, on the other hand, were unlikely to care about the intention behind the atrocity.

Not only were prisoners of war sacrificed. From Seibal in the lowlands of Guatemala, ritual burials of children who were apparently slaughtered as a human sacrifice are known. The mortal remains of four children were arranged according to the cardinal points and provided with burial objects of obsidian and jade. These gravesites in Seibal are dated to the Early Classical period.

The Maya did not even spare themselves when performing creepy rituals. Self-chastening was highly regarded. On certain occasions, they drained themselves of blood to sacrifice it to the gods. The piercing of the penis with the sting of a stingray was a favorite, as it is shown in various illustrations. But ears and other parts of the body were also starting points for the piercing or cutting tool. In one case, there is a depiction in which the wife of a ruler of Yaxchilán pulls a string of thorns through her tongue - a thick string with long thorns! The bloodshed on these occasions was collected with strips of paper - similar to blotting paper - and then burned in honor of the gods.

The Maya were also not averse to the enjoyment of intoxicating substances. Diego de Landa describes various festivals where alcohol was consumed in large quantities. Even today, on the name day of the patron of San Juan de Chamula, in this indigenous community in the Chiapas highlands, such a feast can still be observed. During the festival, which lasts several days, the inhabitants consume a drink called "Posch," corn schnapps made from maize, in enormous quantities and often to the point of senselessness. Alcoholic beverages were not only made from corn, but also from honey and cocoa.

The Maya also knew tobacco, which they smoked in the form of cigars during the ceremonies. The use of hallucinogenic substances, such as psychoactive fungi, was also recognized. Some Maya researchers believe that some of these shamanistic ceremonies were administered the mind-expanding substances by enema.

As far as the way of life of the ordinary population in the classical period is concerned, research naturally remains in the dark. No one has bothered to record the lives of these people in inscriptions. If it wasn't wartime, then one can assume that it was a relatively peaceful country life, with all its ups and downs. The simple houses stood together in small groups and had the character of farmsteads that were probably inhabited by several generations of a family. The buildings around the cities were regular but scattered. Often it is difficult to detect the border to a neighboring town at all because the settlements merge into each other. When the construction of new palaces or sacral buildings was requested by the aristocracy, the entire rural population was undoubtedly called upon to perform compulsory service.

Section 4 – The Maya Calendar, Scribe and Language of the Maya

INTRODUCTION

In addition to their splendid architectural monuments and pottery, the Maya left a large number of written evidence. These inscriptions can be found on the buildings, but also together with murals indoors, on painted ceramics or jewelry made of jade.

In the classical period, many stone stelae were erected on which, in addition to the pictures of the rulers, additional written information can be found. These inscriptions cover a mixture of dates and events that had particular importance to the ruling class.

Take a look at Image No. xxx from Edzná at page 56. The stele from the 8th century shows one of the rulers of Edzná. The date in the upper left corner of the stele is the date September 17, 726 AD

The Maya Codices

Books were widely used by the Maya, the so-called codices. By the 5th century, the Maya had invented the production paper that they fabricated using tree bark. They called the material Huun and used it for the production of clothes as well.

The codices consisted of pages of about 20cm in height. These single papers were joined together in the manner of a concertina. They could reach a length of several meters in the unfolded state.

Only four of these Maya codices have been preserved. When the Spaniards reached Yucatán, there must have been hundreds maybe even thousands of these books, but the Christian monks burned them wherever they could get hold of them. Diego de Landa, the second bishop of Yucatán, was personally responsible for such a book burning and noted this in his records. But many books, that might have existed once have just fallen victim to the ravages of time.

Books have been found as grave goods in several Maya burials. Due to the hot and humid climate in the Maya region, only rotten remains are left over.

Precisely because only a few written evidence has survived to this day, the inscriptions are of particular importance for the understanding of the ancient Maya culture.

The decipherment has only been successful in recent decades. For a long time, the research community was puzzled, and archaeologists argued about what significance the signs might have. Basically, since 1863, they had the key in their hands but didn't realize it.

At that time, a handwritten copy of the previously lost work of Diego de Landa from 1566, the "Report from Yucatán" was discovered in a Spanish library. Unfortunately, this is just an incomplete copy of the original, made up of 3 different incomplete copies.

But not only does Diego de Landa provide the "De Landa alphabet," the key to the Maya script, he also describes parts of the calendar presented below and a very in-depth description of the postclassical history of northern Yucatán and beyond. De Landa wrote down everything of importance to him, producing a relatively accurate description of the Maya's environment, as he could observe.

Of course, Diego de Landa was not an anthropologist and indeed not a linguist. No, as can be seen in several passages in his book, he was a typical Christian committed to the Catholic faith of the late Middle Ages, the same faith that accompanied the Spanish conquest, which took place under the guise of proselytizing.

His report is written from this point of view, but quite benevolently describes the simple people. On the other side, by nature, it has nothing but contempt for the original religion of the Maya.

At the same time, he gave no particular effort in the description of the writing so that the researchers kept his notes for a long time for fantasies.

Figure 94-1 - Part of the Dresden Codex – Pages 58 – 62

I suppose that a combination of antipathy, because of the burning of the codices, and a good dose of bias, because of his Spanish-Catholic origin, played a significant role during the early period of decipherment and led to a complete disregard of de Landa's work.

After all, it was the Russian linguist Juri W. Knorosow based in the Soviet Union who succeeded in decoding the code using the Landa alphabet in 1952.

If only they had looked closer!

The Inscriptions of the Maya

About 800 individual hieroglyph symbols have been identified so far and most of them can be read nowadays.

An excellent book dealing with the historical and scientific aspects of deciphering has been published by Michael D. Coe: Breaking the Maya Code.

But before I start describing the script, I want to introduce the calendar system of the Maya, because it is the basis for many of the inscriptions.

At the end of this series of articles, you will be able to decipher simple calendar data in inscriptions on your own so you can figure out what time period such an inscription is supposed to be from.

The Maya Calendar in the New Age movement

In 2007, when I made a stopover in Austin, Texas on my return from a trip to the Yucatán Peninsula, I was very impressed by the number of books about the culture of the Maya that I found in what is said to be the largest bookstore in the USA.

A year later, when I revisited the same bookstore returning from a trip to Guatemala, I was almost overwhelmed at the same spot by a large number of pseudo-scientific and spiritual-esoteric treatises on the alleged prophesied end of the world on 21.12.2012.

So-called "Maya experts" explained in long essays their New Age interpretation of the Maya calendar, its impact on human history and the fate of the world in general. There have been speculations about the effects ranging from the end of the world to tremendous raising consciousness of the human race.

In the meantime, several years have passed, and everyone should have noticed:

The "date of fate" left by the ancient Maya carved into a stone slab more than 1000 years ago has passed the world without leaving any traces. The world has not gone down, and humanity is still as stupid or smart as it was before that date. The only thing that might have changed by this doomsday hype was the balance of the doomsday experts.

The Maya Calendar – a System of Calendar Cycles

Nonetheless, the Maya calendar, which dates back its origins to the mysterious Olmec culture, is a fascinating phenomenon. And a relatively complicated one, due to the fact that it is not a single calendar, but several, different interlocking calendar cycles.

Like many other cultures whose livelihood was agriculture, the Maya developed a calendar system that allowed them to set recurring dates for sowing their crops. Findings made in the area seem to indicate that the Maya adopted an earlier form of the calendar from the Olmecs and then developed it to their purposes.

Parts of the Maya calendar are still in use in Maya communities in the highlands of Guatemala, and in northern Yucatán as well. In Guatemala, the so-called "calendar bearers" are appointed for this behalf. They act as advisors in their village communities, administer the calendar knowledge and pass it on to the next generation. In Yucatán, traditional Maya ceremonies include various activities related to sowing and harvesting.

Later, the calendars evolved into a system of prophecies and interpretations of fate, comparable to the classical methods of astrology. De Landa suggests this fact in his report from Yucatán.

In the following chapters, I will try to explain the Maya calendar system in as simple a way as possible so that even non-mathematicians understand how this complex system worked.

HAAB - A CALENDAR FOR THE SOLAR YEAR

The calendar closest to our solar calendar is the "Haab" calendar. The word in Yucatecan Maya, the Mayathan, means merely year. This calendar, like our Gregorian calendar, is aligned with the solar year and lasts 365 days.

The original purpose of the Haab calendar was to predict or incorporate the recurrent events that were important in the life of the Maya. Sowing and harvesting, dry or rainy seasons or even dates for the beginning of the hunting season or the collection of honey were indicated by the Haab calendar.

In his book, Diego De Landa describes numerous ceremonies, rituals, and festivals, which were performed in the various periods by the Maya under the guidance of their priests.

The Haab calendar is divided into months similar to our calendar. These months are called Winal or Uinal in Mayathan. Each Winal period has a duration of 20 days. That's why you need 18 Winal to fill up the year. As a result, you get 360 days.

20 days x 18 Winal = 360 days

The remaining 5 days are called Wayab, the nameless days, and finally added as a separate period. Thus the 365 days of the solar year are complete.

360 days + 5 days of the Wayab = 365 days of the Haab year

The ancient Maya used a unique hieroglyphic symbol or sign for each month. The tables above show the months in their order, with the

symbols used and a few notes from the records made by Diego De Landa for each month. The names of these Haab months or Winals are:
Pop, Uo, Zip, Zotz', Tzec, Xul, Yaxkin, Mol, Ch'en, Yax, Zac, Ceh, Mac, Kankin, Muan, Pax, Kayab, Cumku, Wayeb.

The individual 20 days of the month have no names but are numbered from 0 to 19.

7 Pop or 14 Zip are therefore certain days in the Maya calendar, such as August 1st or December 24th for us. The Mayathan word for"day" is Kin.

The Maya year in the Haab calendar starts with the date 0 Pop. The second day then is 1 Pop and so on. The last day of the Haab cycle is 5 Wayab.

According to the records of Diego de Landa, the cycle always started on July 16 (Julian calendar) or on July 26 (Gregorian calendar). A reminder that at the time of Diego de Landa, the Julian calendar was still in use.

But, at this point, Diego de Landa may be wrong. According to his report, the Maya used a calendar correction, which he calls a leap year. An additional day was inserted every 4 years according to our leap year.

Leap Year?

Due to this hypothetic additional day in a leap year, the Maya year on the Haab calendar would actually have started on the same day every year.

However, the content of this statement is called into question by modern Maya researchers because it would not explain the synchronization of the various calendar cycles, as used in the inscriptions.

The actual opinion of the Mayanists is that the Maya used no leap year, at least not during the period in which the inscriptions were created.

The lack of a leap year would have shifted the beginning of the Maya year every four years by one day.

So it remains a mystery. The Maya may have reformed their calendar at the time Diego de Landa noted his findings, as it was the case with the switch from the Julian to the Gregorian calendar system in Europe.

After all, between the time of the last classic inscriptions and the conquest by the Spaniards more than 600 years had passed, a time about which we are only sparsely informed.

For every month of the Haab calendar, the Maya used a unique symbol. The following tables show these symbols , their names and possible meaning.

	No	Month	Meaning	Cholan
	**0**	**Pop**	**Mat**	**K'anjalab**
	Symbol for community and marriage. The first month of the year. After an extended fasting period of at least 13 days, the year started with a New Year celebration.			
	**1**	**Uo**	**Frog**	**Ik'at**
	Consecrated to the god Itzamna, the god of magic, medicine and the priest. Ceremonies were initiated by a fasting period, especially priests and medicine men.			
	**2**	**Zip**	**Deer**	**Chak'at**
	This month was probably dedicated to the god of hunting, Zip. Hunters and fishermen performed certain ceremonies and fasted.			
	**3**	**Zotz'**	**Bat**	**Sutz'**
	This month, beekeepers started to prepare the ceremonies for the next month.			
	**4**	**Tsec**	**Death**	**Kasew**
	This month the beekeeper ceremonies took place.			

Table 4 - Haab Calendar - Pop, Uo, Zip, Zotz, Tsec - Months 0 to 4

No	Month	Meaning	Cholan
5	**Xul**	**Dog**	**Chikin**

In the month of Xul, the festival "Chicc Chaban" was celebrated in honor of Kukulkan. Comedians went from house to house collecting donations for the temples.

6	**Yaxkin**	**New Sun**	**Yax K'in**

Time for preparations. Instruments were cleaned and items were painted blue. Children were given 9 light blows on the ankles, which would make them as skilful craftsmen as their parents would.

7	**Mol**	**Water**	**Mol**

With great care, new images of the gods were carved from wood this month. The activities were accompanied by blood rituals.

8	**Chen**	**Cave**	**Ik' Sijom**

This month, the images of the gods created the previous month were brought to the temples and blessed.

9	**Yax**	**Green**	**Yax Sijom**

In the month of Yax or the month of Chen, a feast called Ocná was celebrated for the renewal of the temple. Earthen idols were renewed.

Table 5 - Haab Calendar - Xul, Yaxkin, Mol, Chen, Yax - Months 5 to 9

No	Month	Meaning	Cholan
10	**Zak**	**White**	**Sak Sijom**

This month, the hunters celebrated a second festival to soothe the gods for the shed blood

No	Month	Meaning	Cholan
11	**Keh**	**Red**	**Chak Sijom**

De Landa has not left any records for this month.

No	Month	Meaning	Cholan
12	**Mac**	**Capstone**	**Mak**

The elders of the community brought animals they had caught to the top of the temple, where the animal hearts were burned in a ceremony. The fires were extinguished with water from pitchers dedicated to the rain gods.

No	Month	Meaning	Cholan
13	**Kankin**	**Yellow Sun**	**Uniw**

Also for this month, Diego de Landa has left no records.

No	Month	Meaning	Cholan
14	**Muwan**	**Muwan Bird**	**Muwan**

Thanksgiving ceremonies were held by owners of cocoa plantations this month. Iguanas and dogs were sacrificed.

Table 6 - Haab Calendar - Zak, Keh, Mac, Kankin, Muwan - Months 10 to 14

	No	Month	Meaning	Cholan
	**15**	**Pax**	**Planting Time**	**Paxil**

A month dedicated to the warriors. Dogs were sacrificed and future happiness was prophesied.

	No	Month	Meaning	Cholan
	**16**	**Kayab**	**Turtle**	**K'anasiy**

De Landa has not left any records for this month.

	No	Month	Meaning	Cholan
	**17**	**Kumku**	**Ripe Corn**	**Hul Ol**

Also for this month, Diego de Landa has left no records.

	No	Month	Meaning	Cholan
	**18**	**Wayeb**	**5 nameles days**	**Uway Hab**

In this only 5 days lasting month no enterprises were started. They stayed home because it was assumed that these days would bring bad luck.

Table 7 - Haab Calendar - Paxa, Kayab, Kumku, Wayeb - Months 15 to 18

THE TZOLKIN CALENDAR

In addition to the Haab calendar, the Maya used a second calendar, which is known as Tzolkin calendar. Tzolkin or Tzolk'in means "count of days."

The Tzolkin consists of two different cycles that were used in combination to designate a single day. For this purpose, two lists were linked together. On the one hand, these were the numbers 1 to 13 and on the other side, the twenty day names.

13 times 20 then results in the length of the Tzolkin year thus determined by 260 days. After that, another year started.

The Tzolkin calendar is also given the name "Sacred Calendar." The reason for this is that it is the calendar that is still used today for ceremonial or prophetic purposes in some areas of the Maya region, primarily by ethnic groups in the highland region.

Looking closer to the Tzolkin, a reference to agriculture can be seen, similar to the Haab. Some researchers assume that the Tzolkin is a calendar that has developed independently of the Haab calendar and that originally this calendar was used to determine the exact days for various activities in maize cultivation.

As mentioned above, research of the inscriptions has shown that the entire calendar system of the Maya was mobile and not anchored as ours that is fixed and synchronized with the actual position of the sun. How this can be reconciled with the purpose of the calendar as a tool for growing corn is puzzling.

The names, symbols, meaning and order of the days are shown on the following pages: Imix, Ik, Akbal, Kan, Chicchán, Cimí, Manik, Lamat, Muluc, Oc, Chuen, Eb, Ben, Ix, Men, Cib, Cabán, Etznab, Cauac, Ahau.

To define a day, a number between 1 and 13 was combined with a day's name. Then the number was increased by one and at the same time, the next day's name was used.

So if one year started with 1 Imix, then 2 Ik followed the day after, then 3 Aakbal, then 4 kan, and so on.

When the 13 was reached, the numbers started all over again but continued with the names in the order above.

13 Ben was followed by 1 Ix, then 2 Men, until the 20th day named 7 Ahau was reached.

At this point, the numbers were continued and the day names began again from the start point. One could consider to name a cycle of 20 days a month or a week. I call them Months in the table below.

7 Ahau was followed by 8 Imix, then 9 Ik and so on.

Sounds complicated, but it is not. The following table shows how it works.

First, take a number and combine it with a day sign. Then increase the number by one and connect it with the next day's name.

Month 1	Month 2	Month 3 ...
1 Imix	1 Ix	1 Manik
2 Ik'	2 Men	2 Lamat
3 Ak'bal	3 Kib'	3 Muluk
4 K'an	4 Kab'an	4 ...
5 Chikchan	5 Etz'nab'	...
6 Kimi'	6 Kawak	... and so on
7 Manik'	7 Ajaw	
8 Lamat	**8 Imix**	
9 Muluk	9 Ik	
10 Ok	10 Ak'bal	
11 Chuwen	11 K'an	
12 Eb'	12 Chikchan	
13 Ben	13 Kimi'	

Table 8 - Tzolkin Calendar – Combining numbers and days

It takes exactly 260 days until the combinations repeat again. This defines a Tzolkin year.

Initially, the Tzolkin calendar seems to have been anchored, which means that it always began on the same day in the year.

And indeed, in the highlands of Guatemala, it is still used today to determine the exact dates for maize cultivation.

However, anthropologists have also discovered other uses of the calendar, such as determining the length of pregnancies or merely astrological reference prophecy calendars. Anyway, the Mayanists agree that the Tzolkin was not anchored when used in inscriptions.

A significant amount of recent archaeoastronomical examinations of buildings of the classical Maya period have shown evidence, that these buildings were aligned in a way that corresponds to the 260 days of the Tzolkin calendar.

The following tables show the symbols that were used by the Maya in their inscriptions.

No	Day*	Meaning	Cholan

1 Imix Water Lily Imux

Imix' , the first day of the 20 day cycle is represened by a sign that depicts the water lily. The sign itself reads Ha', what means water in ancient Mayan. The water lily is considered by the Maya as a symbol of the hidden. Other depictions show a reptiloid monster known as the "water lily monster".

2 Ik' Wind Ik'

The T-shaped structure inside the symbol represents the wind. Ik 'also serves as a symbol for the wind, life, air, breath and voice.

3 A'k'bal Night Wotan

Ak'bal means night or darkness. Inside the cartouche you can see the detail of a serpent body viewed from the side with the lower belly scales and an overhead spine mark.

4 K'an Yellow K'anan

The word K'an can mean both yellow and ripe maize. The symbol in the center of the Tzolkin sign has two different readings ind the inscriptions. Most widely it wwas used for waaj, what means "tamales" or oohl, what means as much as "maize dough".

5 Chikchan Snake Nachan

This day is represented by the depiction of a snake head. Chikchan could be a synonym for Kukulcan, the feathered serpent. Just the symbol itself reads Kaan in the inscriptions, meaning "snake". In Yucatecan Maya, Chikchan could mean "snakebite". Other symbols used for this month mean "vision" or "halluzination".

Table 8 - Tzolkin Calendar – Imix, Ik, Akbal, Kan, Chikchan - Days 1-5

No	Day	Meaning	Cholan

6	**Cimi**	**Death**	**Cham**

The symbol is similar to a percent sign. It means "death" On other Cimi symbols is a skull with the% sign on the cheek. In classic texts the symbol reads as Cham = Death or to die .

7	**Manik**	**Deer**	**Chi**

The back of a human hand. The symbol reads Chi, meaning "deer" .

8	**Lamat**	**Star**	**Ek'**

Shows the symbol Ek' - star or Venus

9	**Muluk**	**Water**	**?**

The sign Muluk shows the syllabogram for u what simply means "he"and sometimes the symbol for b'ah, head sign showing a pocket gopher or probably a kinkajou, a small mamal living in the forests. In addition b'ah could mean self, first or head as well.

10	**Ok**	**Dog/ Opossum**	**Ok**

The symbol shows the head of a dog or opossum. Ok means opossum, dog or foot.

Table 9 - Tzolkin Calendar – Cimi, Manik, Lamat, Muluk, Ok - Days 6-10

	No	Day*	Meaning	Cholan**
	**11**	**Chuwen**	**Howler Monkey**	**B'atz**

According to traditions of the Maya, the year of the Tzolkin calendar begins with 8 Chuen. It symbolizes a the open mouth of a roaring monkey. Other symbols show the head of a monkey- Chuwen is also the title for scribes. In connection with Sak, the word is used as a title "Sak Chuwen": brilliant, glorious or outstanding scribe.

	No	Day*	Meaning	Cholan**
	**12**	**Eb'**	**?**	**Eb'**

Shows a skull. On the back of the head is sometimes the sign of Kawak, the 19th Tzolkin symbol.

	No	Day*	Meaning	Cholan**
	**13**	**B'en**	**?**	**B'in**

There are very different opinions regarding this sign. Some think it shows the stylized side view of a throne. Others think it might mean "reed" or simply "traveling"

	No	Day*	Meaning	Cholan**
	**14**	**Ix**	**Jaguar**	**Hix**

Is the sign for Jaguar, symbolized by the three dots.

	No	Day*	Meaning	Cholan**
	**15**	**Men**	**Eagle**	**Men**

Shows the head of a bird, possibly an eagle. Other symbols show a head with headband. Men means eagle in Yucatecan Maya.

Table 10 - Tzolkin Calendar – Chuwen, Eb, Ben, Ix, Men - Days 11-15

	No	Day*	Meaning	Cholan**
	**16**	**Kib'**	**Wax**	**Chib'in**

The word Kib means candle or wax in the language of the Yucatecan Maya. The symbol sometimes resembles an inverted Kan symbol.

	No	Day*	Meaning	Cholan**
	**17**	**Kab'an**	**Honey**	**Chab**

The Kab' symbol used for this day sign means earth, land, region or world, but honey and bee as well. It might show two beehives attached to a tree.

	No	Day*	Meaning	Cholan**
	**18**	**Etz'nab'**	**Flint**	**Tzanab?**

The symbol shows the prepared surface of an obsidian or flint blade in a stylized way.

	No	Day*	Meaning	Cholan**
	**19**	**Kawak**	**Rain**	**Chac**

Kawak represents storm and rain. The central symbol means Tun = year or stone. It shows a grape-shaped rain symbol on the left and a symbol for a rainbow or maybe the wind force on the right.

	No	Day*	Meaning	Cholan**
	**20**	**Ajaw**	**Lord**	**Ajwal**

Ajaw means lord in the sense of a title for a ruler. It is also a symbol of the sun god.

Table 11 - Tzolkin Calendar - Kib, Kaban, Etznab, Kawak Ajaw - Days 16-20

THE CALENDAR ROUND

The calendar round is the third type of calendar used by the Maya. It is basically nothing more than the combination of Haab and Tzolkin.

For this purpose, the two calendars were turned against each other like two interlocked gears, and the respective calendar entries were combined.

First, the date from the Tzolkin calendar is noted. Second, the corresponding day of the Haab calendar is added.

A simple date of the calendar round would look like this:

2 Ik 0 Pop

The next day would be

3 Akbal 1 Pop

And the next following day would be

4 Kan 2 Pop

The easiest way to understand the Calendar Round is to imagine the days of Tzolkin and Haab located on two different sized, meshing gears. Every day, both wheels turn further by one tooth.

Since the two cycles of the Haab and Tzolkin have different lengths, the combination of the two calendar systems gives unique day names. These

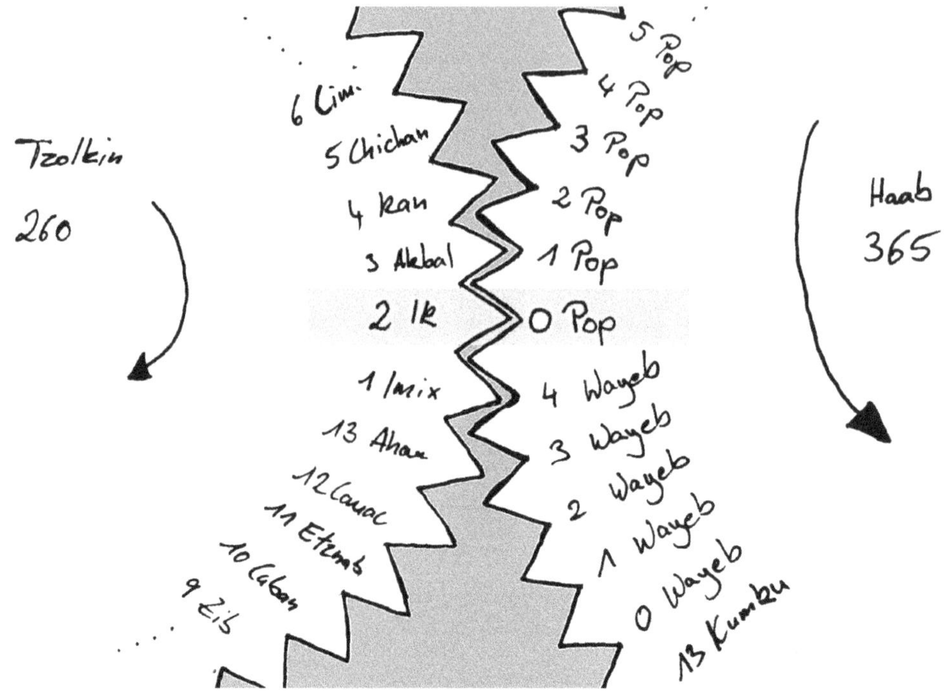

Figure 94 - The Maya Calendar – The Calendar Round – how the date is created

day names repeat only after 52 Haab years or after 18,980 days.

This method is quite useful for recording short periods of time. But if you want to document more extended periods over several generations, then the system reaches its limits soon. Therefore, the Maya used an additional system: The Long Count.

THE LONG COUNT IN THE MAYA INSCRIPTIONS

For exceptional long periods of time, the Maya used additional units. The entire system that is available for date calculation is nowadays called "The Long Count" by researchers. With the Long Count, time periods could be calculated beyond the 52 years that are possible in the calendar round.

For this purpose, in addition to the already mentioned units, Kin, Winal, and Tun, some more units were added to the list and all in all, the time that had passed since the day of creation was noted. Further below, I will explain what the creation day is all about.

This corresponds to our partitioning of time in centuries or millennia. The time periods of the Maya, however, had a completely different length than our time units because, as mentioned in the previous posts, they used a vigesimal number system. The following list shows these time units, their names, and duration.

The names of the minor periods are known from the early colonial records. Kin, Winal, Tun, Katun, and Baktun were named by the Maya in the same way. For the positions 6 to 9, Pictun, Calabtun, Kinichiltun, and Alautun, the Maya researchers invented their own terms based on the Mayan language. The latter is rarely used.

Note that except for Tun, the numbers always contain 20 values, while for Tun it is only 18, so the actual counting always starts at 0 and ends at 19 or for the Tun at 17.

Kin, Winal, Tun, Katun, Baktun – Time structures

Let's take a closer look at the system:

- Kin: The smallest unit is Kin, the equivalent of one day.
- Winal: 20 Kin form one Winal, which corresponds roughly to one month.
- Tun: 18 Winal result in a Tun, which corresponds to about one year. It has 20 x 18 = 360 days. Note! The Year in the Long Count has not 365 days!).
- Katun: If you summarize 20 Tun, you get a Katun, twenty years.
- Baktun: 20 Katun make a Baktun. This covers a period of 400 years.
- Piktun and the rest: The next longer period, the Piktun, would then be 8000 years. Since most of the inscriptions deal with historical events and all of them took place in Piktun 0, the large units hardly ever appear in

Place	Value	Calculation	Number of days
1	Kin	1	1
2	Uinal	20 Kin	20
3	Tun	18 Uinal	360
4	Katun	20 Tun	7,2
5	Baktun	20 Katun	144
6	Pictun	20 Baktun	2.880.000
7	Calabtun	20 Pictun	57.600.000
8	Kinchiltun	20 Calabtun	1.152.000.000
9	Alautun	20 Kinchiltun	23.040.000.000

Table 12 - Long Count - Time Units

inscriptions. I continue without further description of them.

Notation of the numbers in the Long Count

To describe a date with our modern signs, the values are written from left to right, from the larger units to the smaller ones, in a similar way as we would note a number in our system.

For example, 2001, the thousands digit is on the left. Then on the right the hundreds, tens and ones are written in order.

Let's take a Maya calendar date. The number that I use here

9 Baktun 9 Katun 2 Tun 4 Winal 8 Kin

identifies a unique date.

In short form, you would write:

9.9.2.4.8

These 5 numbers define a common Maya calendar date of the classic period. But what does it mean?

The Calendar Calculation

Attention, let's do some math. The multiplication tables of the Maya calendar calculation, so to speak.

If you do a calculation according to the table above, what I do here, you get the number:

1361608

I did the calculation in this way:

(9*20*20*360)+(9*20*360)+(2*360)+(4*20)+(8*1)= 1361608

This is the number of days that have elapsed since day zero in the Maya calendar. What does day 0 mean in the Maya world? Obviously, nothing else than the mythological creation day of the Maya universe.

Accordingly, 1361608 days have passed since the creation day of the Maya to the date 9.9.2.4.8.

Conversion from the Maya calendar to the Gregorian calendar

You might like to know at which time in our calendar 9.9.2.4.8 occurred. Therefore a bunch of conversion calculations has to be done.

By the way, converted to our calendar, the date of the sample calculation results in the 26th day of the month July in the year 615 AD.

The date is an important one and well known from inscriptions. On that day, Pakal the Great ascended the throne of Palenque, just 12 years old.

But how do we get from the number 1361608 to 26-7-615 AD?

The easiest way to convert the day number into a Gregorian date is to use a computer program. On the Internet, numerous web pages offer similar calendar conversion.

Rough calculation when you don't have a computer at hand

You can also use a calculator or use the calculator on your smartphone to determine the year (roughly). A sheet of paper and a ballpoint pen do the same. The formula for this is simple and provides at least a rough result:

Year = (number of days / 365.25) – 3112.31

If we use the number 1361608, this results, in fact, in 615,569535. Just ignore the decimals. The result is 615.

The method is not exact. Depending on whether leap years are involved, the value can differ by one year from the actual year. But for someone who just wants to estimate an inscription on site, this formula is perfect.

There is more information the Maya left in the inscriptions. In addition to the Long Count, they also recorded the exact day of the Calendar Round, the day of Tzolkin and Haab. Therefore, a complete inscription would have consisted of the following values:

9.9.2.4.4.7 5 Lamat 1 Mol

The number 13 in the calculation of the Baktun

There is a special feature to consider when counting the Baktun. The Maya did not use the number 0 for the first Baktun, as we would expect, but started their count with 13. The second Baktun was the one with the number 1, but after 19 Baktun the counter does not jump to 20 and not to 13 too but to 0.

The number 13 had a special status with the old Maya and was worshipped as a holy number. At least that's how you can explain this oddity.

The Creation Day – August 13, 3114 BC

The day of creation can actually only have taken place on the first day of the Maya era. That would be the date 13.0.0.0.0 so the 13th Baktun, which, as I have just said, corresponds to the Baktun with the number 0.

In fact, this number can be found in some inscriptions throughout the entire Maya area of the classical period. A particularly impressive example was discovered at Stele C in Quirigua in Guatemala. (I show this in part 7 of this series)

Converted to the Gregorian calendar, the creation date of the Maya was August 13, 3114 BC. According to the count of the calendar round, it was 4 Ahau 8 Kumku.

The complete date therefore was: 13.0.0.0.0 4 Ahau 8 Kumku

From this date on, the days are counted, sometimes even into the future.

The Correlation

A big problem was the synchronization of the Maya calendar dates with our Christian-Gregorian calendar in order to be able to determine when exactly an event recorded by the Maya actually took place.

For a long time, there was disagreement about this correlation. When the Spanish conquerors began to document the Maya culture, the Long Count as it can be found in the inscriptions had long since ceased to be used.

From the sparse records of colonial times, be it from Spanish clergymen or documents written by Maya, from various astronomical records in the codices and on the basis of astronomical observations (super-nova, special planetary constellations) recorded in the inscriptions, it was nevertheless possible to link the two calendars with each other.

Most researchers are following the so-called Thompson correlation currently. Due to its correlation number, the beginning of the Maya calendar was put on August 13, 3114 BC.

It remains to be seen how long this correlation number will last. But of course, it makes sense to agree on a single kind of time calculation, so that you can at least compare different books with each other.

The symbols of the long count time units

The Maya used special symbols in their inscriptions for the cycles of the Long Count. Each of these time units had its own head sign. Since they were always noted in the same order, you can identify the date just by the position of the character, even on damaged columns on which the symbol can no longer be recognized. Assuming you can decipher the number in front of the head sign.

Figure 95 -Period Glyphs – Symbols and Head Signs – Baktun, Katun, Tun, Winal, Kin

NUMBERS AND COUNTING OF THE ANCIENT MAYA

Before we turn now to the presentation of the date in the inscriptions, I would like to briefly present the numbers and explain some of the calculation rules used by the Maya. No date can do without numbers.

As we have already seen in the introduction to the calendar, the ancient Maya were meticulous arithmetic artists. Dates were standard in the inscriptions, but also distance numbers between two days to indicate a previous date were interspersed into the texts.

In the counting that underlies the Haab and Tzolkin calendar, you've already seen that the Maya used 20 numbers to determine the days. Mostly 0 to 19. If that surprised you, here is the explanation:

The Maya had no decimal system with tens, hundreds and thousands like us. Their system was vigesimal..... which means it was based on the number 20 as opposed to decimal, which is based on the number 10.

In fact, they not only used their ten fingers to count them (but also used their toes additionally...) A vigesimal system may seem unusual to us, but vigesimal seems to have been widespread in Europe too.

Such "base 20 numeral systems" were not only known in the more exotic European cultures, such as the Basques and Scots. Also in the languages of Slovenes, Danes, Georgians, Welsh, Albanians or Irish there are at least remnants of this number system.

And anyone who was allowed to learn French at school will remember the confusing quatre-vingt-dix-neuf (twenty-four-ten-nine), which expresses the number 99.

Here is how: $(4\times20)+10+9 = 99$

Evil tongues claim that vigesimal systems were widespread mainly in barefoot cultures because they had made it easier for them to include their ten toes in the calculation system.

THE PRESENTATION OF THE NUMBERS

Let us first consider the representation of the numbers as they are handed down in the Codices and as they can be found in many inscriptions.

You will find 3 number symbols to express numbers. A dot has the value 1, a dash has the value 5 and for the 0 the Maya used the symbol of a shell.

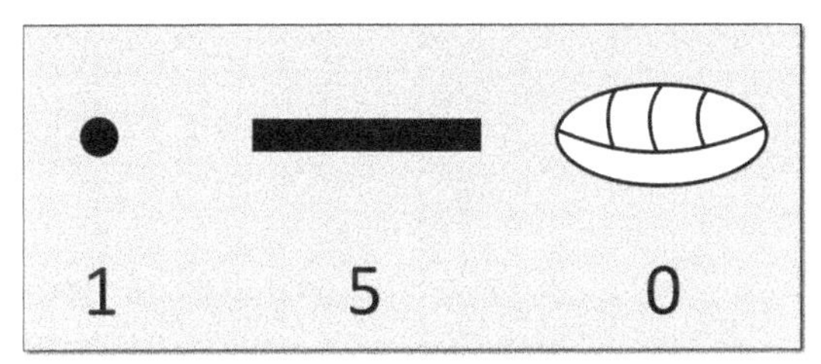

Figure 96 - The Maya Calendar - Number Symbols

In the inscriptions, it was customary to use so-called head signs for individual numbers in addition to this dot-dash notation. You can find a list of these head signs at the end of this chapter. Let's take a closer look at the way of counting first.

The dot-dash notation works similarly to the beer coaster notation famous in German beer gardens. In this case, each beer is counted with a vertical line. The fifth beer, however, is represented by a horizontal line that crosses the first 4 lines. Then the waiter begins with a new group of dashes until he reaches 5. By this notation, the guests and the host are able to calculate the beverage costs correctly even at an advanced hour and under considerable alcohol influence.

The Maya did the same thing. With 1 to 4 points, the numbers 1 to 4 were expressed. For the number 5, they used a simple line. It should be noted that in inscriptions, the number symbols could also be rotated by 90

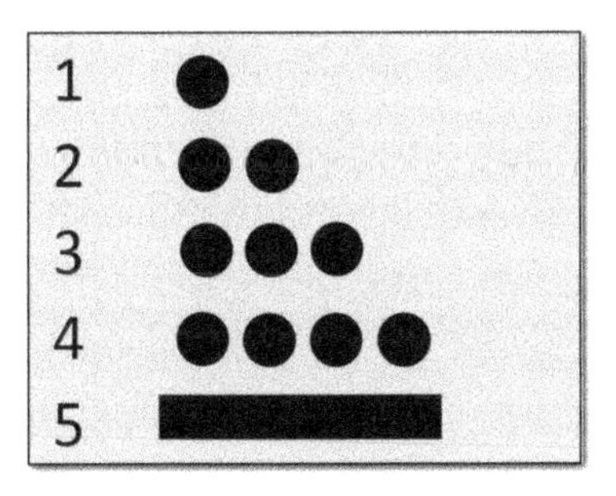

Figure 97
The Maya Calendar - Numbers 1 to 5

degrees.

Once the five had been reached, additional points were added.
Here the number 8:

Figure 98 - The Maya Calendar - The Number 8

To express the number 10, two lines were used:

Figure 99 - The Maya Calendar - The Number 10

Up to four lines were used to express numbers until 20. Numbers larger than twenty can also be recorded in this way. For this purpose, as with us, additional positions are used for the larger units.

In our decimal system, the number 312 is made from right to left out of two ones at first, a ten at second and 3 hundred at third place.

So:

$3 \times 100 = 300$

1 x 10 = 10

2 x 1 = 2

In total: 312

The Maya also used a system of positional notation. However, since it is a vigesimal system, there are other values and positions in incremental counting. Mathematics speaks of digits and numerals.

The place-value notation of the Maya was such that the smaller units lay below, the larger ones above them followed. Instead of going from right to left, they wrote their numbers from bottom to top.

The first digit was used to express the one and additionally the numbers 10 to 19, the second digit to denote the 20s, the third digit to denote the 400's and so on.

The following figure shows an example. By adding further digits, you can display numbers of any size.

8000	•	1 x 800	8000
400		0 x 400	0
20		8 x 20	160
1		10 x 1	10
		Summe:	8170

Figure 100 - The Maya Calendar - The Place - Value - Notation

As we had already seen above in the description of the Long Count, the calendar systems always counted from 0 to 19. But there is an exception for the time unit Tun (a solar year) for which only numbers from 0 to 17 were valid. Therefore, numbers showing a calendar date would be

7200	•	1 x 7200	7200
360		0 x 360	0
20		8 x 20	160
1		10 x 1	10
		Summe:	7370

Figure 101 - The Maya Calendar - The Place-Value-Notation for Calendar entries

calculated slightly different than in simple counting.

Here is the corresponding table:

THE REPRESENTATION OF THE NUMBERS IN THE INSCRIPTIONS

In addition to the dot-dash notation, the Maya used a whole series of head glyphs to represent their numbers. There are also illustrations for zero, which differ from the simple shell of dot notation.

The tables on the following pages show the most common head signs for the numbers 0 – 20, denoted in the Mayan languages Mayathan and Cholan.

Now, we basically have all the essential information together, so that we can deal with the actual date inscriptions carved in stone, as they were left by the Maya.

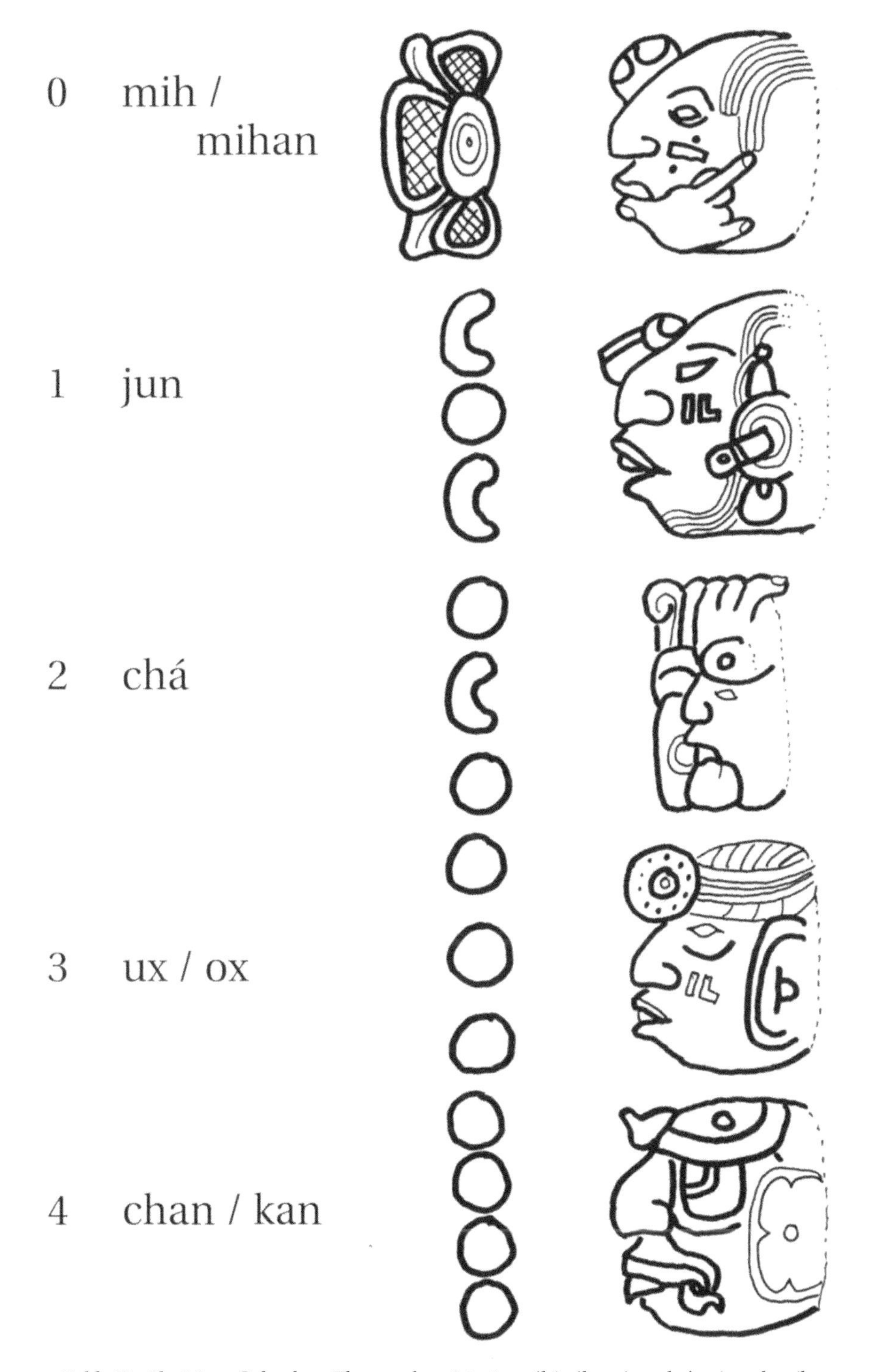

Table 13- The Maya Calendar - The numbers 0 to 4 – mih/mihan,jun,cha',ux/ox, chan/kan

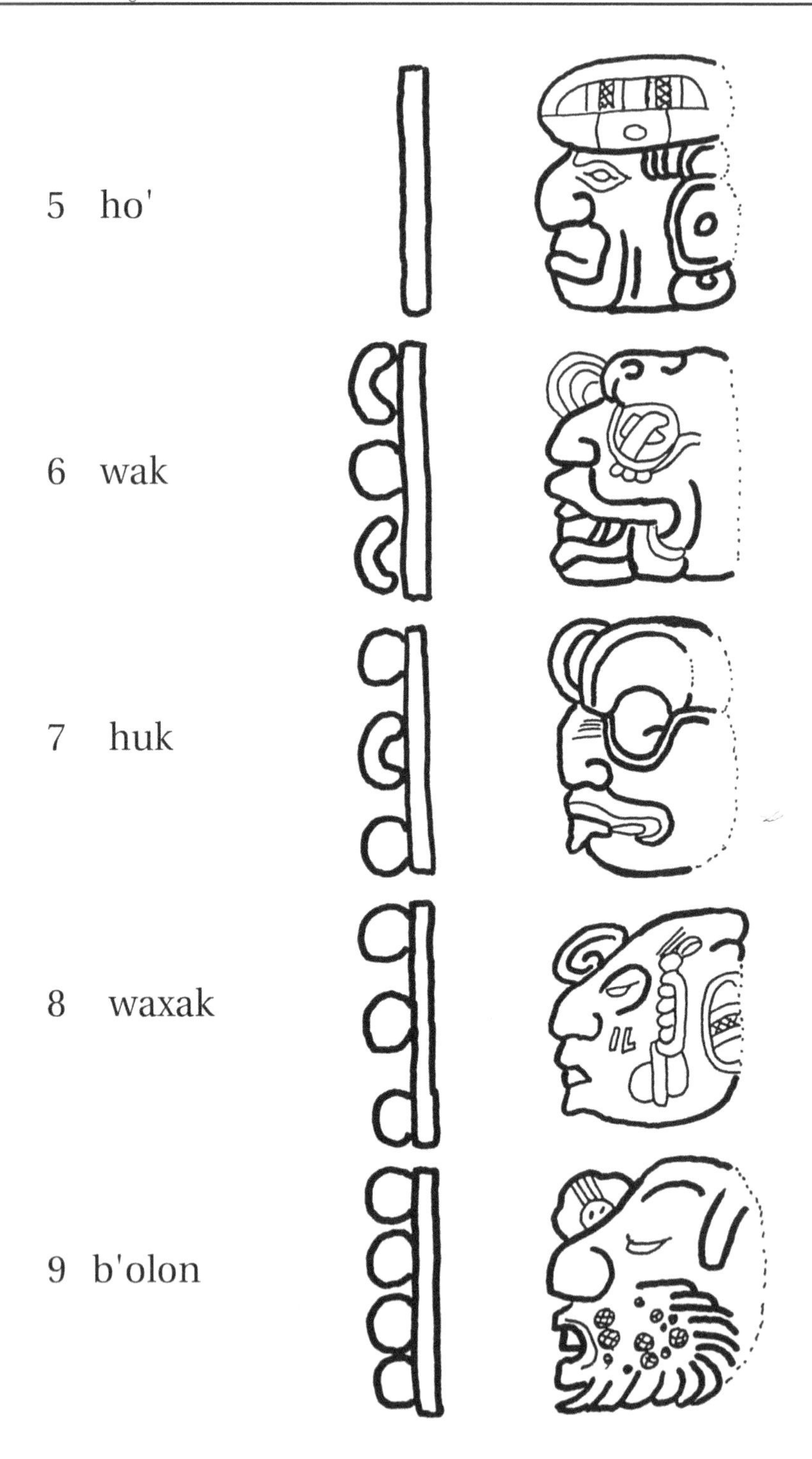

Table 14- The Maya calendar - The Numbers 5 to 9 – ho', wak, huk, waxak, bolon

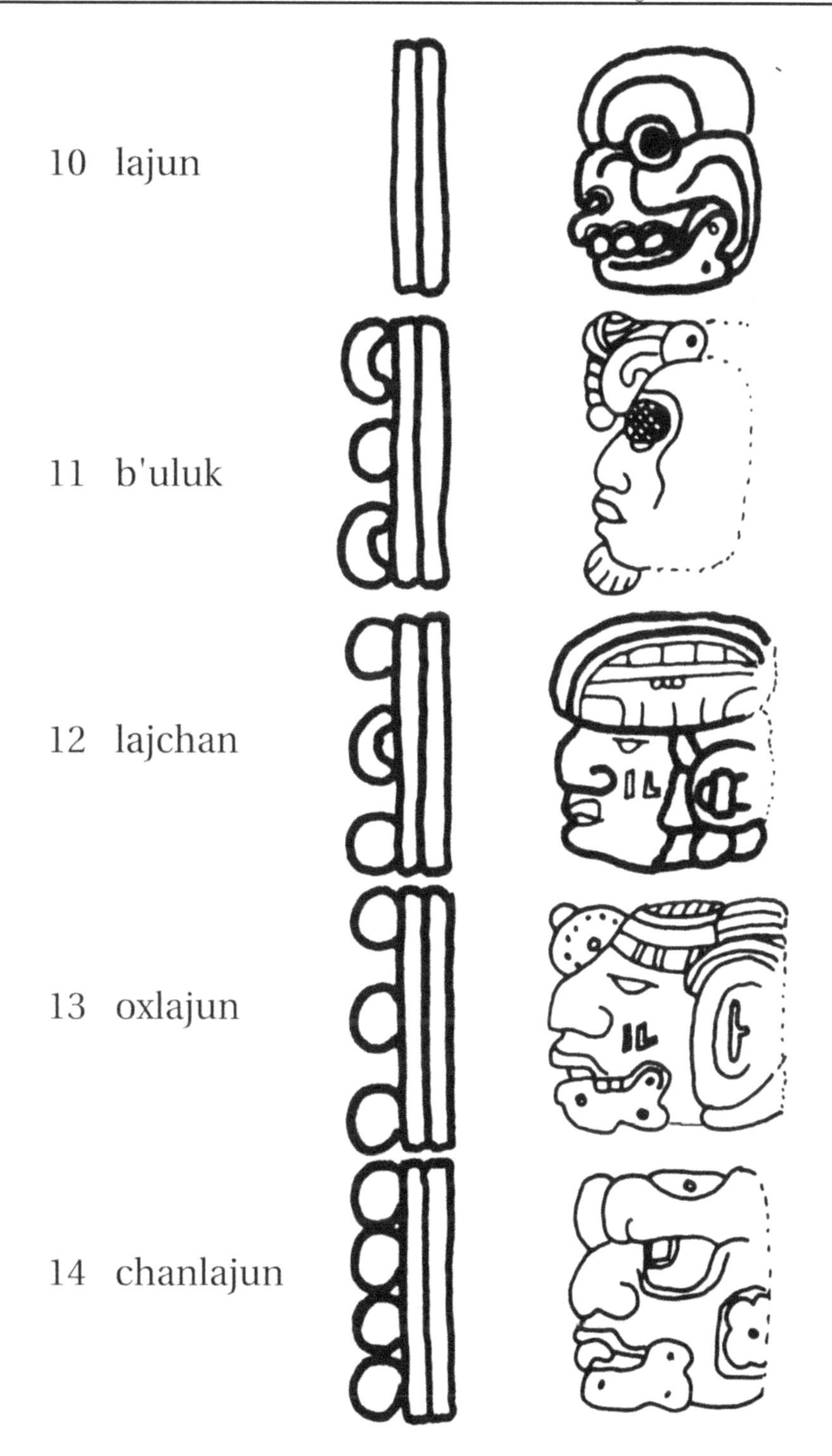

Table 15 - The Maya Calendar – The Numbers 10 to 14 – lajun, buluk, lajunchan, oxlajun, chanlajun

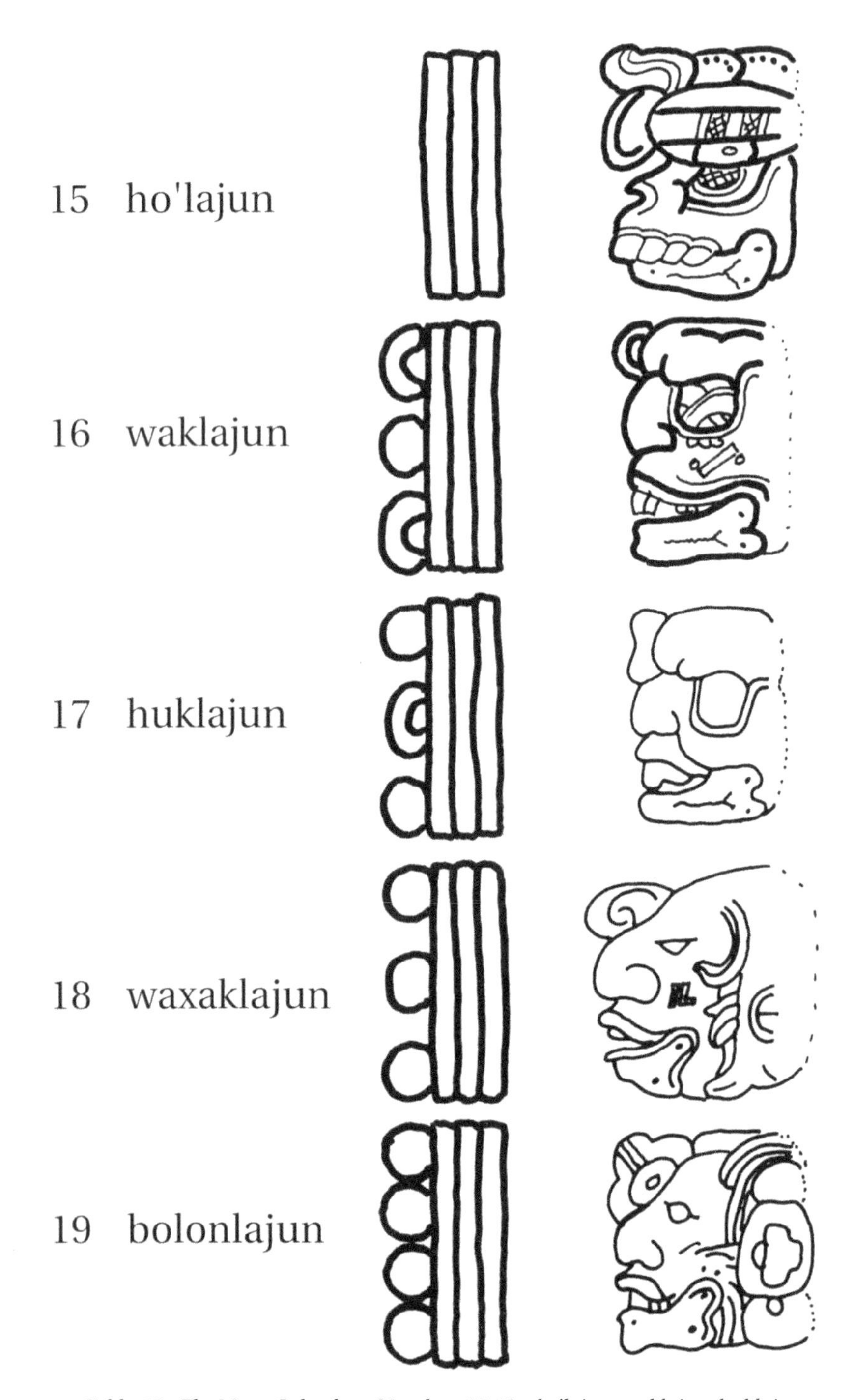

Table 16 - The Maya Calendar – Numbers 15-19 – ho'lajun, waklajun, huklajun, waxaklajun, bolonlajun

THE DATE IN THE MAYA INSCRIPTIONS

THE READING DIRECTION OF THE INSCRIPTIONS

The reading direction of the inscriptions was clearly defined. The Maya used (mostly) two columns to arrange their glyphs. These were read line by line, starting at the top from left to right. The diagram illustrates this process.

I don't want to hide the fact that there were also other arrangements. The Maya were artistically imaginative. If the images were arranged in several columns with an odd number, i. e. 3 or 5, then at first only the first column was read on its own, from top to bottom. Columns 2 and 3 followed then as described above. However, horizontal and even diagonal arrangements have also been detected.

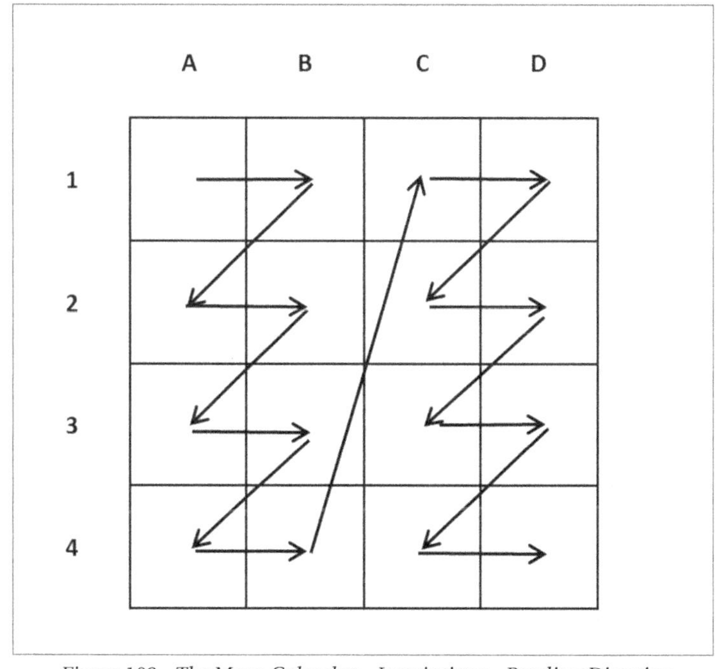

Figure 102 - The Maya Calendar – Inscriptions – Reading Direction

COMPONENTS OF DATE INSCRIPTIONS

Now we have almost all the ingredients together used in the classical Maya period for a date inscription. But before I present the missing parts, I would like to briefly explain the basic structure.

A date in the inscriptions usually consists of two sections or sequences, the Initial Series and the Supplementary Series. The Initial Series is always present. The Supplementary Series is optional and therefore not always used.

The Inital Series consists of:

- Introductory Glyph - ISIG
- Date of the Long Count
- Day of the Tzolkin Calendar
- Day of the Haab Calendar

If the inscription contains a supplementary part, this is inserted between the Tzolkin and Haab entries.

The inscription then consists of the following, additional parts. The Haab entry is moved to the bottom:

- Introductory Glyph - ISIG
- Date of the Long Count
- Day of the Tzolkin Calendar
- The Nine Lords of the Night
- The Lunar Series
- Day of the Haab Calendar

Furthermore, I have renounced the representation of the symbols of the Lords of the Night and the Lunar Series.

In addition to the previously mentioned cycles, the Maya also used cycles in their inscriptions for 7 and 819 days. Interesting in the latter case is the fact that 819 is the product of the numbers 7, 9, and 13, so you get 819 when multiplying those 3 numbers. These cycles were rarely used and I will not go deeper here.

Now let's take a closer look at the single items:

ISIG – The Initial Series Introduction Glyph

In many inscriptions, before the actual date inscription begins, a glyph is found, which in Maya research is referred to as ISIG, an acronym for "Initial Series Introduction Glyph" or simply Initial Glyph.

This glyph marks the beginning of the text. It often extended over two columns. However, sometimes it takes up only one column.

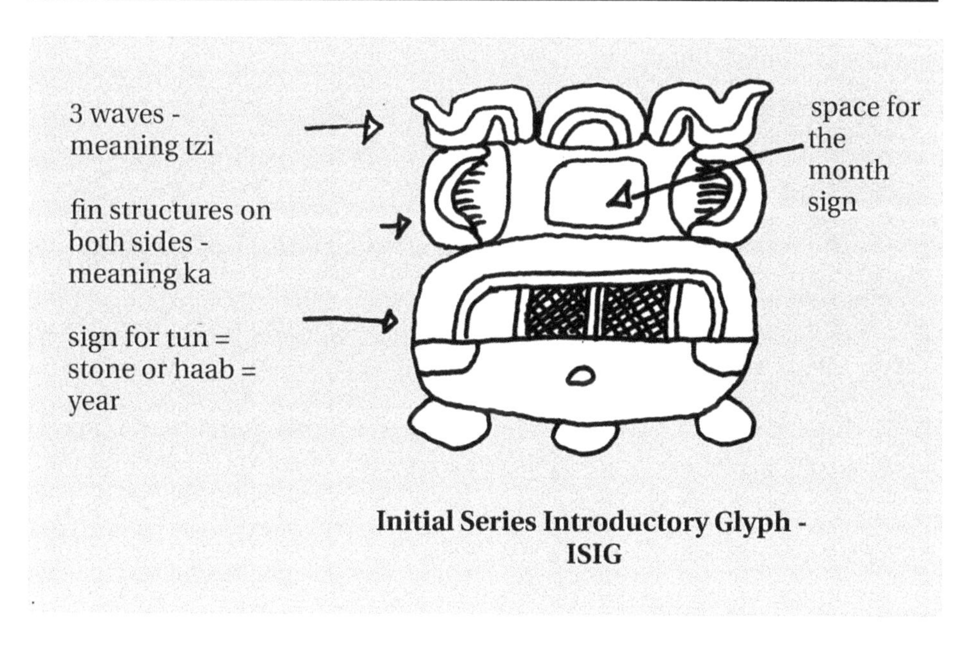

Figure 103 - The Maya Calendar – ISIG – Initial Series Introductory Glyph

The ISIG consists of various elements. At the top, a wave structure marks the glyph – Mayanists call it "Volutes" because it reminds one of the similar structures of the same name found at the capital of Ionian columns. Their meaning is "tzi".

On the sides, the structures are called "fish fins" by the researchers sometimes referred to as "comb" structures, menaing ka.

The lower part is occupied by the symbol for Tun (stone or year). In the central area, there is a variable position. The month sign of the event has been entered here.

Altogether it might read as tziik haab, what usually is translated as "Year Count" or simply as "On the day...".

The Date of the Long Count

The glyphs for the Long Count follow immediately after the ISIG. In most cases, the Long Count starts with the Baktun glyph.

So you have to expect five glyphs in the order Baktun, Katun, Tun, Winal, Kin.

By the way, because the arrangement and sequence of a Long Count date are strict, it is possible to determine the numerical value of the periods without knowing the hieroglyphs exactly. This is helpful if parts of the inscription are destroyed.

The Tzolkin Date

The Long Count glyphs are followed by a single glyph naming the Tzolkin date.

The Nine Lords of the Night

If the Supplementary Series is present, the glyphs for the Lord of the Night are depicted next. The Lords of the Night are nine deities of the Maya. Every night is under the protection of another "Lord."

We know what these glyphs look like, but nobody knows their names yet. That's why they are merely named G1-G9. So this is another cycle with 9 units.

Usually, the G Glyph is accompanied by the so-called F Glyph. Sometimes, G and F Glyph are conflated. The F Glyph is read as "was in the office."

The Lunar Series

The lunar series consists of 4 glyphs containing specific information related to the moon phases. The lunar phase of the Maya began at new moon. The glyphs denote the lunar age, the last phase of the moon, the lunar deity and the length of the current phase.

- The age of the moon phase represents the number of days that have passed in the current moon phase.
- The number of phases of the moon: How many phases have already passed during the year.
- The lunar deity that was responsible for that night.
- The Moon phase length can be 29 or 30 days

Haab date

A single glyph names the day of the Haab calendar and indicates the end of the date entry.

Now we have everything we need to read a Long Count date. We know the numbers, symbols of the periods and the symbols used in the Haab and Tzolkin calendars.

Here are two examples:

The two examples I cite here, are often used in the literature about the Maya. The first is a date from Stela C in Quirigua. Quirigua is a Maya site located in Guatemala near Copan and the border to Honduras. This inscription is a beautiful example of the creation date.

Since in this case there are no entries with the supplementary series, the entry for the day of the Haab follows immediately after the day of the

Figure 104 - The Maya Calendar – Creation Date - Stela C – Quirigua

ISIG	
Baktun	Katun
Tun	Uinal
Kin	Tzolkin
Haab	Lord of the Night

<<< Figure 105 - The Maya Calendar - Schema of Stela C - Quirigua / Guatemala

Tzolkin calendar. For the illustration, I used a drawing by Morley as a template.

You can see from this example that you don't necessarily need to recognize the symbols for the time periods to read the date. The position of the number within the inscription indicates whether you are dealing with Baktun, Katun, Tun, Winal or Kin.

The second example shows the lower part of stele 11 in Yaxchilán. In this case, the supplementary series is inserted between the Haab and the Tzolkin entry. In this case, I used a photo as a template for the drawing.
The meaning of the calendar entry is as follows. My translation of Stela

Figure 106 - The Maya Calendar - Yaxchilan Stela 11

11 is based on the interpretation:
"Yaxchilán: The Design of a Maya Ceremonial City by Carolyn E. Tate."

Under the reign of the month of Zec
It was 9.16.1.0.0.0 (Long Count)
It was 11 Ahau (Tzolkin)
The Lord of the Night was (G8)
It was the 12th day of the moon phase

The 5th phase of the moon was over
His holy name was... <unknown>
The moon phase had 30 days
It was 8 Sek (Haab)

	A	B	C	D
1	ISIG		Lord of the Night G8	Lunar Serie
2	9 Baktun	16 Katun	Lunar Serie	Lunar Serie
3	1 Tun	0 Winal	Lunar Serie	8 Zek
4	0 Kin	11 Ahau		

Figure 107 - The Maya Calendar – Yaxchilán – Stela 11 – Scheme of the date

Now we want to know when it was according to the Gregorian calendar. So here is the calculation:

(9*20*20*360)+(16*20*360)+(1*360)+(0*20)+(0*1)= 1411560

Used in the simplified formula we had seen in the part about the Long Count:

Year = (number of days / 365.25) – 3112.31

Year = 752,25

Ok, we know now at least that the events recorded in Stele 11 must have taken place around the year 752 AD.

If you use a computer program for the date conversion, you can get day and month as well.

The date depicted on stele 11 corresponds to May 1, 752 AD. It is the date of the ascent of the throne of the ruler Bird-Jaguar IV in Yaxchilán.

CONCLUSION

Congratulations! If you've followed the text so far, now you know how to read simple date inscriptions. Your fellow travelers will be amazed if you can explain to them what time an inscription talks about.

Well, that's enough for now about the calendar system. In the bibliographical references, you will find several useful textbooks, some of them free of charge on the internet, for all those who want to get deeper into the topic.

Section 5
–
Language and Writing System of the Maya

MAYAN LANGUAGES AND THEIR DISTRIBUTION

More than 30 different languages are still spoken in the Maya area today. These languages have some features in common, making it possible to treat them alltogether as an independent language family. Some of them are closely related and differ from each other, similar to Scottish and British English. Other Mayan languages have moved so far apart over time that their speakers have communication problems with each other as English and German speakers would have.

Linguists assume that the Mayan language was still a unified entity about 3000 years ago. However, as the Maya conquered an ever-

Family	Language Family	Sub Groups			Languages and Dialects
Maya	Chol Tzeltal	Chol	Chol Chont		Chol, Chont
			Chorti		Chorti
		Tzeltal			Tzeltal, Tzotzil
	Huastec				Huastec, Chicomuceltec
	Kanjobal Chuj	Chuj			Chuj, Tojolab
		Kanjobal	Kanjobal Jacaltec		Jacaltec, Q'anjob, Akatec
			Mocho		Mocho
	Quiche-Mam	Mam	Ixil		Awakatec, Ixil
			Mam		Mam, Tacanec, Tekiteko
		Quiche	Kekchí		Q'eqchi
			Pocom		Poqomam, Poqomchi'
			Quiché	Kakchiquel	Kakchiquel
				Quiche-Achi	Achi', K'iche
				Tzutujil	Tzutjil
			Sacapulteco		Sacapulteco
			Sipacapeno		Sipacapense
			Uspantec		Uspantec
	Mayathan (Yucatecan Maya)	Mopan-Itza			Itza, Mopan Maya
		Yucatec Lacandon			Yucatan Maya, Chan Santa Cruz Maya, Lacandon

Table 17 - Mayan Language Families and Groups

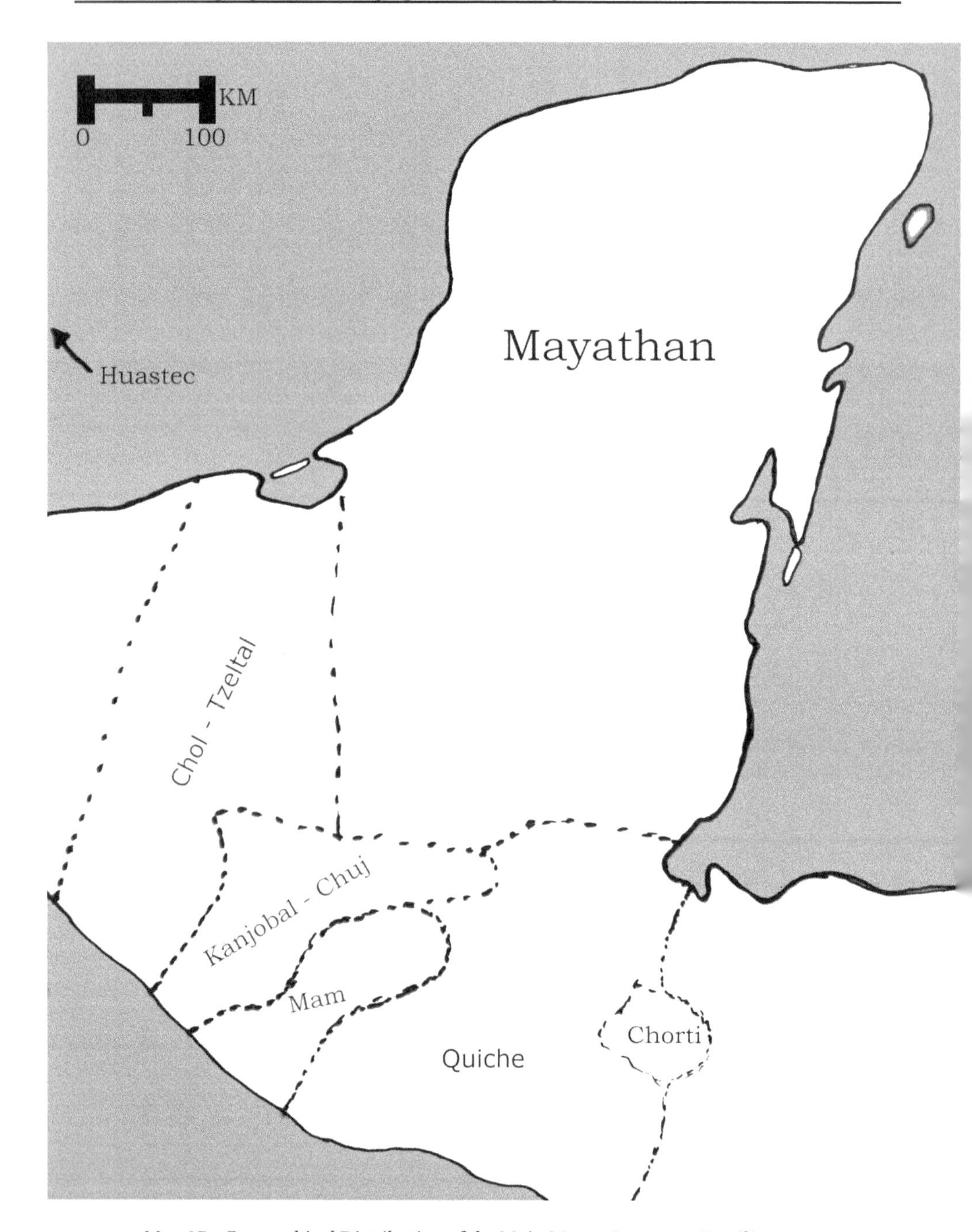

Map 17 – Geographical Distribution of the Main Mayan Language Families

expanding area, the spatial distance and separation of the settlement areas led to the independent development of languages.

The Summer Institute of Linguistics (SIL International) has investigated the spread of the Mayan languages and compiled the following figures.

Today, there are still more than 5 million native speakers who speak one of the numerous Mayan languages. The individual languages of the Mayan are grouped together.

The group "Chol-Tzeltal" includes the languages Chol, Tzotzil, Tzeltal, and Chorti. Nearly 700,000 people still speak one of these languages. The closely related languages Tzeltal and Tzotzil, which are mainly used in Chiapas, form the largest group of them with about 400,000 speakers.

Mayathan, which is mainly spoken in northern Yucatán, still has about

Group	**Speakers**
Chol Tzeltal	673000
Huastec	123000
Kanjobal Chuj	322000
Quiche-Mam	3500000
Mayathan	756600
Sum	**5374600**

Table 18 – Number of Native Speakers - Mayan Languages

700,000 speakers. This group also includes Lacandon in Chiapas, which is only spoken by about 1000 people.

Huastec, with about 130,000 speakers, occupies a unique position. The population of the Huastecs split off from the other Maya early on. They migrated far north to the northern Gulf region of Mexico. Due to their cultural characteristics, it is assumed that they had no contact with the rest of the Maya region.

Kanjobal-Chuj is the name of a language group that is mainly found in the border area between Guatemala and Mexico and there in the highlands. More than 300,000 speakers still speak the languages of this group.

The most significant language group at all is found in the highlands of Guatemala. The Quiche-Mam group comprises 3.6 million speakers, 600,000 of whom are Mam and 3 million Quiche speakers.

CHOLAN - THE LANGUAGE OF THE INSCRIPTIONS

We now need to take a closer look at one of these languages. It is the Mayan language Chorti, which is taught together with Chol in the group of Chol languages. It is striking that the Chol languages are concentrated in two areas far apart from each other. Populations that speak Chol and Chontal, two of the languages in this group, can be found in Tabasco and Chiapas in the far west of the Mayan region. The group of people who speak Chorti live at the opposite edge of the Mayab in eastern Guatemala on the border with Honduras. About 30,000 native speakers of Chorti still live in this area near the ancient Maya city of Copán.

After the research succeeded in deciphering the classical inscriptions, it became clear which of the numerous Mayan languages were used at that time. It was a language that Mayan researchers today call Proto-Chol, Cholan or simply "Classical Mayan."

In the Classical Period, this language seems to have been widespread throughout the southern lowlands. I say this because there is also the view among Mayan scholars that this was a high-level language dominated only by the scribes and the ruling class, but that the ordinary people used other dialects. This view is supported by the fact that over the course of time, more and more proportions of Yucatec Mayan were interspersed in the inscriptions and that written testimonies from the period of the postal classics are almost exclusively available in this language.

Well, of today's modern Mayan languages, the language Chorti bears the most considerable resemblance to what is known as Proto-Chol, the classical Mayan language. A peculiarity of the Chorti is that the letter "l" was almost completely replaced by the rather unusual "r" in the Mayan languages.

SOME FEATURES OF THE MAYAN LANGUAGES

Attention! The following explanations are not intended to be a language course! I speak here about some elements of the Mayan language that can be found in the ancient inscriptions and in the modern day's dialects as well. It is helpful to understand these concepts for the decipherment of Maya inscriptions.

Regardless of which of the Mayan languages you look at: They are characterized above all by high complexity, but primarily by various elements that are entirely foreign to us (mostly) speakers of an Indo-Germanic language, which makes learning an adventure. This begins with pronunciation and the letters they used, continues with exotic word and sentence constructions and culminates in an almost unmanageable number of tenses with which an activity can be described.

But you can also find your way through this jungle. After all, every Mayan child manages to learn its Mayan mother tongue.

Unfortunately, there is just a recent effort to unify the spelling of the

Mayan languages. Especially in the literature on the classical Maya, there are as many spelling systems as there are authors, depending on whether the author has applied the German, English or Spanish spelling system to the Mayan language. Of course, this does not lead to an increased understanding, and sometimes one has the feeling that the Babylonian language confusion was a piece of cake compared to what one finds in professional articles.

These explanations and examples serve only to introduce you to the principles of language. They all come from the Yucatec Maya, the Mayathan, and follow the spelling as defined in the "Diccionario Maya Cordemex."

Pronunciation

Particular attention must be paid to the following:

ch like ch in Chicago - so chichan (yuk: small)

x like sh - so Uxmal (x spoken like sh in cash)

ts like ts in arts

h and j is exchanged by some authors but is pronounced as h like house

y as in yes

Plosives - Explosive Sounds

The plosives or explosives are a particular kind of consonants and a distinctive feature of the Mayan languages. Some consonants are first formed in the oral cavity and then suddenly ejected. The letter is clearly distinguished from the following word.

There are plosives for the following consonants: ch', k', p', t', ts'

That sounds like you're vehemently pronouncing the sentence, "You suck!" or something similar... Now remove all the letters before the k-sound, and you have already formed the plosive consonant k'. Plosives are marked by an apostrophe to distinguish them from regular consonants.

The voice paragraph after the explosive can be imagined in the same way as the English in the word "acknowledgment," where you usually add a small break between ack.. and ..nowledgement. This short pause not only occurs after consonants but is also often inserted between vowels and then sounds something like a'a in "Ah, Aras!" or o'o "Oh, oranges!" As with the explosive sounds, the structure is marked with an apostrophe.

Double Vowels

In the case of double vowels, these are pronounced a little longer than usual, without a paragraph. At the same time, the voice is raised áa or lowered àa.

Yucatec Mayan nouns with a double vowel and explosive sound:

K'áan - Hammock
T'àan - Language
K'áax - Mountain

An explosive sound with the following paragraph:
P'u'ul - Cup

Plural

The Plural of a noun is formed by appending the ending o'ob behind:
K'áano'ob - Hammocks
K'áaxo'ob - Mountains

Vocal Harmony

Vocal harmony is a phenomenon that is common in the Mayan languages. If an extension must be appended to a word, the Maya like to use a variant of the extension with a vowel corresponding to the root word.

Affixes – tension and more

Some call Mayathan an onion language because the meaning of a word as well as its tension results from the addition of new layers of affixes, similar to the peel of an onion. Affixes are small syllables or sequences of syllables that are attached to the word before, after or around the root. They are called prefix, suffix or circumfix. Prefixes are added before the word stem, suffixes behind, while a circumfix will enclose it.

Pronouns

The use of pronouns is somewhat unorthodox. Personal pronouns, possessive pronouns, and reflexive pronouns are the same in the Mayan language. In the 1st person plural, depending on the origin of the speaker, it is distinguished whether the person addressed is included in the group formed by "we, our or us." That means that “we, with you”and “we,without you”is expressed by different pronouns.

The Maya use two different sets of pronouns, set A and B. The set that is used depends on the verb that followed the pronoun. More about this can be seen in the paragraph about the verbs.

Personal	Possesive	Reflexive	Set A	Set B
I	my	me	in	-en
you	your	you	a	-ech
he, she, it	his, her, ist	him, her, it	u	-i
we (with you)	our	us	k	-o'on
we (without you)	our	us	k...-e'ex	-o'one'ex
you	your	you	a...e'ex	-e'ex
they	their	them	u ...-o'ob	-o'ob

Table 19 - Personal and Possesive Pronouns

Possessive Pronouns

To identify the owner of an item, Set A is used, and the word is placed behind or enclosed by the pronoun. In the 1st person plural, depending on the origin of the speaker, a distinction is made as to whether the person addressed is included in the group formed by "our."

And there is a little bit more to know: If the word in question starts with a vowel, then in the 1st and 2nd person singular and in the 2nd person plural a “w,” is used but in the 3rd person singular and plural, a “y” is placed in front of the noun.

k'áan	hammock	otoch	house
in k’áan	my hammock	in wotoch	my house
a k'áan	your hammock	a wotoch	your house
u k'áan	his hammock	u yotoch	his house
k k'áan	our hammock	k otoch	our house
a k'áane'ex	your hammock	a wotoche'ex	your house
u k'áano'ob	their hammock	u yotocho'ob	their house

Table 20 - Examples for Possesive Pronouns

There are also words that have a new ending in connection with possessive pronouns:

nah - house becomes "in nahil" - my house

By the way, we saw two forms for the word house or home now. “Nah” means house, cottage, while the meaning of otoch is rather home, apartment.

Prepositions

There's only one preposition in Mayathan used for spatial data. By, for, on, to, near, at and many more are expressed by the prefix ti’. However, ti’ does not occur alone, but always in connection with a personal pronoun.

To your home - ti' a wotoch

Adjectives

Adjectives always appear before the noun to which they refer.

sac nicté - white flower

chak ch’iich’ – red bird

nohochnah - big house

hanilek’ – bright star

Adjectives can also be formed from nouns. By the vocal harmony, the corresponding vowel plus "l" is attached to the word, and an adjective corresponding to the original noun is obtained.

k'u'uk' - feather becomes k'u'uk'ul - feathered

In connection with káan - snake it becomes:

k'u'uk'ul káan - the feathered snake

Sentence Structure

Before we look at the verbs now, we have to look at the syntax of Maya sentences.

In English, the following order, called SVO, is common for a sentence:

subject - verb - object

The Maya, on the other hand, usually use the order VOS

verb - object - subject.

If there is no object, the order is verb - subject.

Instead of "The boy paints a picture," a Maya would say:

"Paints a picture of the boy."

Verbs

The Maya came up with something extraordinary to talk about activities. First, the Maya speaker considers whether the action needs an object or can stand alone. Without an object, it is an intransitive verb, with an object it is a transitive verb. So in one case targeted, in the other aimless.

Examples:

The child plays – intransitive

The man writes a book - transitive

Just like in English, a verb can be both. “To write” can be used with or without an object. In the sentence: "The man writes." the verb is used accordingly intransitively.

In the next step, a Maya considers whether the action has already been completed or if it continues, that is, whether it is finished or unfinished, whether it is a permanent state or whether the speaker refers to a planned action. Linguistic research describes this as "aspects of action."

complete
incomplete
ongoing
intended

In this way, expressions describing actions are divided into eight groups. In simple terms, it looks like this:

Transitiv	completed incomplete ongoing planned	-ah –ik –mah -e
Intransitiv	completed incomplete ongoing planned	-ah -al (or vocal harmony) -a'an -ak (or vocal harmony)

Table 21 - Mayan Languages - Categories of Verbs

Depending on which of these categories an action falls into, different suffixes are appended to the word.

Only now does the Mayan spokesman consider who (I, you, he...) is performing the action and at what time this action is, will be or has been.

With the pronouns above, we had seen that there are two different sets, Set A and Set B. If you were wondering what these are good for, here's the answer:

In connection with verbs, the pronouns of Set A are used as personal pronouns for transitive verbs, but those of Set B are used for intransitive verbs.

Now we have listed almost everything necessary to make a meaningful sentence in Mayathan. Only the tenses are still missing. And at this point at the latest, you will not be able to avoid linking the synapses in your brain in a new way.

For although the Maya speaker naturally thinks in regard to the present, future, and past, he considers it necessary to reorganize these tenses in a way that is somewhat unusual for us. This is done by a prefixed time word, as we will see in a moment.

The first time word k, which we are about to see, fuses with the personal pronoun in Set A to form a single word, unlike all the others. K and in become together kin.

Let's look at the tenses for presence. While it is easy for us in English to answer these questions:

What are you going to do now?

What are you doing?

What are you doing tomorrow?

What else do you do?

...with a simple sentence in the present tense, like:

"I play football."

A Maya will give a different answer to each of these questions. The following examples all have one thing in common. They are incomplete, i.e., the action is not complete, and they are transitive, i.e., purposeful because they need an object. Similar differentiations have to be done for other tenses as well and of course, depending on “aspect” and verb type.

For the following examples I will use these words:

manik - buy something

kanik - learn something

k'áana - Hammock

Màaya t'áan - Mayathan (language)

The verb is now preceded by the affixes that define the tense and the person. In our case, this is always the first person, singular.

In the first case, this would be k and in for the first person. But as mentioned, the two merge into a single word: kin. The ending -ik corresponds to the aspect "unfinished" for intransitive verbs.

Question: What are you doing now?

Kin manik le k'aana - I buy this hammock

Question: What are you doing?

Táan in kanik màaya t'aan - I am learning Mayathan (right now)

Question: What else do you do?

Suuk in kanik Màaya t'aan - I learn Mayathan (regularly)

In the examples above, I used three different time words, k(in), táan,and suuk.

k(in) – the action just happens and has not ended yet

táan – the operation is performed now

suuk – the activity is done on a regular basis

Of course, there are many more forms, depending on whether the action is in the past or in the future...and a few more. But all this would go beyond the scope of this booklet as a travel guide, and I end my small excursion into the jungle of Mayan languages at this point.

After you have a basic understanding of some aspects of the Maya language now, you are prepared to take a closer look at the Maya writing system, as you can find it at numerous inscriptions at the Maya sites.

THE WRITING SYSTEM OF THE MAYA

Fortunately, the Maya have left us numerous writings, and although most of them are only short inscriptions on ceramics or stone monuments, they allow us to take a look at their world and life.

At the time of the Spanish conquest, the Maya noted the information vital to them in folding books, for the production of which they manufactured a paper-like fabric made of various types of ficus plants. They called this material Huun. Formerly there must have been hundreds, possibly thousands of such books. But the codices still in existence at the time of the conquest were collected by order of Catholic clergymen and burned or destroyed directly by the soldiers. But even without this destructive fury, these original codices would have had a hard time surviving under the climatic conditions prevailing in the Maya region. Many graves of classical times have been found with rotten bundles of paper, which are thought to be the remains of books. Because of their poor condition, they are unfortunately no longer decipherable.

Nevertheless, four of these books have survived to this day. Three of them have been known for a long time. They are kept in various museums in Europe. The fourth, the so-called Grolier Codex, has only recently become known. The codes differ in length and content.

The codices:

- Dresden Codex (74 pages, 3.56 m)

- Madrid Codex (Tro-Cortesianus Codex) (112 pages, 6.82 m)

- Paris Codex (Peresianus Codex) (22 pages, 1.45 m)

- Grolier Codex (10 pages)

The picture texts recorded in the codices contain astronomical calculations on the one hand, but also information of more religious significance on the other.

Also, there are countless short texts written on the surface of ceramic vessels. Some describe episodes from mythical events, others just specify the content for which a pot or dish was intended.

A significant group of texts comprises the inscriptions made by stonemasons on stelae and altars. They report on the life and death or deeds of the ruling upper class. Some of them make it possible to trace

Figure 108 - Writing - Several Variations of the Word "Balam - Jaguar"

the development of ruling dynasties through the time and even their relationship to other Maya cities.

The basic unit of the Maya script is a block or cartouche. It has an approximately square shape. In the chapter about the representation of calendar dates, there is an illustration which shows the arrangement of these blocks in an inscription and their reading direction. The blocks are usually read two at a time from left to right and then from top to bottom. However, there are numerous exceptions to this rule. Especially on ceramics, but also in the stone inscriptions, the writers were quite creative about the order of the blocks.

The Maya used two different types of characters for their writing. On the one hand, certain images were used as logograms to represent at whole a specific word. For the word "Balam" – Jaguar, the image of a Jaguar head was used.

Besides the pure logograms, a syllabary was used. Two-letter syllables consisting of a consonant and the following vowel, i.e., ba or ma, were symbolized by a picture. These are called syllabograms.

If you take the consonants that occur in the Mayan language and combine them with the vowels a, e, I, o, u, you get a syllabary, a table of all possible syllabograms.

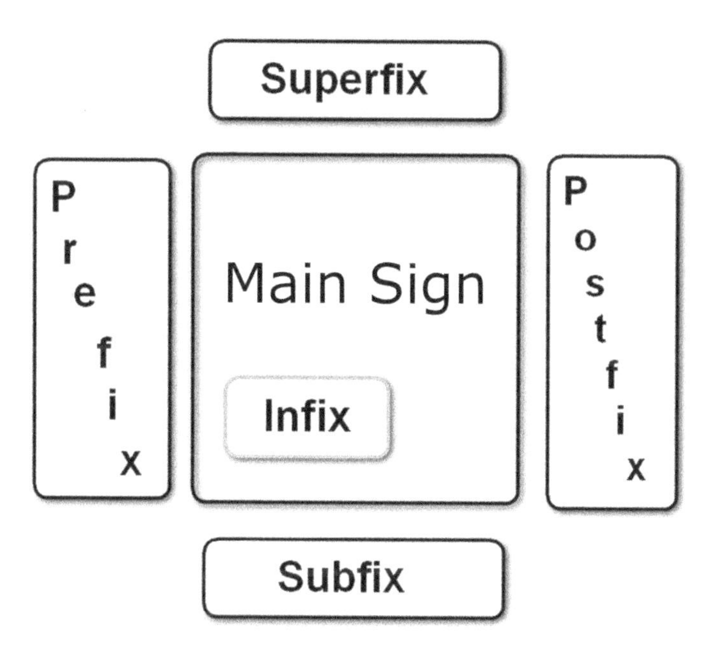

Figure 109 - Writing - Positioning of Affixes

For most of these consonant-vowel combinations, the corresponding symbols have been identified in the inscriptions.

If a word did not end in a vowel, a syllabogram beginning with the corresponding consonant was added to the word, but the final vowel was not pronounced.

The following figure shows the logogram for Balam in the first

Figure 110 - Part of the De Landa Alphabet

position, in the last place you see the same word written out with the syllabograms only. The syllabogram "ma" was used for the terminal m, taking into account the vocal harmony and stripping the "a".

The variations in between show a peculiarity of the Mayan typeface. Although the logogram already shows the word, Balam, the characters for the start and/or end syllable are added before and below the symbol. This seems to have served the Maya writers to specify a logogram more precisely and to support a reader of the text in deciphering and also in pronunciation.

Combining different symbols into one block was a standard procedure. Similar to the spoken language, affixes were added to the central word stem. With the help of these affixes or additions not only additional words could be generated, but also grammatically necessary changes of the word could be made.

The following graphic shows the basic positions of the affixes. Depending on their location in relation to the main character, these affixes are called prefix, postfix, superfix or subfix. A unique feature is the infix, which represents a symbol that merges with the main character. The order in which the glyph is read is, as in the general reading direction, from left to right and from top to bottom. But also here, the Maya writer could break the rules according to his personal taste and let his imagination run free.

Some of the syllable characters were already known from Diego de Landa's description. However, he and his Indian informant were talking at cross-purpose while they were writing down the alphabet. Diego de Landa seemed to have asked for individual letters according to the Latin or Spanish alphabet and did not pronounce the letters differently, as we still do today and as we learned it in school. A, B, C... becomes A, Be, Ce and so on.

The literate Maya, apparently unaware of this characteristic of the Latin alphabet, heard the two-letter syllables and provided a symbol that stood for an entire syllable.

Here is an example from the manuscript de Landas. Many of the signs actually correspond to the symbols that have been found in inscriptions so far.

Meanwhile, a large number of syllabograms from the inscriptions have been identified. They are usually summarized in tables, the so-called syllabary. Unfortunately, there are relatively many syllabaries that differ depending on the focus of the creators, their artistic skills and their love of detail.

Below you will find a syllabary I created myself. In some of the signs, you can see from the shaky lines that I had previously drunk two strong espressos. I also confined myself to the rather dull syllables and omitted a few complex characters.

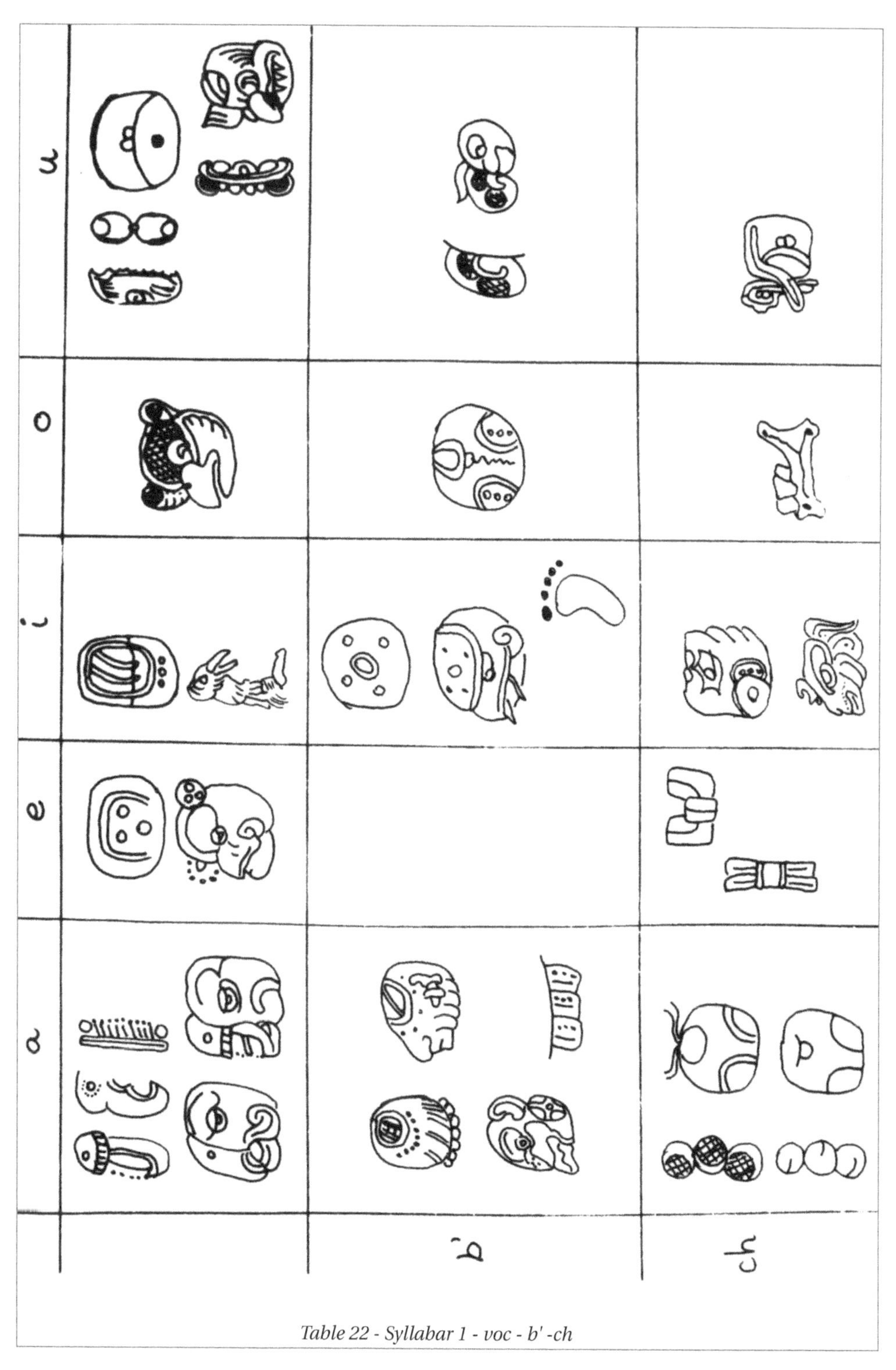

Table 22 - Syllabar 1 - voc - b' -ch

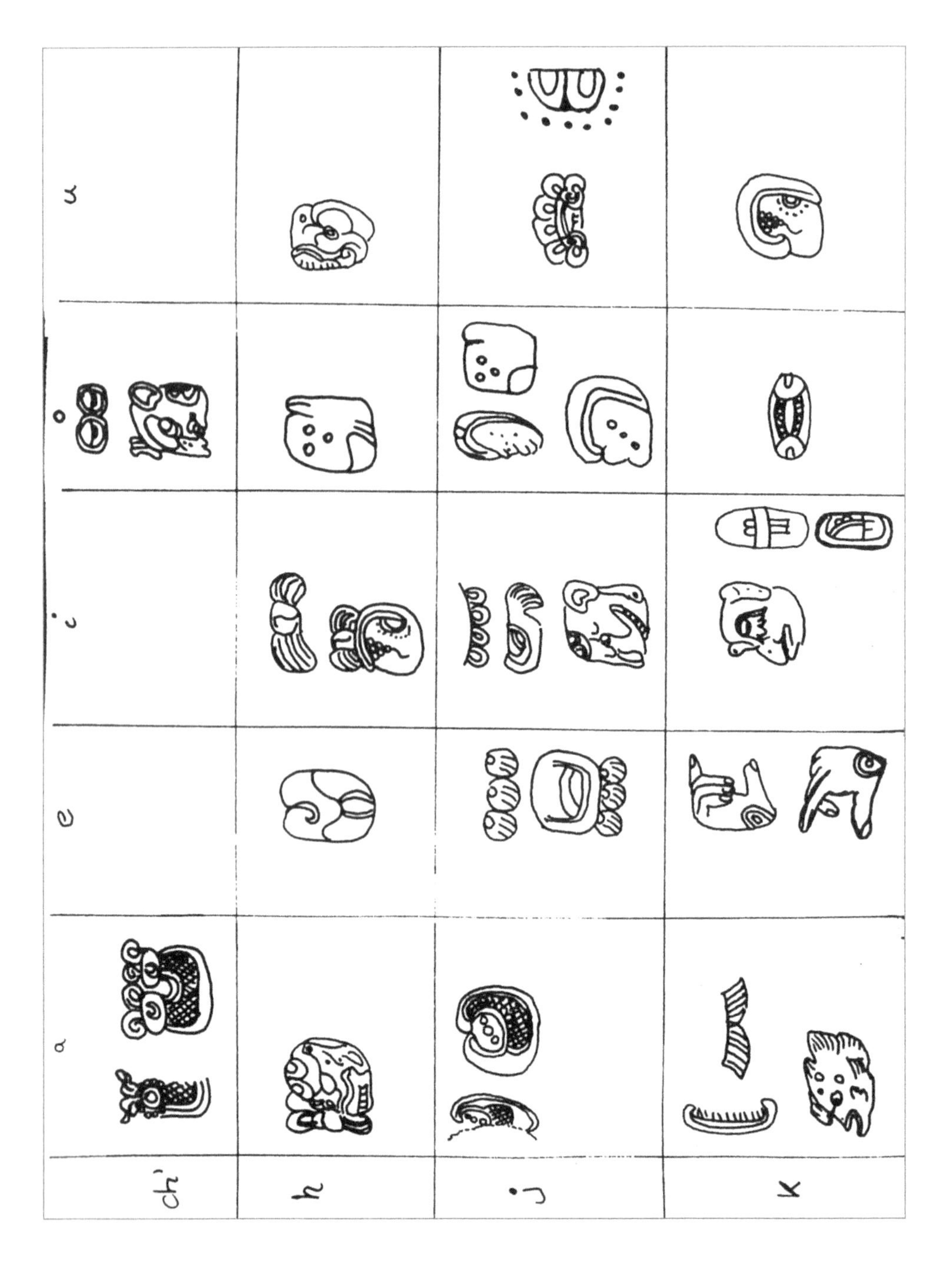

Table 23 - Syllabar 2 - ch' - h - j - k

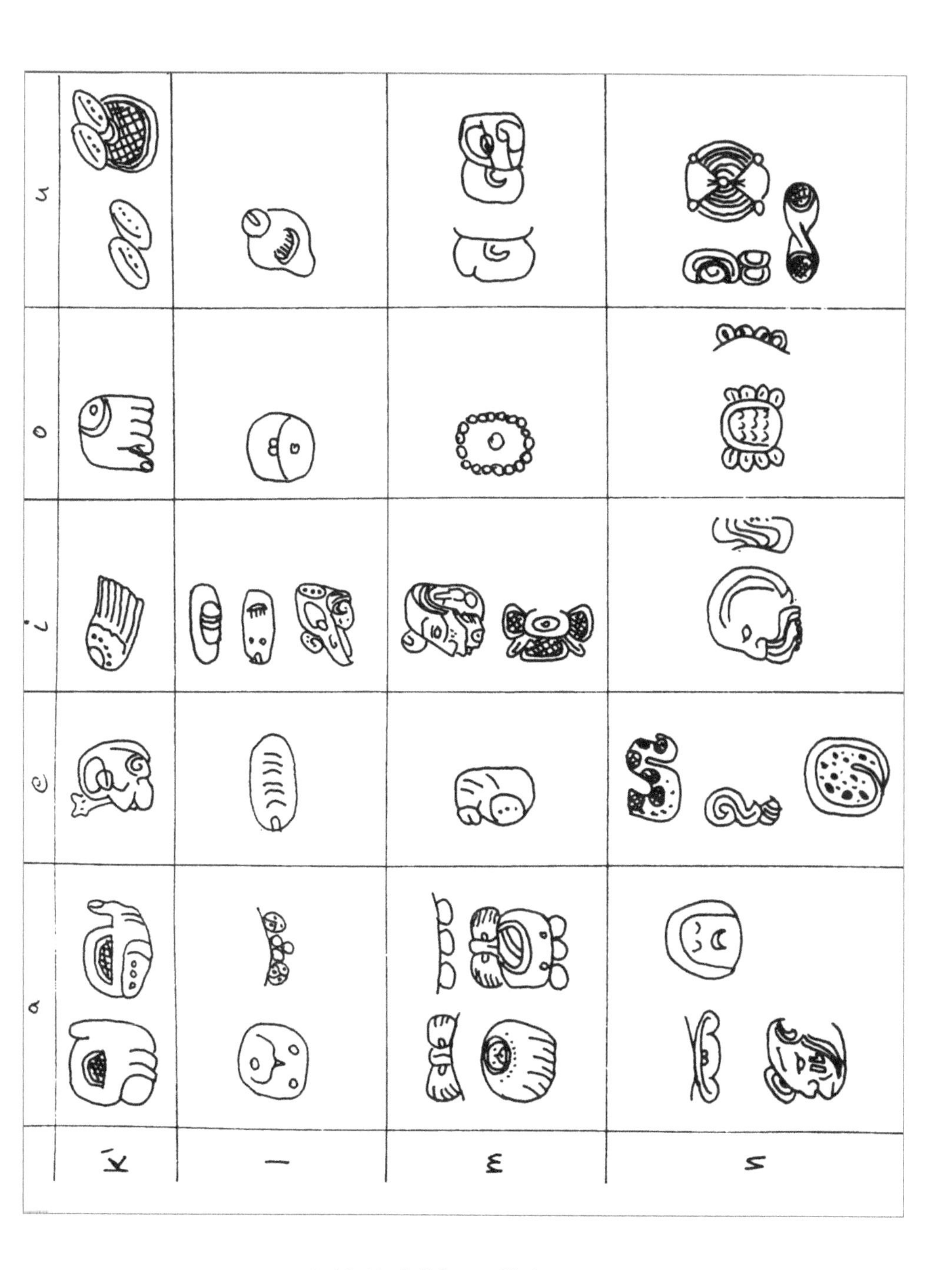

Table 24 - Syllabar 3 - k' - l - m - n

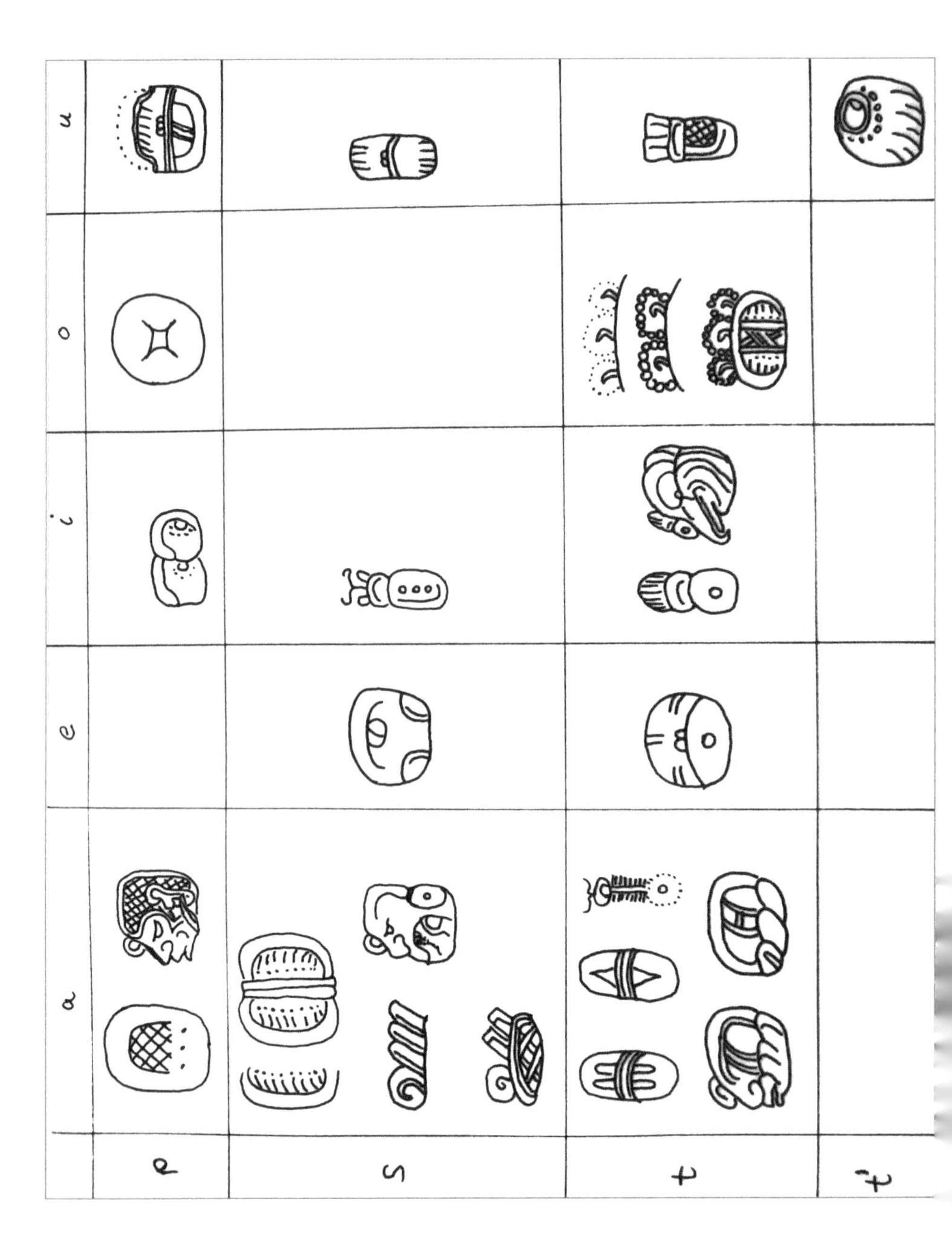

Table 25 - Syllabar 4 - p -s - t - t'

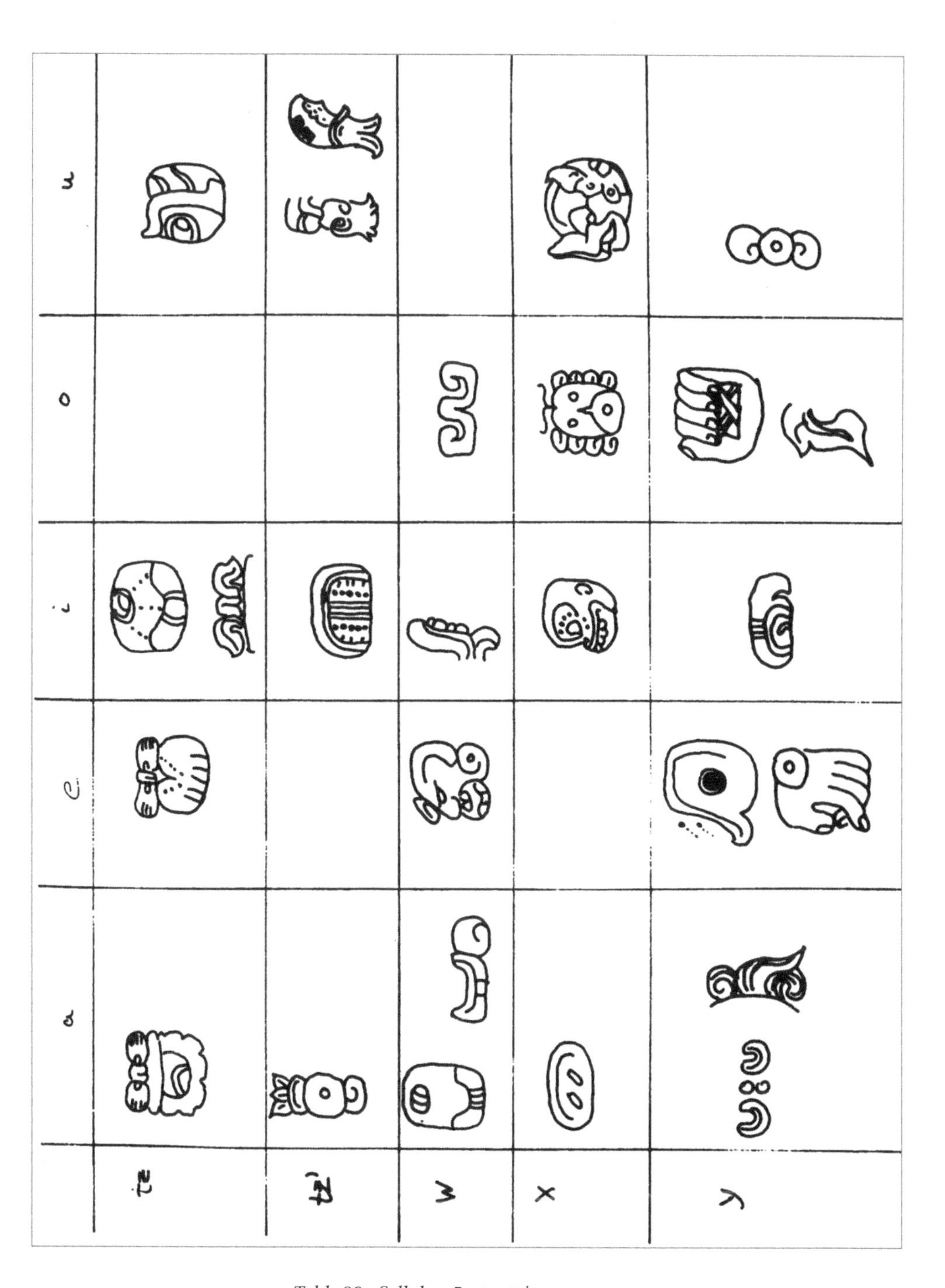

Table 26 - Syllabar 5 - tz - tz' - w - x - y

Epilogue

I did not know what I should expect when I entered the Mexican ground for the first time many years ago. First, I had to overcome the culture shock, this jump from snow-covered Germany into subtropical Mexico.

Some routes I have traveled more than one time, and often I just stayed in the same location for several weeks.

Later on, I began to document the sites I had visited on my website "Amazing Temples and Pyramids".

With this book, I have decided to process my travel experiences and publish the information obtained by me in the form of this document.

This booklet is intended to help the interested traveler in planning his journey through the land of the Maya as efficiently as possible. It was made to give those interested in historical Maya sites a list of places whose visit is most worthwhile.

Archaeologists assume that about 2,000 pyramids or buildings from the period of the Maya culture exist in the Maya region. Most of them are hidden in the forest, overgrown by lush greenery beyond recognition. Few of the submerged sites have been studied in detail, and even fewer of them were liberated by the vegetation. Just some of them were repaired and restored in a way that one can get an idea of its former appearance.

I have added only those Maya sites in my book that I have visited on my own. For this reason, some celebrities like Calakmul in Campeche or Copán in Honduras are missing - I just was not there - yet.

Those looking for recommendations for restaurants or hotels should better look out for the standard works of the travel industry or directly obtain information on the Internet.

Appendix

FURTHER READING

The following books are recommended for those who are looking for details. If you have the eBook, you can just click on the link that leads you to the relevant page at Amazon.

An Account of the Things of Yucatán – Diego de Landa

1566, after he had burned the documents of the Maya, Diego de Landa, a Franciscan monk and bishop of Yucatán, published this book. Today, it is an irreplaceable document of the Maya culture. It describes customs and traditions of the ancient Maya at the time of the Spanish conquest. His description of the letters/glyphs and the Maya calendar have contributed significantly to the modern research and understanding of these indigenous people.

Breaking the Maya Code – Michael D. Coe

The history of Maya research is also a history of the decryption of the hieroglyphic system of Maya. Coe follows the researchers through the centuries and describes their ways and wrong ways in this book.

Incidents of Travel in Yucatán – John L. Stephens

With maps, plans and numerous partly colored illustrations by Frederick Catherwood

This is a pioneering work in which Stephens has documented the experiences of his travel in Central America of 1839. Actually, Stephens traveled in his role as a US Diplomat to visit the government of Central America. Due to the revolutionary turmoil at this time, he could not achieve his goal but used his time to visit the Maya ruins in this area instead. He was accompanied by Frederick Catherwood, an architect, and painter to whom the origin of the very first images of Maya ruins is credited.

There are several editions of this book; some include Catherwood's paintings, others unfortunately do not.

The Maya – Michael D. Coe

Amazon Description: "The Maya has long been established as the best, most readable introduction to the New World's greatest ancient civilization. Coe and Houston update this classic by distilling the latest scholarship for the general reader and student.

This new edition incorporates the most recent archaeological and epigraphic research, which continues to proceed at a fast pace. Among the finest new discoveries are spectacular stucco sculptures at El Zotz and Holmul, which reveal surprising aspects of Maya royalty and the founding of dynasties.

Dramatic refinements in our understanding of the pace of developments of the Maya civilization have led scholars to perceive a pattern of rapid bursts of building and political formation. Other finds include the discovery of the earliest known occupant of the region, the Hoyo Negro girl, recovered from an underwater cavern in the Yucatán peninsula, along with new evidence for the first architecture at Ceibal.

213 illustrations, 28 in color"

This is one of the best books about the Maya.

PLANNING

TIMETABLE, NORTHERN YUCATÁN

Location	**Activity - Visits**	**Min. estim. Days**
Arrival / Cancún	Airport	0
Riviera Maya	Acclimation	2
	San Gervasio	1
Travel to Tulum		1
Tulum	**Tulum**	1
	Cobá	1
	Valladolid / Ek Balam	1
Travel to Chichén Itzá		1
Chichén Itzá	**Chichén Itzá**	2
Travel to Merida		1
Merida	**Merida**	1
	Uxmal	1
	Izamal	1
Back to the Riviera Maya		1
	On the Road: 4 Days	
	Total Time	**15**

Table 27 - Planning - Time table, Northern Yucatán

TIME TABLE FOR CAMPECHE AND CHIAPAS

Location	Activity - Visits	Min. estim. Days
Travel to Campeche		1
Campeche	**Edzná**	1
	Campeche	1
Travel to Palenque		1
Palenque	**Palenque**	2
	Toniná	1
	Yaxchilán	1
	Bonampak	1
	Villahermosa	1
Travel to San Cristobal de las Casas		1
San Cristobal de las Casas	**San Cristobal de las Casas**	2
	Chamula	1
Back to Palenque		1
Back to Riviera Maya		1
	On the Road: 5 Days	
	Total Time	**16**

Table 28 - Planning - Time Table for Campeche and Chiapas

TIME TABLE PETÉN / GUATEMALA

Location	**Activity**	**Min. estim. Days**
Travel to Flores		1
Flores	**Flores**	0
	Tikal	1
	Yaxhá	1
	El Mirador	5
Back to the Riviera Maya		1
	On the Road: 2 Days	
	Total Time	**9**

Table 29 - Planning - Time Table Petén / Guatemala

TIME TABLE – TOTAL

Location	**Activity**	**Min. estim. Days**
All	**Without El Mirador**	33
	With El Mirador	38
Result:	**On the Road (total)**	9
	Visits (total, with El Mirador)	29
	Visits (total, without El Mirador)	24

Table 30 - Planning - Time Table – Total

INDEX OF FIGURES

INDEX OF TABLES

INDEX OF MAPS

ACKNOWLEDGMENT

First of all, I want to thank Dr. Gad Sobrino in Mexico, who initiated the interest for the Maya culture in me and also to Anna Pal and Magdalena Sorger, two scientists from Austria. Without them, the jungle walk would not have been half as enjoyable. And especially, I thank Heike Schaffhauser for editing the original manuscript.

THE AUTHOR

Christian Schoen was born in Freiburg i.Breisgau in the Black Forest in Germany. Traveling has always been a unique experience for him. The biologist and IT manager refers to getting to know other cultures as his lifeblood. On numerous trips through southern Mexico, the highlands of Chiapas and the hot and humid jungles of Guatemala, the globetrotter dipped deep into the ancient Maya culture. After publishing the highly successful blog project "Amazing Temples and Pyramids," he now decided to publish his findings in this book.

Last word:

Visit me on http://AmazingTemples.com

CPSIA information can be obtained
at www.ICGtesting.com
Printed in the USA
LVHW071203190119
604490LV00017B/18/P